Sexual Consent

4/3/98

Sexual Consent

David Archard

WestviewPress
A Division of HarperCollins*Publishers*

Copyright © 1998 by Westview Press, A Division of HarperCollins Publishers, Inc.

Published in 1998 in the United States of America by Westview Press, 5500 Central Avenue, Boulder, Colorado 80301-2877, and in the United Kingdom by Westview Press, 12 Hid's Copse Road, Cumnor Hill, Oxford OX2 9JJ

A CIP catalog record for this book is available from the Library of Congress.
ISBN 0-8133-3081-5 (hc)—ISBN 0-8133-3082-3 (pb)

The paper used in this publication meets the requirements of the American National Standard for Permanence of Paper for Printed Library Materials Z39.48-1984.

10   9   8   7   6   5   4   3   2   1

To Bernarde with love

Contents

Preface and Acknowledgements

THIS IS A BOOK ABOUT SEXUAL CONSENT. It is not an account of sexual morality in general; it is directed to one particular theory of the sexually permissible. But it is not a full-blown defence of that theory. Rather, it is an exploration of how that theory should be understood and of the implications of that understanding. It is also about consent—what is consent, what counts as the giving of consent, and when consent is not real or valid. These kinds of issues are general in import and have application outside the specific domain of sexual activity. Although the book is sensitive to the meaning consent must have within that domain, it cannot help but broach broader matters. Consequently, it is hoped that the reader will gain a clearer idea not only of one account of sexual morality, but also, generally, of consent and its relationship to the morally permissible.

The format of the book is as follows. The early chapters introduce and elaborate a popular view about sex, namely, that whatever is consensual and harms no one else is permissible. Chapter 1 considers what consent is and how it can be given. Chapters 2 and 3 examine the role of consent in sexual activity, why consensual sex might be thought permissible, and what conditions, on a standard view, are sufficient to render consent invalid. Chapter 4 looks at a number of cases in which that standard view seems inadequate. Chapter 5 reviews the overall plausibility of the popular view that the consensual is permissible, and Chapter 6 treats the feminist critique of consent. The final three chapters address particular areas of sexual conduct in an attempt to assess the limits of the popular view. Chapter 7 is concerned with incest, prostitution, and sado-masochism; Chapter 8 with the age of sexual consent; and Chapter 9 with rape.

This book arises from my long-standing interest in sexual morality reflected in earlier articles on prostitution and the consensuality of sexual relations between professionals and their clients.[1] Chapters 2 and 3 incorporate material from an article in *Legal Theory* on the role of conventions in

ix

sexual consent.[2] In the book's writing debts to various people have been incurred. Sue Miller was a most encouraging (and very patient) editor at Westview. Susan Mendus and Jim Brown provided me with invaluable comments on the first drafts of early chapters. Alison Diduck read and commented helpfully on Chapter 6. Sandra Marshall and Tony Duff informally discussed and thereby improved greatly my own appreciation of a number of themes in the book. Hugh LaFollette provided me with incisive comments on most of the chapters and discussed these with me over several most enjoyable meetings. I am grateful to all of these people, who are very definitely owed the usual disclaimer. The views expressed here are my own, and I am sure they would not wish it to be otherwise.

My greatest debt is to my partner, Bernarde Lynn. My views on the subject of this book—as on so many other matters—have been immeasurably influenced by her. Her love and support through its writing have, as always, been extraordinary and ill-deserved. The book is dedicated with much love to her.

David Archard

◀ 1 ▶

Questions of Consent

IN JUNE 1994 TWO READERS of the British newspaper the *Independent on Sunday* reacted angrily to the previous week's column by one of that paper's regular contributors, Geoffrey Wheatcroft. He had suggested that men were fast becoming the victims of a sexual game whose rules were changing. Understandably, they were no longer able to understand what these rules were. Wheatcroft had been discussing the vexed issue of 'date rape' with particular reference to the cases of the American boxer Mike Tyson and the English solicitor Angus Dibble. Wheatcroft's view was that such men were only guilty of the crime of rape to the extent that they had found themselves stranded and vulnerable in the minefield that the game of sexual relationships between men and women had become. The letter writers protested that unconsented sex is nevertheless rape and that it remains the responsibility of men to be sure that consent is given. The newspaper's subeditor gave the two protesting letters the heading 'There is only one rule in the sex game, and that's consent'.[1]

This statement rather neatly and accurately summarises a common view, and one which is reflected in popular judgements about sexual matters. This is that consent makes a difference to whether some sexual activity is seen as immoral or not. Indeed it will be said to make all the difference between the permissibility and impermissibility of some practice or activity. On the one hand, a sexual practice which is not consented to is immoral. Rape, for instance, is wrong, and it will always be wrong, because the victim of rape does not consent to the sexual advances of her assailant. On the other hand, a sexual practice which is consented to is permissible. Whatever people do sexually as 'consenting adults' should be allowed, even if the rest of us find a particular practice disgusting or shocking. An example discussed in Chapter 7 is that of consensual adult sado-masochism.

1

It should be obvious that the common view is not a simple one. Equally it should be evident that it is not endorsed by everyone; nor need people endorse both of its halves. This book is not a defence of the 'common view' that consent is the 'only rule in the sex game'. It is generally sympathetic to that view, and its approach is to proceed on the basis of such a general sympathy. There are other understandings of the morality of sex, and at various points in the book these other views are signalled. However, the purpose of the book is not to show that the common view of sex is the only correct one. Rather, it is to explore the implications of holding the common view, to spell out the common view, and to try to understand what it claims, why it has plausibility, and what its implications might be in particular instances. What, for instance, is consent, and what is it within the context of sexual activity? Does consent have a particular significance in the area of sexual activity, and if so, why should this be? Why should we think that consent plays the role that it does in the legitimation of some practice?

These and other questions will be addressed in due course. But by way of a context to this discussion, the general view, as it has been called, should first be given a more formal statement. Let me suggest that the general view consists of two principles. The Principle of Consensuality states that 'a practice, P, is morally permissible if all those who are parties to P are competent to consent, give their valid consent, and the interests of no other parties are significantly harmed'. The Principle of Non-consensuality states that 'a practice, P, is morally impermissible if at least one of those who are parties to P, and who are competent to consent, does not give their valid consent, even if the interests of no other parties are significantly harmed'. The first principle is a formal statement of the view that whatever consenting adults do is all right; the second formally expresses the view that something is not all right if somebody does not agree to it.

Some of the terms of these principles—such as 'third parties' and 'competent to consent'—will have to be explained. For the moment attention need only be drawn to the phrase 'valid consent'. Clearly the common view holds that not every instance of what appears to be consenting should be taken as sufficient to legitimate a practice. This is because what appears to be consent is, on occasion, not really. Most obviously agreement at the point of a gun is not. There is a need thus to make clear what does and does not count as valid consent. This may well be done by means of a Principle of Valid Consent which states that 'the consent of a person, X, to some practice, P, is not valid if . . . ' or 'is valid only if . . .' where what follows is a statement of the conditions whose occurrence invalidate or validate the consent of that person. Since it is plausible to hold that the consent of a person competent to consent is valid unless some condition can be shown to hold (and it is more useful to operate with such a presumption), most attention will focus on the statement of invalidating conditions. This statement is likely to be a disjunction. Consent, for example, is invalid if obtained by coercion or given in unavoidable ignorance of some significant relevant fact or given by someone who is temporarily mentally disturbed. Whether a complete disjunctive statement of invalidating conditions can be agreed upon is obviously a crucial and difficult question to resolve.

With all of the foregoing in mind let us move to address a series of questions about consent. In answering these questions, I am trying to be clearer about what consent is—what is its moral significance, what is its scope, and how may it be given. In subsequent chapters I will examine the role of consent in sex and what it is about consent that may be thought to make any activity permissible. Still later chapters will examine some worries about the relationship between consent and permissibility, before exploring some practical applications of the understandings gained.

What Is Consent?

For present purposes there are four claims about consent that need to be identified and elucidated.[2] First, the giving of consent is something which makes a difference to the situation, normatively characterised; it alters the normative relationships between individuals in that situation. Consent has been described as 'morally transformative', as displaying a certain 'moral magic' in the way that it can suddenly make an otherwise wrong action right.[3] If I consent to the doing of something, I put myself under some sort of obligation in respect of that doing. It may be that I consent to do the thing in question—I agree to organise the meeting, and I should then take steps to realise that end. It may be that I consent to someone's else doing of something, in which case I am obliged not to obstruct their doing of it or to assist their doing of it in a manner indicated by the giving of the consent. If I agree to a friend's using my house while I am away, I should give them a key, not change the locks or move others in beforehand. Those to whom I give the consent thereby acquire rights or legitimate expectations in respect of what it is I have agreed to do or allow to be done.

Second, there are actions which are 'morally transformative' but which are not the giving of consent. That is to say, consent is sufficient but not necessary to generate obligations and permissions. If, for instance, Smith has stolen goods from Jones, then Jones can take certain steps to recover these goods, and Smith is under an obligation not to prevent her from doing so. There are also behaviours of which one might say that it is almost 'as if' consent had thereby been given. Smith may not have consented to Jones's doing something. Nevertheless, what Smith did do was sufficient for Jones reasonably to believe that she could do it and that Smith was under an obligation not to stop her or to assist her. Cases like this will be discussed later under the category of 'quasi-consent'.

Third, the giving of consent needs to be accomplished in and by a positive, intentional act. Consent is an act rather than a state of mind.[4] Consent is something I do rather than think or feel. When I give my consent, I may do so in ways other than by a public expression of the form 'I consent to . . . .' Whether consent can be given tacitly is moot. Whether what is argued to be tacit consent can be distinguished from other kinds of behaviour which may incur an obligation is also open to question. However, it is assumed that consent, whether express or tacit, is *given* rather than simply assumed in the absence of any sign to the contrary. I do not, normally, give my consent by my failure to perform some action which indicates dissent. There are, to be sure, circumstances in which being silent constitutes consent. If the chair of some meeting announces that she will take silence to betoken agreement, and pauses to permit any declaration of disagreement, then staying silent is something I can be described as subsequently deciding to do, and doing. But plainly this is not a mere failure or absence of voice.[5]

The view of consent as something that is done rather than as a state of mind is normally expressed by the statement that consent should be understood in 'performative' and not 'psychological' terms. Nevertheless, it is surely reasonable to expect that the person who consents, in the performative sense, will have, as a psychological state, the right kind of attitude towards that to which she is consenting.

The fourth claim about consent concerns the relevant mental states. When I say 'I consent to X', must I think to myself 'I consent to X'? There are three types of relevant mental state, cognitive, dispositional, and volitional, whose character determine, respectively, whether I know I am consenting, whether I agree with what I am consenting to, and whether I intend to consent.

It seems, first, that someone consents only if they are aware that they are consenting. One gives one's consent deliberately and knowingly. If I say 'I do' in a foreign language, believing myself to be saying something quite different, then I am not properly described as giving my consent by mistake. Rather, I have simply failed, in virtue of my linguistic incompetence, to give my consent. However, I do not, second, have to want or to approve of what I consent to. I can consent to P while having no view about P's desirability, or even while disliking the very thought of P. Someone could consent to sex that is unwanted. A wife may have uncoerced, willing, and knowing sex with a husband in the knowledge that she will not enjoy it and preferring that it not take place. There is reason to condemn such a sexual interaction but not in virtue of its being non-consensual.

Consent is to be distinguished from assent. Etymology alone indicates that they are closely related. But while consent is essentially agreement *to* something, assent is essentially agreement *with* something. Agreeing with something is like Joseph Raz's 'consenting in one's heart': 'Consenting in one's heart is not a performative consent but a psychological state akin to coming to terms with. The core use of "consent" is its use in the performative sense'.[6] When I consent to the holding of a party in my house, I agree that it may be held there. When I assent to holding the party, I agree that holding it in my house is a good idea.

My consent to the holding of the party in my house is 'morally transformative'. If I consent to have the party in my house, then I have no right that others not hold it there. Before I gave my consent, I did have such a right. If I assent to having the party in Smith's house, I do not thereby strip Smith of his right that it not be held there. It is for Smith to give his consent to holding the party in his house. Saying 'I agree' when it is the giving of consent is a performative utterance as saying 'I do' is in the context of the marriage ceremony. Saying 'I agree' only as an expression of assent is not.

Assent, unlike consent, can be both an act and a state of mind. I can express my approval of some state of affairs or merely wish for it. I can, in a single act, express both my assent and consent. To the question 'Is it OK to hold the party in your house?' I reply, 'Yes' and thereby both consent and assent to its being held there. Dissent may be taken as the contrary of both consent and assent. In the absence of further explanation or context an expression of dissent from P is both an explicit withholding of consent to P and the signalling of one's disapproval of P. Dissent, like assent, can be both an act and a state of mind. However, a person may give her sincere and willing consent to that from which she dissents, that is, does not approve of. Equally, consent need not be given to that from which no act of dissent is expressed. When Smith submits sexually to Jones in real fear of her life, she makes no protest, but she does not consent.

When I consent to X, I must, cognitively, be in the state of knowing that I consent to X. Consent need not require the dispositional mental state of agreeing with X. The third type of mental state, the volitional, governs what I really will to be the case. Do I have to mean what I say when I say 'I consent'? If I say these words in jest or with the intention of misleading the other, even though I know what the words mean, then am I actually giving my consent? In short, is an insincere consenting a consenting nonetheless? J. L. Austin suggested that something goes wrong when somebody who says 'I promise' does not have the corresponding intention to promise. The 'performance' is not 'void', but it is 'unhappy', an 'infelicity'; it is given in 'bad faith'.[7] John Searle stipulates that a speaker makes a promise in uttering certain words only if he intends to do that which he promises to do and intends that the utterance will place him under an obligation to do what he promises to do.[8]

It does seem true that if I know what I am doing when I say 'I consent', then I put myself under an obligation to honour the commitments that are normally made by a sincere utterance of these words. I intend that my words shall be understood by the other as the giving of my consent. Moreover, since we would normally expect the utterance to be accompanied by the appropriate intentions and there is nothing in my behaviour to indicate that this is not the case in this particular instance, I lead others to believe that I am sincere in my utterance. If in saying 'I consent' I do not actually intend to consent, it is nevertheless the case that I intend to be responsible for the consequences of its being as if I did intend to consent. The man who insincerely but deliberately and knowingly answers 'I will' at the appropriate moment in the marriage ceremony does thereby and to all intents and purposes enter into the marriage.

What Is Consented To?

This is the second question we need to try to answer. This is a question about the scope of any act of consent. If I agree to your borrowing my car, I accord you the right to drive it. I do not alienate my right of ownership; nor do I, normally, allow you use of the car for more than a limited period. I also do not consent to you using the car in certain ways, for instance, as the getaway vehicle in a bank robbery. Many of these limits have to be understood as governed by informal conventions of usage. I should not have to say that you should not break the law when driving my car. There may, however, be disagreements. I did not say you should not take the car abroad when you asked to borrow it for a week, but I would have expected you to ask if you might. Any state of affairs or outcome or action that we consent to is thus limited in ways that any reasonable person, understanding the informal conventions in question, could be expected to acknowledge. These conventions, it should be emphasised, govern the question not of whether a person has consented or not, but of what, in having consented to something, a person has precisely or in full detail consented to. There *is* a question of whether in doing one thing a person is consenting to something else, and whether the inference from the first to the second is governed by conventions. But that is something that will need to be examined when we turn to the question of how consent is given.

It should be clear that in consenting to something, I do not consent to its being accomplished in any manner whatsoever. If I agree to have sex with you, I do not thereby agree to the form of sexual activity that you may prefer. If I consent to sexual intimacy in general, I do not consent to each and every possible particular sexual act. If I consent now to an act of sexual intimacy, I do not thereby consent to sex on each and every subsequent occasion that might arise. On the other hand, notoriously, it has been believed that through the act of marriage and its first consummation a woman thereby consents to all future sexual activity between herself and her husband. This belief has given support to the law's refusal, until recently, to recognise the crime of rape within marriage. This refusal does of course have other explanations—that a wife, on marriage, becomes the property of her husband or only a constituent element of a single legal agent, husband-and-wife, whose decisions are made by the husband alone. Nevertheless, the idea of consent to future sexual activity in general being given through the single act of agreeing to marry is an influential one.

How Is Consent Given?

In answering this question, we need to distinguish, first, between types of consent and, second, between consent proper and ersatz consent.

Tacit Consent

A first distinction can be made between express and tacit consent. Express consent is the making of a public, explicit sign of agreement to something. At its most basic express consent can be given by someone saying 'I consent to . . . ', or by signing one's name under a written statement of the form 'I consent to . . . ', or by responding to an inquiry as to whether one does consent with words such as 'I do'. 'Tacit' or, as it is sometimes also described, 'implicit' consent is consent which is implied by, or can be understood from, a person's action. With tacit consent an action can be taken to mean something other and more than it would normally, and taken strictly in itself, mean. The most notable philosophical defender of the idea of tacit consent was John Locke. He thought that every citizen 'that hath any Possession, or Enjoyment, of any part of the Dominions of any Government, doth thereby give his *tacit Consent*, and is as far forth obliged to obedience to the Laws of that Government, during such Enjoyment, as any one under it'.[9]

How does this work? The simplest and most plausible model is that of 'playing by the rules of the game'. If I take part in an activity which is constituted by some set of rules, then I may be taken as agreeing to abide by those rules. More generally I may be taken as agreeing to accept what, normally and reasonably, may be expected to follow from taking part in this rule-governed activity. Somebody who plays a sport thereby agrees to play by its rules and to accept what standardly befalls those who play it. 'Consent to bodily contact and to violence is inferred from participation in play subject to rules and the working culture within the game'.[10]

It is proper to insist that tacit consent can only be given in this manner if somebody knows both that they are participating in the activity in question and that participation entails accepting its rules. It must also be the case that the person takes parts voluntarily. We have seen that consent must be given knowingly and willingly. If these conditions are met, there is no reason to think that consent could not be given tacitly.[11] However, a familiar criticism of the kind of tacit consent to political authority which Locke had in mind (and, before him, Socrates in the *Crito*) is as follows: Because an individual citizen has no real choice but to 'enjoy' his government's protection or cannot be expected to know that his 'enjoyment' entails his consent to that government's authority, then his consent is not valid.

The model of 'playing by the rules of the game' is a case where one action, taking part in the game, implies another, consenting to its rules. Now it is easy to imagine that there should be agreed conventions whereby consent can be inferred from some action which is not, in itself, a public or express declaration of consent. The conventions can be such that the action and giving of consent are related arbitrarily in the same way that linguistics would argue the signifier and signified to be related. Imagine two persons construct and agree to some set of conventions whereby the consent of one to various proposals can be inferred, For example, Smith agrees in advance with an auctioneer a system of bidding signals. Scratching her nose shall mean an increase in the bid of $500, a tugging of her ear lobe shall mean an increase of $1,000, and so on. Her actions may be taken as the appropriate bids only within the context of the auction and only in consequence of the convention agreed to between her and the auctioneer. There is nothing otherwise about her actions that would allow them to be read as bids.

Other conventions are not so artificial and are such that an action and its meaning are related in a less arbitrary fashion. Indeed there may be an obvious and direct connection. If I respond to your request to borrow my car by wordlessly tossing you the keys, then you may reasonably take my action to signify agreement. The keys are related to the car in such a way that I may be said metonymically to be giving you the car. We are familiar with a whole range of non-verbal behaviours which, in the appropriate context, constitute the giving of consent. In response to a request to enter the room, the respondent steps back, sideways, and makes a sweeping gesture of invitation with her arm. Asked if she will sign a document, someone stretches out her hand to receive it. Nodding and shaking one's head to indicate, respectively, agreement and disagreement are the most familiar and apparently evident behaviours of this kind. Yet even though people in very many different cultures express agreement by nodding, nodding and shaking one's head are not culturally universal expressions. That they are so nearly universal suggests an etymology. A nod signifies agreement because it derives from a curtailed bow, which, in turn, represents a ritualised submission to the other. Shaking one's head to mean 'no' may originate, it has been suggested, in the baby's refusal of proffered food by turning its head away.[12]

The fact that even the simplest conventions may not apply everywhere (to the embarrassment of the inexperienced traveller) reminds us that it should not be assumed that a person's behaviour can be read as consent. This is particularly true where there is a dispute about whether a convention applies or which convention does apply. It should be evident that this has particular relevance to sexual interaction, and the problems that arise in this regard will be considered again in the next chapter. Let us for now assume that tacit consent can be and is given in those instances where there is a clear agreed convention of which the person is aware and which permits the consent of that person to be inferred from her deliberately chosen action. It is still important to separate the distinction between tacit and express consent from another distinction.

Indirect Consent

On one use of the expression of 'tacit consent' John Locke can be understood as arguing that if you expressly consent to P, then you may be taken as tacitly consenting to Q—'if it would be generally taken that consenting to P involves consenting to Q'.[13] Why might it be 'generally taken' to involve this? One answer, already given, is that there exists a convention to the effect that consenting to P has this implication. Another line of argument might point to the nature of the connections between P, which is consented to, and Q, consent to which may be inferred in the light of these connections. Some have thus argued that I implicitly consent to what must follow from what I do expressly give my consent to: 'A person consents to all the consequences that he knows are necessary effects of his voluntary acts'.[14] There are a number of ways in which P and Q might be appropriately connected. First, Q could be an accompaniment of P, that is, it is not possible to do P without at the same time doing Q. If I let you watch television in my house while I am away, I also let you consume my electricity. Second, Q might inevitably succeed P. If I consent to a medical procedure, then I consent to its outcome. Third, Q might be a precondition of P. A patient who agrees to a particular operation consents to the administration of the general anaesthetic that must precede it. We might call all three cases instances of *indirect* consent whereby consent is given to that which is connected to that which is directly consented to. In each of the three cases—as accompaniment, consequence, and precondition—the connection between what is consented to and what is thereby indirectly consented to is a lawful one. It must be such a kind of connection if the indirect consent is to be properly inferred.

However, since it was also argued earlier that a person must be aware of giving their consent, indirect consent will count as consent only if the person is aware of the connection between P and Q. A person who consents to sexual intercourse with another person who has a sexually transmittable disease does not thereby consent to acquiring the disease, which may be the inevitable outcome. She does not consent to this outcome if she does not know that, in this case, sexual intercourse leads to the acquisition of the disease. They do not do so precisely insofar as they are unaware that in this instance such an outcome follows from sexual intercourse. It might further be claimed that a person should not only be aware of the connection between P and Q but also be aware that consent to P constitutes indirect consent to Q. This claim seems too strong. It is surely reasonable to presume that someone who knows that Q cannot but occur if P does may be taken as agreeing to Q in consenting to P.

Consider, though, what might be called 'Portia's argument'. In Shakespeare's *The Merchant of Venice* Antonio consents to give Shylock a pound of his flesh in forfeiture should he be unable to repay a loan. When Shylock demands the forfeit, Portia argues in court that Shylock is entitled only to the flesh and not to any blood. 'This bond doth give thee here no jot of blood: The words expressly are "a pound of flesh". . . . Therefore, prepare thee to cut off the flesh. Shed thou no blood, nor cut thou less nor more. But just a pound of flesh; if thou tak'st more . . . thou diest, and all thy goods are confiscate'.[15] The argument serves to deny Shylock even his pound of flesh since he cannot take that with 'no jot of blood'. Of course no reasonable person could be unaware that bleeding accompanies or inevitably follows excision, and Portia's argument has the appearance of legal sophistry. Since she uses it when a plea for mercy fails, we can acknowledge that its effect, if not its form, is just. Nevertheless, the argument serves to remind us that someone might claim not to have consented to what is nevertheless a necessary accompaniment to or inevitable consequence of that to which they have consented.

In his interpretation of John Locke, John Plamenatz has also argued for a distinction between direct and indirect consent. This, for him, is not the same as that between express and tacit consent which marks the manner in which the consent is given. Direct consent can be express or tacit, as when a convention permits silence to be taken as consent to a proposal. Indirect consent must always be tacit since I can expressly consent only to that which is connected to the object of my indirect consent. His example of indirect consent is as follows: 'When you vote for a person or party that wins an election, you directly consent to his or to their authority, and you also consent indirectly to the system of government'.[16] The example is interesting since the relationship here between P and Q is not evidently one of precondition, inevitable outcome, or accompaniment. Plamenatz's argument would seem rather to be of this form: Someone who does P in a proper understanding of its full significance may be taken as thereby giving their consent to Q, which is entailed by that proper understanding. Individual acts of voting are clearly, in the first instance, the formal expression of personal preferences for some candidate, party, or policy. Their full significance, however, is that individuals thereby participate in a process whereby an overall outcome is determined by the voluntarily expressed preferences of everyone who votes. Knowing this to be the case, anyone who chooses to vote in an election commits herself to an acceptance of the means by which that outcome is determined. Her consent to the electoral system is real enough even if indirectly given.

It is arguable whether voting does have this significance.[17] What is crucial is how we are to understand the 'full significance' of an act such as voting. It is not part of the *meaning* of 'voting' that in voting, one endorses the electoral system. Someone could vote to express a preference for a candidate while repudiating that system. Imagine a person resigned to the victory of Party A and thoroughly disillusioned with the democratic procedures that render this inevitable who nonetheless thinks it important to vote just on the grounds that Party B should be seen to garner as many votes as possible. The disillusioned voter intends that her vote should be added to those of others who are expressing a preference for Party B. But, unlike the others, she does not intend by so voting that she should play her democratic part, even as a member of the losing side, in the determination of a winner. She does not express a preference for Party B as the possible winner of this democratic game, and she does not endorse the game which others are taking part in.

There is a reason to be careful of any use of a notion of the 'full significance' of some action in order to show that consent has been given indirectly. This is that the 'full significance' of some action may be open to disputed interpretation. I take you to have indirectly consented to what I, but not you, understand to be the full significance of your action. Of course if you are not aware of the significance of what you do, then you cannot be taken to have consented. Nevertheless, I may think it reasonable to assume that you do appreciate the significance of your action and thus have consented. This possibility will be of considerable importance in the area of sexual behaviour.

A related point can be made about cases where one thing 'normally' succeeds or accompanies another. Again this will be of special importance in sexual activity. Consider that sexual intimacy admits of varying degrees or increasing levels. It should be evident that consent to some degree of sexual intimacy is not indirect consent to a greater degree of intimacy on the grounds that such an escalation is what could 'normally' be expected. The 'Sexual Offence Policy' of Antioch College, which received such widespread attention in the media in 1993, requires that 'if the level of sexual intimacy increases during an interaction (i.e., if two people move from kissing while fully clothed—which is one level—to undressing for direct physical contact, which is another level), the people involved need to express their clear verbal consent before moving to that new level.' The requirement that consent be given expressly and verbally is a distinct matter (to be considered in due course). The important point to note here is that the code of practice acknowledges that when an activity, such as sexual interaction, admits of levels, consent to one level is not indirect consent to another higher one. And that is true even if the higher levels normally succeed the lower.

Quasi-consent

Imagine that there is such a thing as tacit consent. Imagine that my behaviour in a given context is such that any reasonable person could have been expected to recognise that they were, in behaving this way, giving their tacit consent. I do not think of my behaviour as tacit consent. I have not consented, but I have put myself under an obligation in regard to what would have been tacitly consented to. That I should be aware that I am tacitly consenting is not sufficient to make it the case that I am in fact consenting. But it is enough to give rise to duties on my part and legitimate expectations on the part of others which are as if I had consented. Peter Singer has thus spoken of *quasi-consent*, since 'under certain circumstances, actions or failures to act may justify us in holding a person to be obliged *as if* he had consented, whether or not he actually has'.[18] His own example is of someone who participates in the practice of buying rounds of drinks to the extent of accepting drinks from others, but who then protests, when asked to buy his own round, that he did not agree to be a part of the round. He can certainly claim not to have agreed, even tacitly, to take part, and he can claim to have been unaware that his participation constituted any such agreement. However, he cannot acquit himself of the obligation to buy his round which he has incurred in consequence of the well-grounded expectation others in the practice have that he will do so.

Singer is clear that quasi-consent is not real consent, either express or tacit. The usage is helpful only so long as it does not lead us to think of quasi-consent as a type of actual consent. As Ronald Dworkin has remarked in another context, 'A hypothetical contract is not simply a pale form of an actual contract; it is no contract at all'.[19] It is also true that what Singer understands by quasi-consent is captured by the legal principle of estoppel *in pais*. This principle can be expressed as follows: When, by saying or doing something, I induce another to believe that I can be depended upon to perform some further action, and the other relies upon this expectation, then I cannot subsequently claim that I did not represent my future actions in the way the other came to

believe. I would thus be liable for losses incurred by the other in acting in reliance upon the expectation that I would so act. For the principle to apply, it
must be the case not only that the second party does rely on the first party's
future performance, but also that there should be an intention on the first
party's part to induce an expectation of reliance, or at least a lack of care
with regard to the forming of such an expectation.

If Smith sits down at a restaurant table and gives her order to the restaurant owner, Jones, she intends Jones to believe that she will pay for the meal
ordered, and in supplying the meal Jones expects Smith to settle her bill.
Smith is liable for payment and cannot claim to avoid payment by arguing
that she did not expressly agree to pay. Smith puts herself under an obligation to settle the restaurant bill. But she does not do so by consenting to do
so. Nor does her action, in placing an order, fall under a convention which
allows it to be read as tacitly consenting to pay. If she did expressly consent
at the outset to pay the bill, or if there was a convention whereby she did
tacitly consent to do so, then she would have put herself under an obligation to pay. That she is under an obligation to pay by the principle of estoppel does not mean that she did consent to pay.

Quasi-consent, in turn, needs to be distinguished from the likelihood of
actual consent, either express or tacit, where this likelihood is grounded in a
regular succession of behaviours. An action, P, may be regularly succeeded
by a further action, Q. This is not to say, nor does it licence us in saying, that
there is a convention which allows a person's consent to Q to be inferred
from her voluntary performance of P. I regularly leave a tip after dining in a
restaurant. My choosing to dine in a restaurant does not represent an agreement to leave a tip. Of course regularities of behaviour lead people to make
predictions and to have confident expectations about future performance.
This can give rise to obligations, but it does not do so as a result of consent
having been given. I may be led to believe that you will consent to Q, and I
may be led to believe this because you did P and because your performance
of P has been regularly succeeded by your willingness to do Q. But there is
all the difference between a rule which allows us to make this prediction and
a convention which allows us to say that doing P *is* consent to Q.

How Do We Know That Consent Is
Being or Has Been Given?

Here we are concerned with what shall count as evidence that consent has
been given or withheld. This question should be carefully distinguished

from the preceding one. Of course an answer to the question of how consent can be given will determine what shall count as reasons to think that it has. But evidence sufficient for someone reasonably to believe that another has given their consent will not conclusively establish that it has. It may on occasion be eminently reasonable for somebody falsely to believe that another person has given their consent.

Where and when the question arises of whether consent has been given, we should normally presume that it has not been given. That is, we should seek to show that someone has given their consent rather than presume, in the absence of any sign to the contrary, that it has been given. This is appropriate since consent, as has been argued, is both a positive intentional act and one which changes the moral situation. Assuming that consent is not forthcoming is not of course the same as assuming that the person dissents, that is, that she is positively withholding her agreement. This might be the case. But it could also be true that she would consent if asked. What is true is that the more importance there attaches to the giving or withholding of some specific consent, the more reason there is for presuming not simply the absence of consent but the presence of dissent.

This brings us then to the question of how high we should set any probative requirement, that is, how much evidence we should require of someone who acts in the belief that consent has been given. Remember that if you have consented to let me use your car, then I have a right to do so and can legitimately expect you not to prevent me from doing so. If I have every reason to believe that you have agreed to let me use your car, then I will proceed on the basis of that expectation. If you have not consented, then harm may be done to you by my using your car against your wishes. Or I may be harmed if, having made arrangements on the assumption that I could use your car, I am now left without its use. A plausible principle is then that the greater the harms that would result from acting on the false assumption that consent has been given, the better grounded should be the belief that it has been.

A second principle derives from the consideration that not everyone may understand the convention in the same way, or believe that a particular action is governed by any convention. A behaviour which I regard as meaning something else need not be seen in the same way by another person. It is plausible then to demand that the more likely it is that a behaviour is open to different interpretations, the more certain we should be that it can be interpreted as conveying consent.[20]

A third principle is given by the consideration that it may be possible to confirm or confute the belief that consent is forthcoming in a more direct and unmediated fashion than through simple reliance upon the convention. We can often directly ask if the nod did mean 'yes'. Each principle should be separately acted upon. Taken together they yield the following requirement: If a convention is not generally accepted, or if there is disagreement concerning its existence, and if acting in reliance upon it may result in great harm to someone, and if it is possible directly to confirm the belief inferred from acceptance of the convention, then someone who acts in the light of a belief inferred solely from the convention may be judged to have behaved unreasonably and culpably. In short it is wrong to rely exclusively on a risky and uncertain convention when doing so is not necessary.

Can Consent Be Revoked?

This is the final question to which we need to attempt an answer. There do seem to be imaginable scenarios in which consent would be revoked, and further, it is reasonable to believe that the consent would justifiably be revoked. I agree to you using my car. But it turns out that you use it for purposes that I had not envisaged your doing. You plan to run a taxi service. Or I find that circumstances are changed and that I now have urgent need of my car. I need to visit a close relative who has suddenly fallen seriously ill. Or it transpires that I gave my consent only because you misled me in some significant regard. You told me that without the car you could not get to an extremely important interview when no such interview had been arranged. In all these cases we might say that I could withdraw my agreement to your using my car and that I would be right to do so.

However, it is more correct to say that, in two of the imagined instances, I did not really give my consent and that, in the third, other considerations outweigh the obligations that have arisen in consequence of the consent. In agreeing to your using my car, I am understood to agree to your using it for certain purposes only and on certain conditions. Even where these are not made explicit, they may be understood to govern the usage. If you exceed these limits, then you do what I have not consented to your doing. If you deceived me at the time that I gave my consent, then my consent was not really given. Duping a person into giving their consent is a standard ground for regarding that consent as invalid. In both of these cases then it is more proper to say not that the consent is revoked but that it was not given in the first instance. My 'revoking' of the consent is in fact a public declaration of this fact.

In the third case you do have a right to make use of my car, but you ought also to be moved by the thought that exercising this right in the changed circumstances has a serious cost, namely, that you deprive me of the only realistic means I may have of helping my sick relative. I cannot claim that I am not under an obligation to let you continue to use my car since my consent was indeed given to this use. However, you ought to recognise that this obligation is now outweighed by a more pressing and substantial duty on your part to allow use of the car to revert to the one who has much greater need of it.

However, what of a case where I consent to your using my car and then simply change my mind without there being anything in the circumstances of the original giving of consent or subsequent use of the car that would fit with the previous examples given. I just decide that I do not want you to use the car. Here it seems that we should insist that consent is not the same as assent. I have agreed to your using the car, and that agreement does not require my liking the fact that you do so, either at the time that I agreed or during the period of use licensed by that agreement. You have a right to use the car, and I am under an obligation to let you use it. The right and the obligation have arisen from the giving of the consent, and they cannot now be willed away by some further act of revocation. To say that they cannot may seem overly stringent, but our thoughts here may be influenced by an assumption that any such case must be one of the three discussed before.

Or consider that I now try to act out my revocation of consent by making it very hard for you to exercise the right to which that consent gave rise. I come and retrieve the car using a spare set of keys. I immobilise the car. You should consider the costs of persisting in the exercise of a right that you continue to have but that can now be exercised only with difficulty. You will of course be entitled to compensation since the disappointed expectation that you might use my car was a legitimate one, and I am responsible for creating but then frustrating that rightful expectation.

Let me address these issues in the context of sexual interaction. Can a woman revoke her consent to intercourse having initially given it and penetration having already occurred? American courts have answered in the negative.[21] I will consider this issue further in Chapter 9, where I discuss rape. Here I want to make some comments about revoked consent to sex which parallel those made previously about the borrowing of a car. The nature of the sexual interaction may change from that which the woman understood herself to be consenting to at the outset. It may proceed with violence on the part of the man. It is then appropriate to say that she did not consent to that kind of intercourse. Or she may have consented to penetration but not to full coitus and intra-vaginal ejaculation. It may be thought reasonable for a man to believe, in the absence of explicit signs to the contrary, that consent to penetration is consent to full intercourse. That is something to which we will need to return. But the reasonableness of his belief apart, it is certainly possible for a woman to consent only to penetration.

Let us say that a woman did consent to full intercourse but now, after penetration, changes her mind. It is obviously possible that intercourse could become extremely painful for the woman. This is analogous to the prior case in which changed circumstances mean that the continued exercise of any right that has arisen from the initial consent now has a serious cost. There are good reasons which derive from the particular character of sexual activity—and which will be discussed in the next chapter—for thinking that persistence in sexual activity against the current wishes of someone, even if within the terms of their originally given consent, incurs a very serious cost. Indeed it is such as to make persistence deeply morally objectionable.

I think that similar comments apply even when the change of mind on the woman's part is not attributable to any such change of circumstances. A man may reasonably claim to be disappointed in legitimate expectations of sexual satisfaction that have arisen from an originally given consent. But—again for the kinds of reasons that will be discussed in due course—it would be unreasonable of him to insist upon that satisfaction in the face of a woman's dissent. That is not to say that the consent has been revoked or that it was not really ever given. Rather, it is that the costs of securing that satisfaction are not now warranted by that initial consent.

◀ 2 ▶

Sexual Consent

Why Does Sexual Consent Matter?

Is consent specially important in sexual relationships? That is the first subject of this chapter. Let us grant the truth of the Principles of Consensuality and Non-consensuality—namely, that whatever is consented to is permissible and whatever is not consented to is impermissible. There is a question of whether these principles apply to sexual activity. This will be the subject of subsequent chapters. The distinct question considered here is whether in being applicable to sexual activity, these principles have a particular importance. Is it worse for sexual activity to be unconsented than it would be for other kinds of activity? And is it better, compared with other activities, for sexual activity to be consensual? If this is the case, what is it about the nature of sexual activity that makes this the case?

Let me suggest that there are at least three plausible reasons for thinking consent important in sexual activity. The first concerns the relationship between consensuality and pleasure. In the last chapter it was pointed out that consent is not the same thing as assent. I can agree *to* what I do not agree *with*. Further, it need not be the case that what I agree with I find agreeable in the sense of taking pleasure in. If I consent to become secretary of a society, I need not agree with the idea of doing so in the sense of having a favourable attitude to the idea. I do consent because I promised some years ago to do so when my turn came and recognise that now, whatever my feelings, I must honour that promise. Even if I think that becoming secretary is a good idea and one with which I wholeheartedly agree, it does not follow that being secretary is something I derive pleasure from. I think it

19

best that I do the job because I know that I will do it better than anyone else, but I do not enjoy my secretarial duties.

In the case of sexual activity, however, it is plausible to think that individuals will normally only consent to what they believe they will find pleasurable and only find pleasurable what they consent to. In the first place, sex is mainly engaged in for its pleasure. Sex may be freely practised out of duty, habit, boredom, curiosity, defiance, revenge, the impulse to procreate, and, almost certainly, many more motives. But it is chiefly done for and in the expectation of pleasure. This of course is not to say that pleasure need be the sole motive, or that sex engaged in for another motive need not also be pleasurable, or that pleasure is always the outcome even when sought. Individuals may often seek to give pleasure to those they love without any regard for their own satisfaction. The point is simply that it is unlikely that individuals should always voluntarily engage in sexual activity with no aim or hope of deriving pleasure from doing so.

Second, the pleasurableness of a sexual encounter is closely tied to its being one in which the parties willingly engage. Sexual activity is not normally something that can be enjoyed in the face of or despite an unwillingness to participate. It is also plausible to suggest that sex is the more pleasurable the more that persons willingly take part in it. Sexual activity is one in which the individual gives herself over to its pleasures, surrenders or abandons herself to its enjoyment. Such language, which admittedly exaggerates, nevertheless serves to emphasise the centrality of voluntariness. Someone might never derive pleasure from the sex that she chooses to have, and someone might always find pleasure in sex that was unconsented. But these are rare individuals, and for the majority of us the pleasure and consensuality of our sexual experience are closely tied together.

The second reason for thinking consent important in sex derives from the consideration that at stake in any sexual encounter is the individual as an embodied self. Sex is an opening up of one person to another, a mutual disclosure in circumstances of particular intimacy and vulnerability. Sex is also carnal, and as incarnated beings we have a very strong interest in regulating and controlling access to our bodies. This interest is rooted in considerations of self-esteem, integrity, and personal dignity. There are, in consequence, special dangers and possible harms attached to sexual interaction. Someone can be particularly damaged by a sexual experience, and this is most likely to occur when that experience is not of the person's own choosing.[1] Victims of unconsented sex thus frequently speak of the strong feelings of personal violation and of the abiding loss in self-respect that can result from the violation of their bodily integrity. It seems evident, as Tony Honoré says, that 'bodies deserve better protection than goods'.[2]

The third reason that consent is important in sexual activity has to do with the fact that sex matters to us, that it is something over which we do want to exercise choice, and that the denial of such choices in this area as we do want to make is deeply frustrating. There are a number of ways in which our sexuality, and thus our being able to exercise choice over it, matters to us. It is a source of pleasure. As H. L. A. Hart observes, to punish the consensual achievement of sexual satisfaction is to create 'misery of a quite special degree'.[3] Sexual activity may in itself be valuable to us. Each of us may wish to express a particular sexual identity. Sex is one way in which a relationship with another human being may be explored and possibly deepened. Sex is a way in which our affection, our love for another person can be expressed. Sex is a means to the procreation of offspring. For all these reasons it matters to us that we can make sexual choices.

Can Sex Be Consensual?

Sexual consent is, in short, vitally important because sexual pleasure is linked to consensuality, sexuality implies our personal integrity as incarnate persons, and it matters that we can exercise choice over our sexuality. However, is it in the nature of sexual activity that talk of consent is inappropriate, or at best very difficult? There are three different worries about the very idea of sexual consent, the least significant of which I will tackle first.

The Privacy of Sex

This first worry derives from the fact that sexual activity is in essence a private activity. If it takes place publicly—in the sense not merely of occurring in a public place but of being open or likely to be open to public gaze—it will probably fall foul of the familiar liberal requirement that behaviour not occasion offence. In fact nearly all societies regulate sexual conduct by having taboos on its public expression and by reserving spaces or times in which sexual activity can properly be conducted.[4] These regulations reflect a universal desire that each of us should be able to express ourselves sexually in conditions of intimacy and seclusion. The general existence of such a desire is not disproved by the wish among some for sexual exhibitionism or group sexual activity.

The essential privacy of sexual behaviour presents a difficulty for the securing of any assurance that such behaviour is also consensual. How can we know that some sexual activity is or is not with the consent of those involved when it takes place out of the public view? This is an evidentiary consideration. However, it does not tell against the idea of sexual consensuality. Whether some feature of an activity should be a key condition of its permissibility can be argued about independently of the question of how evidence as to whether or not the feature was present might be obtained. Anyway no one can believe that there is *no* such evidence in the case of sexual consensuality. At most it might be asserted that where there is conflicting evidence, such as results when a version of events is disputed by the only two parties involved, there is no further independent evidence that might decide the matter. However, this is not a problem that uniquely besets sexual activity or any activity in which consensuality is the condition of its permissibility. Was, for instance, the physical confrontation that took place between two friends in private an assault by one on the other, or a consensual rough and tumble?

Consensual Sex Is Passionless Sex

The second, more serious kind of worry about the idea of sexual consensuality arises from the nature of sex itself. Sex, it will be said, is an activity characterised by informality, spontaneity, heightened senses, high feeling, imperatives of satisfaction; it is one in which its participants are taken over by passion and the needs of the moment. It is not, therefore, one in which there is any appropriate space for the seeking of or expression of something as formal, considered, and deliberate as consent.

Now there may be a number of distinct worries expressed here. One is that at no time in any sexual encounter is there any opportunity to elicit or give consent. That seems false. Two persons could agree to the broad terms of their sexual activity in advance. Equally they could communicate during any sexual encounter as to the terms of its further progress. One form of sexual activity which might seem both to need consensuality and to render its giving and taking problematic is sado-masochism. Yet its participants do take care to agree in advance what might and might not be done, and to be responsible in relying on signals and cues given during any encounter. Consider these quotes from SM practitioners: 'SM encounters between consenting adults involve a process of negotiation within the context of sexual pleasure. These negotiations, which are expressed as mixture of prior agreement and the more spontaneous/improvised situations that arise during a sexual encounter, are the means by which the participating individuals attempt to arrive at a "correct" balance in their relationships.' 'SM activity is typically an activity which requires extensive negotiation and planning.' SM sex 'should be fully consensual. . . . And for this consent to be present prior negotiation is essential to ensure that all the acts which a lover instigates are genuinely consented to'.[5]

Another worry is that a sexual activity takes over its participants in a way that precludes the possibility of communicating consent. The 'language' of sexual self-expression, to exploit a metaphor that must be used with caution, cannot 'speak' consent, and yet it is the only language sexual partners can use. This worry seems exaggerated. Any sexual activity which involves more than one person is a complex interplay between distinct incarnated intentionalities, seeking and giving pleasurable experiences. The possibilities of intimacy and openness to another which sexual activity involves mean that it is also the site of a heightened sensitivity to the wishes and feelings of another. That is not to deny that sexual encounters can be selfish, uncaring, brutal, unfeeling affairs. Many are. Nor is it to deny that the use of the 'communicative' metaphor of sexuality may be over-intellectualised.[6] However, sexual activity remains a willed or deliberate (if not always deliberative) activity. The behaviour of its participants can express and be recognised to express feelings—of pleasure, pain, anticipation, reluctance, agreement, dissent, and so on.

Yet another worry might be that the only satisfactory ways in which consent can be secured or communicated will ruin the passion of the sexual moment; they will interrupt the flow, destroy the spontaneity, put a dampener on things. All of these expressions are familiar ones in this context. They suggest that consensually negotiated sex is not impossible but is less satisfactory sex, for being colder, lacking spontaneity. The plausibility of this charge may depend greatly on how someone thinks the consent is negotiated. Defenders of the charge may neglect the ideal of 'negotiation within the context of sexual pleasure' articulated by the SM practitioner just quoted. They may subscribe to a caricatured portrait of consent being formally requested and formally given. (The Antioch College code of conduct unfortunately invited this kind of portrait.) They may, crucially, construe consent in ways that are insensitive to the particularities of any relationship or encounter, something to which I will return.

Importantly, this charge—and, generally, the thought that there is some necessary conflict between 'cold' consent and 'hot' sexuality—runs the risk of endorsing or giving a measure of support to two interrelated ideas. Both of these ideas need to be challenged. The first is that sex somehow comes as a seamless whole; it does not admit of levels or degrees. A related version of this idea is that sexual activity has a single *telos* or goal, standardly genital intercourse and ejaculation. Thus, any form of intimacy is conceived of as a preparation for, prior to, leading up to, but still less than this goal. Less than full intimacy cannot, within this view, be accepted and enjoyed for what it is in itself. The familiar colloquialism 'going all the way', resonates with this idea—there is one way, and it has a terminus. The dangerous, and evidently false, implication of subscription to either version of this idea is that agreement to some form of intimacy is, or betokens some measure of, agreement to full, complete sexual intimacy.

The second idea is of sexual arousal as having an increasing intensity and an increasing degree of involuntariness. The further one goes, the less easy it is to stop. One gives oneself over to a sexual pleasure which increasingly takes one over. The most frequently used metaphors are of an unstoppable train or a fire which once lit cannot be extinguished. These images are both pervasive and insidious. Their use has a number of dangerous implications, all of which are recognisable in accounts of problematic sexual encounters. The most important are that someone in the grip of a mounting sexual passion becomes less in control of and thus accountable for his behaviour and that the other party to a sexual encounter characterised by such an increase of passion should recognise the difficulties of controlling its further progress—it is hard to put out such a fire once it is lit.[7]

The 'climactic' model of sex which is constructed by both these ideas—of sex as having a unique *telos* and as marked by a developing urgency and irresistibility—is also associated with and favours what can be called a 'possessive' model of sex. This displays an asymmetrical understanding of sex as the 'possession' by one party, who strives for the pleasurable *telos* in coition, of the other, who is pleased in yielding to that striving. Both models are not unfairly represented as favouring men's understanding of their own (heterosexual) sexuality at the expense of women's.[8] Both are also models of sex that need to be disputed so that their assumptions and implications are not simply taken as facts of unchangeable nature.

Let me briefly indicate one way in which the models can be linked to understandings of consent and thereby generate serious problems. We saw in the last chapter that direct consent to P might be interpreted as indirect consent to Q when Q is the inevitable outcome of P. If it is thought that some level of sexual intimacy, but short of full coitus, must nevertheless always be followed by completed sexual intercourse, then direct consent to the first may be taken as indirect consent to the latter. Indeed many a man has complained that a woman's consent to some level of sexual activity was taken by him, and with good reason, to betoken consent to full sexual intimacy. However, that 'good reason' may derive from the 'climactic' model. A woman who goes most of the way is not thereby committed to going all the way. It is men who tend to think in terms of a point of no return.

Relationships Beyond Consent

The third and final worry about the very idea of sexual consent is best broached by means of an example.[9] Consider a group of close friends whose joint activities have, over the years, come to be characterised by a very high degree of mutual trust and understanding. They can confidently claim to know what the others think or would think about some matter affecting their interests. This group has co-operated in ways which involve the shared use of individually owned goods. For instance, the friends will on occasions borrow one another's car. It has come to be understood that this is done only when there is a real need to do so—somebody lacks alternative transport and has to get somewhere—and with due regard to the needs of the person whose car is borrowed—it will be used only if the friend does not have a prior, more pressing need, and it will be returned as soon as possible. Now the friends have come to be able to do this without any formal process of consultation or even advance notification.

John, for instance, knows that George is away on holiday, and George has, for security reasons, left a spare set of house keys with John. John needs a car—his own is being serviced—and knowing where George leaves his own car keys, John makes use of George's car. Although John does not bother to inform George until his return and after he has used the car, John feels entirely confident that George would not mind. Indeed he knows that both of them would see this possibility of mutual aid through the sharing of goods as being one of the features of their friendship which they both value highly. It is also true that at no point has George given his explicit consent to John's use of the car and that talk of a tacit consent to be inferred or implied from past behaviours would be a strained interpretation of their interactions. It is truer to say that this is just how their friendship has evolved into a relationship of deep mutual trust and understanding.

Consider now by way of contrast a consortium of taxi drivers each of whom drives the car he himself owns. In recognition of the difficulties they might face should one of their number find himself without his car—through an accident, breakdown, or whatever—they contract to put at the disposal of one another their own cars where this is at all possible. If someone, for instance, is working a different shift which does not overlap with that of the other who lacks a car, the presumption is that the first would be in a position to loan the second his car. The contract is very clear about all the circumstances in which this might be done, and it always requires the explicit agreement of the parties involved. Should there be any room for doubt, an acceptable outcome is subject to negotiation and bilateral agreement.

This example suggests a very familiar contrast between two kinds of social interaction. It is one that has been expressed in a number of ways.[10] Its relevance to the present discussion is as follows: The concern to secure consent seems to represent a requirement of the way in which the taxi drivers must interact, whereas it is not a requirement of the way in which the friends interact. A failure to seek consent for the use of another's car is at odds with the terms of the taxi drivers' association, whereas such a failure is fully consistent with the terms of the friends' association. There is a further point. Should one of the friends start regularly to seek permission for the use of another's car in circumstances where no such permission had previously been sought (or expected), one might reasonably fear that the terms of the friendship had changed and changed in ways that would naturally be described as a loss of friendship or a falling away from a previous level of trust. More strongly one might accuse the friend who starts insisting on the formalities of mutual borrowing as helping to bring about that very fall from grace. In contrasting terms a taxi driver who started borrowing one of his colleague's cars without asking would be breaking the consortium's contract and would properly be accused of undermining its conditions of existence.

Some political philosophers have argued both that there are forms of community which are 'beyond justice' or 'beyond rights'[11] and that an insistence upon regulation of the community's affairs by means of rights or principles of justice will destroy that which made the community beyond the need for such principles.[12] Might we not say that there are relationships which are, in this sense, 'beyond consent'? The friends who borrow one another's cars seem to exemplify this ideal. Are there not loving couples whose sexual relationships are similarly 'beyond consent'? And would it not be wrong to insist that their relationships be or become consensual?

A proper response to these questions contains two halves. The first half is that the idea of a loving couple who are 'beyond consent' is an ideal. That is not to deny that some couples may exemplify the ideal. But three cautions are in order. First, one must be careful to be sure that the behaviour of a couple is evidence of the ideal rather than something very different. In particular mutual trust and understanding should be distinguished from habits of acquiescence and passivity which might pass for the ideal. When nothing is or needs to be said between two people, that can just as easily spring from an exhaustion of the desire or capacity for dialogue as it can from a transcendence, through mutual understanding, of the need for it. This is true in sexual interaction as it is in many other areas. Second, relationships can and do change their character. What was once ideal can become less so. Because there was a time when there was no need for consent, it does not follow that now, under altered circumstances, the need does not press. Indeed it may press all the more strongly since the suspicion and uncertainty that follow upon a loss of trust and love can be all the stronger for arising from that failure of the ideal. Third, even within a loving couple one partner can initiate a new kind of sexual activity which it would be unwise to presume the other is agreed to. Even the most trusting of lovers may, on occasion, need to assure each other that what they are about to engage in is agreeable to both.

The second half of the response is that even the ideal as described may be covered by the Principles of Consensuality and Non-consensuality suitably modified. The relationship which lies 'beyond consent' is one whose parties *would* consent to their sexual interaction even though they do not, in fact, do so. It is true that George would consent to John's use of his car and that we have good reasons for knowing that this is true. We can say this without requiring or expecting of George that he will actually ever give his consent.

What Should We Presume?

The upshot of the foregoing is as follows: General principles of permissibility through consent should not be applied without a due sensitivity to the character of the relationships within which such principles are presumed to operate. The less familiar one person is with another, or the less familiar some practice is to either, the more imperative it becomes to be assured that what is done is consented to. The best context within which to set this thought is that of what we should presume when, using some principle of consensuality, we judge a sexual encounter as permissible or not.

In the previous chapter I said that, when consent is at issue, we should normally presume that it has not been given. That claim can now be made

more precise. For what is now at issue are the different degrees of familiarity that a relationship within which sex takes place may display. And it
seems appropriate to presume different things when we consider different
kinds of relationship or sexual encounter. A simple presumption of non-
consent is not sufficiently sensitive to these differences. Let me suggest then
that there are in fact three levels of presumption, each with a corresponding
question that needs to be asked unless we have grounds for not asking it.
The levels may be summarised as follows. At the first level of familiarity we
should ask if a couple are 'beyond consent' and whether, if this is so, the
question 'Is this relationship consensual?' is somehow inappropriate. At a
second level of lesser familiarity we presume that it is appropriate to ask if
the relationship is consensual, and here we need to ask 'Has the consent actually been given?' At a third and final level we presume that consent is
needed, that it has not been given, and here we need to ask further 'Is the
absence of dissent sufficient to indicate that consent is given?'

At the first level, then, we should not presume that a sexual encounter
takes place between a couple who are 'beyond consent'. Of each such encounter we should insist that it is impermissible if consent is not given. If
we are persuaded that consent is not given because those involved are related to each other in such a way that it is proper to speak of their relationship as lying 'beyond consent', then we can regard their encounter as permissible. Even at this level it is possible to inquire whether for this couple
this particular encounter is such as to be beyond their consent. The corresponding question is, Is there or is there not consent to this encounter? We
do not ask this question if we judge that the encounter lies 'beyond consent'. We will make this judgement of couples whose established relationship displays a certain measure of mutual trust and understanding. Of such
a couple's encounter we are able confidently to say that, although consent is
not given, it would be given.

At the second level of presumptiveness we judge some encounter as permissible or impermissible according to whether consent is or is not given.
Should the presumption be that consent is given, one that is defeated by evidence of its not being given? Or should the presumption be that consent is
not given, one that is defeated by evidence of its being given? If we use the
analogy of contracts, it would be reasonable to presume that consent is not
given. It is absurd to think that somebody is a party to each and every contract he could possibly have signed and to require that evidence of his non-
signature defeat this thought in each and every case. Rather, we look to see
if someone did sign a contract before concluding that he is a party to it.

However, we do not think of some activities that they need to be regulated by an explicit contract. Each party to the activity can rightly normally assume that the other will agree to what is being done unless she gives some evidence to the contrary. This is not a situation which lies 'beyond consent' but rather one that lies beyond the need to give one's consent. It is governed by the requirement of consensuality, but that requirement is normally met and may be assumed to be met. This will be the case where people have become familiar enough with what the other person wants in certain circumstances to feel warranted in making the assumption that they would agree to something and do not need to asked.

Consider the following analogy. Smith and Jones are strangers. Smith removes something of Jones's from Jones's house. Smith cannot claim that, since Jones did not dissent in advance to this removal, he, Smith, is not guilty of theft from Jones. Smith should presume that Jones does not consent to the loss of his possessions. Imagine now that Smith and Jones have participated in a regular co-operative pattern of behaviours. They are not deep trusting friends, but they know each other's character and actions well enough to judge what they would and would not agree to. Sometimes this judgement is simply based upon the fact that some interaction between them conforms to a regular, repetitive pattern. Smith has always borrowed Jones's lawnmower on a Sunday (Jones mows on a Saturday), and the weekly borrowing, which may or may not have begun with some formal request, has never met with a protest. Smith is surely entitled to think that Jones consents to his borrowing the lawn mower this Sunday. They do not, in this context, need a formal contract or declaration of consent.

It would seem to stand in exactly the same fashion with sexual encounters. Between strangers it is proper to presume that consent is not forthcoming. It would be wrong to think that consent is given unless there is evidence to the contrary. However, the initial presumption of non-consent is defeated if we have good reasons for thinking that the relationship is one of sufficient familiarity for consent not to need to be always explicitly given. Again this is a case not of a relationship which is 'beyond consent' so much as one that is beyond the need for the giving of explicit consent. It is a relationship which has need of consent; it is one whose conduct is mutually satisfactory only if each agrees to its terms. It is just that it has been managed over time in such a way as to obviate the need for actual consent to be given to each and every further instance of joint conduct.

The question corresponding to this level of presumption is, In this sexual encounter has consent been given? We should ask this question of every sexual encounter that does not lie 'beyond consent' unless we are satisfied that there is sufficient familiarity or enough of a well-established pattern to the relationship to judge that consent can normally be presumed within it.

We initially presume that a relationship is not 'beyond consent', and that any encounter within it is impermissible if not consented to, unless there is evidence that it is such a relationship and that the encounter fits within the terms of that relationship. We further presume that, if the relationship is not 'beyond consent', then any encounter within it is not consented to unless there is evidence of consent. This presumption is defeated if the relationship displays sufficient familiarity for us to judge that the encounter within it is consensual. However, if we do need to find evidence of consent, what should that be? At the final level of presumption we might presume that no dissent is evidence of consent or presume that only explicit positive signs indicate consent.

A very traditional view holds that a woman who does not protest is consenting. On this view it is evidence enough that she consents that she does not resist or show signs of refusal. Directly opposed to such a view is the claim that an affirmative verbal consent standard is needed. This standard holds that consent is given if and only if an explicit 'yes' or its verbal equivalent is uttered.[13] Let me suggest here that there is a bad reason for not adopting, and a good reason for adopting, the affirmative verbal consent standard. I will return to this question in Chapter 9.

The bad reason is to be found in the very familiar, traditional stereotype of women as essentially demure and passive sexual creatures. Femininity is constituted by a lack of explicit sexuality. This stereotype is attributable to the belief either that women are not sexual beings or that they are but are required not to display evidence of this nature. Women do not have sexual preferences or are forbidden to make them explicit. It may matter little whether such feminine modesty is innate or socially inculcated.[14] Consistent with this stereotype is the understanding of sexual encounters between men and women wherein it is men who must 'make the first move', who must initiate the encounter, and who must try to dictate its further terms; to women falls only the role of resisting or complying with the encounter and its progress. Man proposes; woman disposes.[15]

Are There Sexual Conventions?

The good reason for adopting the standard lies in the dangers of reliance on anything other than explicit affirmative consent. Most obvious in this context is the role that conventions might play in permitting people to express their agreement to sexual relations other than by explicit verbal consent. In the last chapter it was conceded that there could be agreed conventions whereby consent can be inferred from some action which is not, in itself, a public or express declaration of consent. It was noted that the use of such conventions should be distinguished from the regular succession of one behaviour by another and from quasi-consent. It was also noted that problems might arise where there was a dispute as to the existence of any convention.

In an important article Douglas Husak and George C. Thomas have argued that there are social conventions by which women express their agreement to sexual relations.[16] They cite psychological studies of 'courtship rituals' whereby women give non-explicit encouragement to sexual advances from men and indicate their willingness to be sexually intimate with them. The use of such rituals is, they say, understandable inasmuch as women are socialised not to be sexually forward or explicit and fear being characterised as promiscuous or 'loose' if they are. That women do regularly and systematically employ non-verbal solicitation behaviours is a matter for empirical investigation. Crucially the law should concern itself with how behaviour between the genders is currently patterned, and not seek to enforce an ideal of such behaviour which does not conform to the reality.

As we shall see, the crime of rape requires both that the sexual intercourse be unconsented and that the defendant proceed to have sexual intercourse despite his knowing that she does not consent.[17] If there are conventions of the kind suggested, then they will play an important role both in permitting women to express their consent to sex other than by explicit verbal agreement and in giving rise to reasonable beliefs on the part of men that women are consenting to sex with them.

Before we proceed to evaluate their argument, four brief points need to be made. First, it would be absurd to deny that there are no sexual conventions. In Chapter 1 I cited the example of sado-masochistic sexual activity whose practitioners recognise the importance of securing consent but also acknowledge the difficulty, given the nature of the activity, of ascertaining whether or not consent is being given to some practice. SM practitioners will engage in prior negotiation about the limits and terms of any encounter, and this may include prior agreement on conventions or rules by which agreement may be inferred from some behaviour.

Again a loving couple may, over time, have developed a clear understanding of what each party sexually wants and is prepared to do. Such an understanding may rely on conventions which they, but no others, share. Their relationship is all the better for having these wordless, yet conventional understandings of what is agreeable to them both. In the first case strangers can explicitly negotiate and agree on sexual conventions; in the second a loving couple gradually develop such conventions. The claim at the heart of the argument by Husak and Thomas is that *everyone*, including those who are strangers to one another, can reasonably rely on sexual conventions which have not been expressly agreed between them.

Second, it is also plausible to assert that sexually explicit behaviour may be taken as consent to further intimacy if it succeeds a direct inquiry as to whether such further intimacy is acceptable. If a woman responds to a man's question 'Do you want sex?' (or some similar unambiguous formulation) with a wordless but sexually explicit action, then *that* behaviour, in such a context, may be presumed to constitute consent. But it does in exactly the same way as my silently tossing you my car keys may be presumed to signify 'yes' in response to your request to borrow my car. No appeal to sexual conventions is necessary. Rather, it suffices to appeal to a general convention to the effect that some non-linguistic behaviour counts as an affirmative answer to a request for consent when it is that very behaviour (or behaviour clearly and unequivocally related to that behaviour) to which consent is being requested.

Third, no use is or should be made of a sexual convention to the effect that the absence of dissent signifies consent. Silent acquiescence to a man's advances may not thus be interpreted as consent. The argument is indeed that there are some explicit behaviours which constitute consent by falling under a sexual convention. Fourth, the alleged conventions, if they do have presumptive weight in allowing consent to be inferred from explicit behaviour, have such weight only where no explicit dissent has been given. It cannot be that a woman's behaviour falling under such a convention can be cited as evidence that she has consented against the fact that she said 'no'. 'Her lips said "no" but her eyes said "yes"' is a familiar excuse offered by a man who persists sexually in the face of his victim's protests. The claim must be that, in the absence of any other signs to the contrary, consent may be inferred from a behaviour by means of sexual convention.

So there are four large difficulties with the argument of Husak and Thomas. First, they describe the conventions in an ambivalent way. In particular they shift from a weaker to a much stronger construal of the conventions in question. There may indeed be conventions—'courtship rituals'—whereby a woman expresses her interest in another man, her willingness to be approached by him. This is not the same as saying that the woman, if approached, would consent to have sex with him. Nevertheless, there may be conventions governing a woman's behaviour which would give a man a reason to believe that a woman behaving in a certain fashion would consent to sex with him. But the conformity of her behaviour to that convention need not in itself be the consent.

Compare the following two argumentative forms:

A. 1. There is a convention to the effect that anyone who does P is consenting to Q;
B. 2. Smith does P;
C. Therefore, 3. Smith consents to Q.
D. 1. There is a convention to the effect that it may reasonably be believed that anyone who does P will consent to Q;
E. 2. Smith does P;
F. Therefore, 3. It is reasonable to believe that Smith will consent to Q.

There is a clear difference between the two arguments which turns on how the convention is to be understood and which licences quite different conclusions. It may be reasonable for a man, observing that a woman's behaviour falls under a convention, to believe that she would consent to sex. He may not be justified in believing that her behaviour *is* consent, since there is no convention to that effect.

Husak and Thomas shift from one claim to the other, and on one occasion they do so on the very same page. They say it is 'crucial to understand the convention by which women express their agreements to sexual relations', and they speak of convention 'wcs', standing for 'women's consent to have sex'. Several lines later they state that 'conformity with convention wcs is a reason to conclude that the man's belief [in the woman's consent] is reasonable, whether or not his partner has in fact consented'.[18] Of course, if convention 'wcs' is the convention *by which* women express their agreement, then conformity with the convention *is* consent. The man's belief in consent is true, and not just reasonable 'whether or not his partner has consented'.

The shift from one form of convention to another is, perhaps, to be explained by Husak and Thomas thinking of a convention as both a rule, which governs the meaning that can be imputed to a behaviour, and an inductively grounded regularity, which permits someone to predict what will succeed a behaviour. The difference is between a convention that gives a nod the meaning of 'yes' and a convention that says a wink is regularly succeeded by the giving of an affirmative answer. But a wink is not a nod, and there need be no convention that allows a wink to be read as a 'yes'.

The 'convention' is weaker still if it links together not a behaviour and the present giving of consent, but a behaviour and the probability of the giving in the future of consent. A woman's wink now may be regularly conjoined not with her present agreement to sex but with her likely agreement in the future. A man cannot reasonably claim that a woman's behaviour indicates current consent when at most it supports a prediction of probably subsequent consent.

The second difficulty with the argument of Husak and Thomas is that they fail to acknowledge the possibility that men and women attribute different meanings to the same behaviour. Since Husak and Thomas attach enormous importance to empirical evidence,[19] it is surely valid to note the wealth of material that documents cross-gender miscommunication, especially in the area of sexual interaction.[20] Among the most salient findings of this psychological research is that men consistently read behaviour in more sexual terms than women. They interpret friendly behaviour as conveying sexual interest and are more inclined than women to see certain dating scenarios as indicating a willingness to have sex. Men thus see a token piece of behaviour by a woman as indicating more sexual interest and willingness than do women.

It may be the case that women make use, consciously or unconsciously, of conventions whereby their behaviour can be understood in sexual terms. But they are not the same conventions as men use to understand the women's behaviour. What to a woman is just a wink is likely to be seen as a nod by a man. In the last chapter it was argued that a relevant consideration in deciding whether someone is entitled to rely on a convention is the extent to which the convention has a universally univocal meaning—that is, how many people understand the convention in the same unambiguous way. The evidence is that the convention to which Husak and Thomas appeal is not understood by women as it is by men. Moreover, given the same evidence, it is much more likely that women are not consenting when men think they are than that they are consenting when men think they are not. In short, male reliance on a convention of the sort Husak and Thomas favour regularly exposes women, without any obvious compensating rewards, to the risk of unconsented sex.

It may be said that women know the risks and should modify their behaviour accordingly—that is, conform their behaviour to the convention that men, if not they themselves, understand as prevailing. This does not help and merely compounds the problem. In the first place it is not as if men decide to read women's behaviour in one way, and women another. There need not be, and probably is not, conscious awareness of any conventions, or of any difference between those that men and those that women employ. Even those who might be expected to be aware of the difference need not be.[21] Let us assume that both genders do become aware of the difference. Why should women change *their* behaviour? It is men who run the risk of inflicting injury through a mistaken understanding, and it is they who should adopt a policy of caution. Moreover, they are able directly to confirm their understanding of women's wishes by inquiry. In these circumstances, reliance solely on a convention that is known not to be necessarily shared is culpably risky.

Even if there was a general change in women's behaviour to conform with men's expectations under the convention, there would still be merely a shifting of the initial problem to another level. The initial problem is one of co-ordination: A man should act in a certain way only if he can be sure that the woman wishes to go along with his actions. He relies on a convention to the effect that her behaviour indirectly signifies that wish. He learns that women do not behave in conformity with that convention. Even if, subsequently, most women do come to conform their behaviour with the convention, he cannot be sure that *this* woman has changed her patterns of behaviour. There is, in short, still a problem of co-ordination. A man cannot be sure that every woman has acted according to the higher-order convention, that where a lower-order convention is disputed between the genders, a woman will act to conform to the male understanding of the lower-order convention.[22]

The third difficulty with the approach of Husak and Thomas is that there is a certain, irreducible tension between the generality of conventions and the particularity of each and every sexual interaction. When Smith allows Jones to undress her, she is engaging in a particular behaviour with a particular person in a particular situation. The convention 'wcs' of which Husak and Thomas speak abstracts from all these particularities. If allowing oneself to be undressed falls under a convention 'wcs', then Smith is consenting to sex with Jones, as she or anyone would be who did the same thing with any other person in any other set of circumstances. Smith is to be understood as consenting *whenever* and to *whomever* she behaves in this way. However, sexual behaviour, even between a long-standing couple, is rarely of a uniform character. It is likely to be modulated by immediate circumstances, present expectations, just-past events, mood, and disposition to the other. Therein lies the pleasure of discovering the unexpected within the familiar.

It is reasonable to expect someone to be sensitive to these particularities of any sexual encounter, and to regard anyone who relies exclusively on general conventions as grossly insensitive. Husak and Thomas acknowledge that a man, trying to interpret a woman's responses to his own initiative, may operate not only with the social convention 'wcs', but also with a 'specific schema' that reflects how she 'has responded to similar advances in the past'. They argue that his knowledge of her sexual history, 'particularly with him', is relevant to his interpretation.[23] A man may come to realise that the behaviour of a woman with whom he has a sexual history conforms to one or several conventions 'wcs'. However, what should surely matter to him in his relationship to her is not that these conventions, being applicable to all, govern her behaviour towards him. She and he have their own 'specific schema', which just happens to be consonant with the alleged conventions 'wcs'.

He may, on the other hand, come to realise that her behaviour does not conform, entirely or in part, to the conventions 'wcs'. Husak and Thomas cannot surely believe that the man should still give a presumptive weight to these conventions, arguing to himself, as it were, that as a woman-in-general she must mean this by her behaviour even if as this particular woman she does not give her behaviour that meaning. The 'specific schema' simply supplants the conventions 'wcs'. In short, it is not that some 'specific schema' should operate in conjunction with conventions 'wcs'. Such a schema should operate independently of, and without the need for, any such supposed conventions.

The fourth difficulty with the analysis of Husak and Thomas is that they appear simply to discount the duty upon men of seeking to assure themselves that women are consenting when there is a risk of mistake by exclusive reliance upon the convention. In the last chapter it was argued that it is wrong to rely exclusively on a risky and uncertain convention when this is not necessary. Everything seems to suggest that this is how things are in the present context. It is not reasonable to rely upon a convention 'wcs' which is not universally acknowledged or unambiguous. At the same time it is possible for men directly to inquire of women whether or not they are consenting. The harm to a woman of unconsented sex is much graver than that of the loss to a man who refrains from proceeding to have sex without consent.

Husak and Thomas concede that there may be an emerging convention which does impose on men an affirmative duty 'to be more certain that the women [*sic*] is truly consenting'. Husak and Thomas maintain that only 'careful empirical research, not wishful thinking' can confirm the hope that this is happening.[24] However, the duty in question is deducible from a general, natural duty to avoid causing harm to others, where this can be done at no unreasonable cost to oneself. The duty is not a social convention in the way that the convention 'wcs' is, and the duty's prescriptive force is not dependent upon the existence of some social rule which acknowledges it. It may well be that very many men are presently failing to fulfil the duty. That is to be condemned, and the demand that men change their ways does not need to wait on empirical evidence that, as a matter of fact, they are starting to recognise that they should.

Is It Necessary to Say 'Yes' to Everything?

There are reasons then to doubt that there are sexual conventions in the manner alleged. At the very least it is, in general, unreasonable for men to rely on the assumption that there are in their relationships with women. To repeat, the wrongness of relying on such conventions provides a good reason for employing an affirmative verbal standard of consent. However, it should be emphasised that the case for such a standard has been made within the context of an encounter where it is presumed both that such an encounter is permissible only if consensual and that it is consensual only if there is evidence that the consent has been given. The further question then arose of what should count as evidence of consent, and the case was made for presuming that only the giving of an explicit affirmative should count.

That presumption is defeated if there is good reason to think that some particular couple do both understand and operate by an agreed convention of sexual consent. Carefully distinguishing among different kinds of relationship and encounter allows us to specify which presumptions should be made in any particular case. It does not follow from what has been argued previously that in every sexual encounter consent must be given in the form of an explicit verbal affirmative. A relationship may be 'beyond consent' in the manner indicated, or it may be one where it is reasonable to infer consent from a regular pattern of past behaviours, or it may be one where it is reasonable to think that the same conventions of consent are being relied upon by both persons. Where none of this can reasonably be believed to be the case, it is proper to operate with all the levels of presumption outlined.

In short, what is proper to the sexual relationship between strangers need not be appropriate for lovers of long standing. Insistence upon the operation of an explicit verbal affirmative standard if any sex within the latter kind of relationship is to be permissible is mistaken. But the fact that it would be does not show that such a standard is not rightly insisted upon when it comes to the evaluation of an encounter between two people who barely know each other. That it is important sometimes to ask for a 'yes' does not mean that it is necessary to say 'yes' to everything.

◀ 3 ▶

Sexual Consensuality

THIS CHAPTER AND THE NEXT TWO ARE concerned with the plausibility of the Principles of Consensuality and Non-consensuality, which were stated in the first chapter. In other words they are concerned with the plausibility of the general view that whatever transpires sexually between consenting adults without affecting others is morally permissible. The three chapters do not offer a full-blown defence of the general view. They are more interested in exploring how that view might be defended and what sorts of problems it faces. The failure to offer a comprehensive defence is not an admission that the view cannot be defended. The view expresses an understanding of what is and is not tolerable in sexual matters which commands widespread popular acceptance. It is also the case that the defence of the view would be made in terms which are very familiar from contemporary writing in jurisprudence and social philosophy.

It is worth trying to provide an account of what gives the general view its moral distinctiveness. What is it about consensuality that makes consensual sex permissible? What exactly is consensuality? And is consensuality enough? These three questions indicate three broad areas of fruitful discussion: the principles which might underpin the legitimating role of consent, the definition of valid consent, and the question of whether the Principles of Consensuality and Non-consensuality provide necessary and sufficient conditions of moral permissibility. This chapter will take up the first two areas of discussion; the next two chapters will turn to the third area.

What Is It About Consensuality That Makes Consensual Sex Permissible?

The answer to this question, assuming that there is one, can best be approached if one appends a 'because' to the Principles of Consensuality and

Non-consensuality and then considers what, most plausibly, might succeed that 'because'. For the moment let us simplify matters by ignoring third parties and assuming that the consent given is valid. Sue and Harry engage in consensual sex. The Principle of Consensuality states that their sexual activity is permissible. We can now ask why it is permissible by asking what might follow the 'because' in 'The consensuality of the sex between Sue and Harry makes it permissible because . . . ' A parallel form of explanation will apply if the sex between Sue and Harry is non-consensual and impermissible.

Let me suggest that there are three kinds of answer to the question of what might follow the 'because'. The first is of the form 'because neither Sue nor Harry will then be treating the other merely as means'. This answer gives expression to some version of the familiar Kantian principle that individuals are ends and not merely means and should be treated accordingly. The second is of the form 'because this is what Sue and Harry freely choose to do'. This answer gives expression to the familiar liberty principle that individuals should be free to do as they choose, subject to standard constraints (one of which is captured by the proviso that the interests of third parties should not be significantly harmed). The third answer is of the form 'because Sue and Harry own their selves, including most obviously their bodies, and may dispose of these as they wish'.[1] This answer gives expression to a version of the libertarian principle of self-ownership whereby each person belongs to herself.

Before assessing each of these three answers, let me rule out a fourth, which takes the form 'because that is what Sue and Harry want to do'. Even if it were the case that whatever Sue and Harry want to do is permissible, it should be clear that it need not be the case that whatever Sue and Harry consent to do they also want to do. Chapter 1 made the distinction between agreeing *to* and agreeing *with* something, emphasising that a person's consent to some outcome did not imply either their approval of that outcome or their taking pleasure from that outcome. Chapter 2 suggested that 'individuals will normally only consent to what they believe they will find pleasurable and only find pleasurable what they consent to'. However, the use of 'normally' is important. One party may consent to, but not want, some sexual activity. Sue might prefer unwanted sex with Harry to the ending of that relationship (Harry insisting that sexual intimacy is a necessary condition of his continuing to have a relationship with Sue). This suffices to show that unwanted sex is not necessarily unconsented.[2] It is worth adding that this situation need not be one-sided. Sue and Harry might be the willing parties to an agreed marriage and to its consummation, despite failing to find each other attractive and deriving no enjoyment from its sexual side.

Of the Kantian principle two things can be, and often are, said. First, the Kantian principle does not proscribe treating another as a means; it rules out treating the other merely as a means. It is permissible to treat another as a means provided that one also treats them as an end. Second, what is required of treating another as an end, beyond not treating them as a means, is unclear. What positively is required by way of one's attitude to the other or in one's treatment of the other is not made precise by Kant. It might, for instance, be said that only to act towards the other with their consent just is to treat the other as an end. Correlatively, to act towards the other without their consent or in defiance of their dissent just is to treat the other as a means. This is to define treating the other as an end as treating the other as someone whose consent should count as a decisive consideration against treating them in certain ways. However, we want to know *why* a person's consent should count.

Let me suggest a different understanding of what it is to treat the other as a means or as an end. To treat the other as a means is to have regard for the other only insofar as she serves one's own ends. To treat the other as an end is to have regard for her own purposes and desires, taking these into account in the formulation of one's own actions towards her. The following then are paradigmatic examples of sexually treating another merely as a means and treating the other as an end, and from these examples we can see how they relate to the issue of consent. If Harry has sex with Sue solely for the purpose of deriving sexual gratification from the encounter and with no concern for what Sue might get out of it, if Harry pursues this end single-mindedly and never allows himself to think of how it might be for Sue, then Harry treats Sue merely as a means to his ends. If, by contrast, Harry derives pleasure from his sex with Sue but also strives to attend to Sue's pleasure and conducts the encounter in a way that is sensitive to her needs, then Harry does not treat Sue merely as a means.

That the sexual relationship between Sue and Harry is consensual does not mean that neither one of them is treating the other merely as a means. Sue may consent to (and want) Harry thinking only of his own pleasure and in the pursuit of that pleasure to use her as a means. This may be true of some or all sexual encounters within what might be a prolonged relationship, or this may be true of a single sexual encounter. I will return to the question of whether such use of another is morally impermissible. However, the permissibility of a consensual sexual relationship is not to be explained as due to that relationship's not involving either person treating the other merely as a means. Sue may not consent to Harry using her merely as a means to his pleasure. The Principle of Non-consensuality says that this is wrong because one party does not consent, not because one party is treated solely in instrumental terms. The Principle of Consensuality must also say that Sue and Harry's consensual sex is permissible even if one or both use the other merely as means to their own ends.

Is the consensual sex between Sue and Harry permissible because Sue and Harry each own themselves and may therefore dispose of themselves as they wish? Two points should be made immediately. First, a principle of self-ownership is not the same as a principle of freedom.[3] A principle of self-ownership is limited by conditions and considerations which constrain ownership in general, such as those governing permissions to destroy or alienate what is owned. A principle of freedom, on the other hand, is constrained by considerations such as the requirement that all should enjoy equal maximal freedom or that freedom should not be exercised in ways that harm the interests of others. In rough terms, the first principle expresses the ideal that somebody should be in control of their own person; the second, that a person should be in control of how their life is led. The two kinds of control need not coincide. Second, it is not clear what, for sexual ends, it is that a person owns and disposes of—their selves, their bodies, or some power of theirs.

Brief consideration of the example of a prostitute will serve to illustrate these points. A prostitute owns what, in the first instance, she sells or perhaps rents to her client. Even the fiercest critic of prostitution does not deny that. However, it is arguable that, for many of her class at least, she does not act freely precisely inasmuch as what she rents is all she has to offer. The status of the prostitute who is forced onto the street by economic necessity is akin to that of Marx's proletarian, compelled to sell his labour power, which is undoubtedly his to sell, to the capitalist. Both prostitute and proletarian are self-owning but unfree agents.

What is it that the prostitute sells? She does not sell herself; she does not alienate to her client, in the manner of a slave, those rights over herself which constitute her self-ownership. Perhaps she rents the use of her body for a specified purpose and a limited period. Or it could be argued instead that she sells a service. A barber does not rent his hands to the customer; he sells them the skilled use of his hands to a specific end. But perhaps the prostitute does also sell something of wider, more general import, such as a certain image or understanding of women and their sexuality. It is less clear what rights a prostitute has over *that*. In sum, what a prostitute who is said to be self-owning does own, and thus what she may sell or rent, is open to serious question.

Nevertheless, does Sue's and Harry's consenting to sex with each other make that sex permissible because Sue and Harry can dispose of what they own, namely, their own persons? If the example of the prostitute economically forced to sell herself is compelling, then it may be said that what somebody does with their own person is not really free. What is licensed by a principle of self-ownership may not be voluntary, and, to that extent, consensual. On the other hand, what is not consented to may not violate the principle of self-ownership. Imagine that Harry derives sexual gratification from behaving in certain ways towards Sue that do not involve his touching or even being physically close to her but to which she clearly and explicitly objects. Harry exhibits himself, or makes an obscene phone call to her. Harry engages in sexual behaviour harmful to Sue's interests to which Sue does not consent. Yet he does not take from her anything over which she has rights under a principle of self-ownership. It seems then that the permissibility of a consensual sexual relationship is not to be explained as due to that relationship's not involving a violation of the principle of self-ownership.

It does seem much more plausible to think that the permissibility of Sue and Harry's consensually engaging in sex is to be explained by the fact that this is what they freely choose to do. There is a familiar argument which explains this fact. As was pointed out in the first chapter, my consenting to something puts me under an obligation in respect of that thing. If I am obligated to do X, then I am, to that extent, not free not to do X. Sue's agreeing to have sex with Harry amounts to her not standing in the way of Harry having sex with her. Thus, my consenting to something limits my freedom, and it is reasonable to think that my limiting of my freedom should only be done freely. John Locke thought that the contract by which individuals enter into civil society, thereby constraining the exercise of the freedoms they enjoyed in the state of nature, could only be made freely: 'Man being, as has been said, by nature all free, equal, and independent, no one can be put out of this estate, and subjected to the political power of another, without his own consent. The only way whereby any one divest himself of his natural liberty, and puts on the bonds of civil society, is by agreeing with other men to join and unite into a community'.[4]

If the giving of consent is the expression of a freely made choice, it is also true, by contrast, that acting without or against the consent of another is the violation of their freedom. And, to that extent, unconsented sex is wrong because it is unchosen. I say 'to that extent' because, as was argued in the last chapter, a sexual relationship might not be actually consented to and yet be one that would be consented to and one that would be freely chosen. If the permissibility of consensual activities is to be found in the fact that such activities are freely chosen, then we are also directed to one account of what makes consent valid—namely, that it does express the free choice of whoever it is that gives their consent. The problems of such an account can now be explored.

What Exactly Is Consensuality?

This is the question of what make consent valid. The favoured standard account maintains that there are three conditions which must be satisfied if any instance of consent is to be held valid: The consent must be given by someone capable of doing so; it must be informed by knowledge of all relevant, material facts; and it must be voluntary.[5] Let me consider each of these in turn.

Capacity

An individual must have the capacity to give her consent. This capacity comprises both an ability to understand the nature of that to which she is consenting and an ability to make a decision in respect of the matter. The lack of such a capacity may be permanent, as would be the case with someone who is seriously mentally ill or disabled. It may be temporary, as would be the case with someone gravely affected by drugs or alcohol, or who was suffering from a short-lived psychological disturbance, such as serious depression. A child is judged to lack the capacity of an adult but not to be permanently disabled in that she will acquire capacity with age.

Clearly some courses of action are more complex and difficult to appreciate than others; it would follow that they require a greater degree of understanding. The law may wish to reflect that difference by, for instance, fixing a higher or lower age at which consent can be validly given to various activities. The 1957 Wolfenden Committee recommended that the age of homosexual consent be higher than that, sixteen, for heterosexual consent on the grounds that 'a boy is incapable, at the age of 16, of forming a mature judgement about actions of a kind which might have the effect of setting him apart from the rest of society'.[6]

Wherever the age of majority is fixed, we may presume normal sane adults to be capable of giving their consent. This is what others term 'a presumption of global competence'.[7] But how serious must a temporary disturbance of a person's mental state be for any consent she gives to be invalid? Consider the influence of alcohol. Many people engage in drunken sex. It is true, but not telling, that individuals may, when drunk, have sex that they would not have when sober. For it is also true, and telling, that, when sober, they know this to be the case and get drunk in that knowledge. Very many of us deliberately acquire 'Dutch courage' in the awareness of how it is acquired (and can only be acquired). It is also true that people regret what they did when drunk and know that they would not have done it if sober. They may, for that reason, regret getting drunk. But, again, what is true is that individuals know what they are inclined to do when intoxicated and, knowing that, still take drink. What does seem important, then, is that individuals should be aware of what it is that drink does to them and deliberately decide to take drink. That is, they 'consent' to their drunkenness. Insofar as they do, their consent when drunk may be presumed valid. It is clearly otherwise with individuals who do not know what drunkenness entails or who do not agree to become drunk. Someone who is slipped a doctored drink and becomes inebriated in consequence cannot be held accountable for that to which they subsequently might agree.

However, there is a further question. At what point of drunkenness may an individual's agreement to sex be considered beside the point? There must be such a point even if there was an initial willingness to start getting drunk. Somebody may agree to make themselves incapable of giving their consent. Such an achieved incapacity undercuts the validating force of the original first voluntary step. There is a continuum of drunkenness which runs from tipsy to unconscious. Clearly a comatose person is not able to consent to (or even properly to participate in) sexual activity. But, even short of being unconscious, somebody may be so drunk as not to be aware of what they are doing or incapable of making a decision. In the 1993 case of Austen Donnellan, a student acquitted of rape, which attracted considerable press attention, the accuser testified that she had drunk so much as to have passed out. She was barely aware of the sex to which it was alleged she consented. The press made much of the fact that, earlier in the evening, she had behaved in an abandoned way as a result of her drinking. She had been seen dancing with and kissing the accused. The press reported the police forensic opinion, which Sue Lees rightly judges prejudicial, 'that from the amount [she] had drunk—three pints of cider, a vodka and two Drambuies—although her alcohol level would not be enough to induce a coma, drink was an aphrodisiac and she would have been "very very drunk and very very sexy"'.[8] Someone behaves in a less inhibited way because she is drunk, and insofar as she knowingly took drink, she can be held responsible for such behaviour. But when her drunkenness induces a stupor, she cannot be held, within such a state, to consent, even though she may be held responsible for getting into the state. Drink may make someone 'very, very sexy' but someone who is 'very, very drunk' may also be simply incapable of engaging in consensual sex.[9]

Information

Someone who consents must be in the know about what it is they are consenting to and what it entails. Consent must be informed to be valid—that is, the person consenting must be possessed of all the relevant material facts bearing significantly on the decision to consent. The person does not need to know everything, only everything that would make a real difference to whether or not she consented. These facts can concern what is being consented to, prior or background information bearing on that which is consented to, or what may transpire in consequence of the giving of consent. Ignorance of or mistakes in respect of these facts may be no person's fault. Or they may be attributed to the culpable action (or inaction) of either party to the consensual exchange.

The law recognises that consent may be fraudulently obtained through a deliberate misrepresentation of relevant facts. The law also recognises a distinction between fraud in the *factum* and fraud in the inducement. The first constitutes a misrepresentation of the act itself or the identity of the persons involved in the act; the second, of some state of affairs which supplies a motive for the other to consent. An example of the first would be a doctor falsely representing sexual intercourse with a patient as a vaginal examination or surgical operation or of a woman having sex with someone she is deceived into believing is her regular sexual partner. An example of the second would be a doctor falsely representing sexual intercourse as a necessary part of a patient's therapeutic treatment. In the first the person does not know what it is she is agreeing to; in the second she does but is misled as to the reasons she has for doing what she agrees to do.

Examples of the fraud in the *factum* are rare, though there have been recent cases involving impersonation.[10] I could concede that a person might well be misled as to who had entered her bed on a dark night, but add that only the unbelievably naive or ignorant could fail to know that sexual intercourse was taking place. Nevertheless, it is proper to insist that a real harm may be done even to the artless and unknowing, however astonished we are by their ignorance. As to fraud in the inducement to sexual intercourse the law is inclined not to regard it as constituting an instance of rape and rather to provide for a separate crime, such as procuring by deception.[11] Take, for example, the case of a prostitute whose client promises to pay for her services but who subsequently does not (or pays with counterfeit notes).[12] We are inclined to say of such a case that it is not as serious an offence as that of the doctor misrepresenting an examination to his naive patient and that this difference, that between fraud in the inducement and fraud in the *factum*, is to be explained in terms of a difference between 'what is consented to'. Is this an adequate explanation?

We might suggest that the prostitute consents to the act of sexual intercourse, though she does not consent to the terms on which it is conducted, whereas the naive patient does not consent to the act itself, imagining herself to be agreeing to something completely different. But consider that the unsuspecting woman who sleeps with a man she thinks to be her husband, and is deceived in the *factum*, does agree to the act of sex. She does not agree to sex with this particular person. Perhaps the act of sex is inseparable from its object, the person with whom sex is engaged in, in a way that is not true of the relationship between an act and its rewards, such as monetary payment. We might expect the wife quickly to realise that the man in her bed was not her husband, since, for her, sex-with-him is essentially different (and recognisable as such) from sex-with-another. That, of course, need not be so. A wife who engaged in sex with her husband from habit, conjugal duty, or whatever might well have become so indifferent to the act as to be insensitive to its object. And that would be true while it was still the case that she did consent to sex with her husband but would not consent to sex with someone else.

Consider, also, that inducement to the act might be such as to constitute the very act in a certain light. What the act is in itself and what the act means for the person who consents may not be as separable as an act and its monetary payment are. The practised seducer falsely but successfully represents sex to his victim as demanded by the love they both feel for each other, or as a prospect of barely imaginable joy. Neither love nor transport of delight are forthcoming. The woman is induced to consent to that which she then experiences as considerably less and other than her seducer led her to believe it would be. The difficulty here may be simply due to slippage in the notion of 'what is consented to'. Retaining a robust but defensible understanding of the act in itself as distinct from collateral matters will preserve the required separation of the two forms of fraud. However, the discussion does suggest that making the distinction in this way will not obviously explain the difference in gravity between the two.

Joel Feinberg suggests that this difference is to be found in the fact that the sexual relations which result from fraud in the inducement may be presumed to be '*not be very harmful*, if harmful at all'.[13] The plausibility of this suggestion derives much of its force from the contrast between the cheated prostitute and the misled patient. Both suffer harms, but the harm to the former is merely a monetary loss, whereas those to the latter are 'the pains of depression, shame, loss of self-esteem, and tortured conscience, if not pregnancy and more obvious harms'.[14] This is probably true but need not be so. Imagine that the deceived patient never comes to know that what transpired was sexual intercourse, that there are no harmful consequences, and that she experienced what did occur as no more than uncomfortable. She may still be said to have suffered a harm, but it is not one that can be described in terms of the evident or perceived damages Feinberg lists. Imagine, as a corollary, that a woman so despises men and the sexual act that she can only bring herself to engage in sex for money. Is it not evident that she suffers serious harm if she has sex without payment?

Feinberg wants to appeal to the thought that the unwillingness to engage in some sexual act is part of its very (and possibly serious) harmfulness. The cheated prostitute is willing to have sex for money, and thus 'the sexual episode in itself is not a clear harm to her'.[15] The deceived patient is harmed by the very fact of her unwilling (because unknowing) engagement in sex. But the discussion suggests that it may be too simple to speak of a 'sexual episode in itself', which at most has a compensateable cost. Further, by ironic contrast, the 'sexual episode in itself' may, its unwillingness apart, have minor costs for the naive patient. Compare the prostitute with the victim of seduction who will have sex only for love and who is cruelly misled as to the feelings of her seducer. In Laclos's *Les Liaisons dangereuses* (1782) Valmont seduces Madame de Tourvel, a woman of immense virtue and religious faith. She does not renounce her faith and believes Valmont's protestations of his love for her very moral integrity. In the wake of his exposure as a deceiving blackguard she dies of a broken heart. It sounds strange to say that she is willing to have sex for love and thus that 'the sexual episode in itself is not a clear harm to her'. A wrong is done to both the prostitute and the deceived patient, which probably lies simply in the fact in itself of their unwilling participation in the sexual act. This suggests a better way to think about the examples and the two kinds of fraud.

We must be cautious here and not extend too far the application of a wrong of fraudulent inducement. Consider Glanville Williams's rhetorical question 'How many men have caused a woman to yield by deceitfully saying, "I love you"?'[16] What would cause us not to characterise sex obtained by false proclamations of love as unconsented? Such a case needs to be one in which the sex is obtained *only* by such a proclamation—it is not that the woman would have yielded even if he had not said the words—and also one in which the falsity of the proclamation is crucial—a woman may want to *hear* a man say 'I love you' even if she does not believe him when he does. What distinguishes the insincere declaration of love from the false promise of monetary payment are two features which bear on the expectations someone who hears them can reasonably form. The first is the prevalence of a proper and general suspicion of such declarations of love. No one but the most naive believes that every statement of love is sincere. All of us come to learn that protestations of affection and regard will often be well meant but need not be. Second, someone who receives a promise to pay a certain sum of money has a clear and determinate sense of what is being promised. This is not so with a confession of love. It is not just that how love might show itself varies greatly. It is also that what people think of as love is as different and individual as the persons who profess it and the objects of their devotion. How wrong does someone go who really does claim to love a person for just that one night? Whereas the prostitute and client have the same idea of what was offered and is not forthcoming (a particular sum of money), it can never be the same with the love declared by one person to another. Consider that somebody could claim to be misled even by a sincere declaration of love ('But you said you loved me and love is forever').

There are aspects of a sexual act—what, why, and with whom—about which, and there are also degrees to which, a person may be misled in respect of that act. The more completely a person is misled, the less willingly she can be said to engage in that act, and the more wronged she is if she does engage in that act. She is wronged to the extent that her will is not implicated in the act and it does not express her free choices. She is wronged in this way independently of other harms that may result from her unwilling participation. Our intuition is that to be deceived in the *factum* is to be completely misled about an important, indeed probably crucial, aspect of the act. To be deceived in the inducement is to be less than completely misled about the act. That is why we are inclined to think of fraud in the inducement as less grave than fraud in the *factum*. We are inclined to think this not because the 'sexual episode in itself' is the more harmful in the one case than in the other. It is rather that in the one the will of the person having sex is less implicated than in the other, and thus a lesser wrong is done to the agent.

Voluntariness

The preceding discussion of information and fraud has served a further useful purpose. It has drawn attention to the fact that, as Feinberg again notes, 'the voluntariness of actions, including acts of consent, does seem to vary under different kinds of fraud'.[17] An act of consent is valid if it is voluntary. But while there may be degrees of voluntariness, there cannot be degrees of consensuality. Consent is either given or not given. Is there a point then at which an act is so involuntary as not to be consensual? And, if so, where should that point be fixed?

It may be useful to start with paradigm cases of clear involuntariness at the top end of the scale and work downward. The clearest case of involuntariness will be one in which the will of the person is literally forced. If a woman is physically held down, restrained, and sexually violated, then, beyond any possible doubt, she does not consent to the sex. A woman may be coerced into compliant sexual behaviour by threats of harm. She complies from fear, and, again, her consent is invalid. A familiar distinction between threats and offers is that the former are proposals to worsen, the latter proposals to improve, the outcome of the other's choice of action from what it would normally be, the proposal being made with the intention of securing the compliance of the other's choice with the proposer's wishes.[18] For such threats to be considered coercive, we need to say of the consequences threatened that they are significant, proximate, and real.

By significant I mean that a real harm is proposed. A threat to kill or mutilate is coercive; a proposal to poke the other in the arm is not. However, it is important to recognise that the harms proposed may be nonphysical. After all in the classic crime of blackmail the victim is threatened with public exposure of some facts which would seriously damage her status and esteem. In Australian law consent is negated 'by a threat to publicly humiliate or disgrace . . . the person'.[19] English law seems to be less consistent in this regard. A man was convicted of rape who had pretended to be a security officer and secured his victim's submission to sexual intercourse by saying that otherwise he would inform the police and her parents that she had been having intercourse in a public place. In another case a man was convicted only of attempting to procure intercourse with a woman whom he threatened with disclosing to her employers that she had once been a prostitute.[20]

By proximate I mean two things. First, the harm proposed is immediate. More precisely it cannot be avoided before she must decide whether to comply or not. A proposed harm may be distant in time but such that somebody can do nothing between now and then to avoid it. Second, the harm is proximate in that it will befall the person or somebody very close to her. A threat to kill or mutilate a woman's child is coercive; a threat to harm a total stranger is not. By saying that a harm is real, I mean that it is one that it is reasonable to believe the person making the threat can bring about and that it is not one the person threatened can take reasonable steps to avoid. A threat to cause someone spontaneously to combust is not real; nor is one to physically harm the other if made by an unarmed weakling to an armed able-bodied person.

The threat can be explicit or implicit. If I am approached in a dark, deserted alley by two large men carrying baseball bats, one of whom makes the gesture of inviting a contribution from me, no threats are issued; indeed no words are spoken. But I may understand them to be threatening severe violence if I do not hand over my valuables.[21] Note too that consent may be invalid if a coercive threat is reasonably believed to be made, yet none is intended. That is, consent may be invalid in the absence of a coercive threat. Many an anecdote is told of passers-by rushing to the rescue of robbery 'victims' who are, in fact, actors filming on the street. Imagine that an actor playing the role of a mugger accosts someone he mistakenly believes to be another actor but who is in fact a passer-by. The actor's 'threat'—'Your money or your life'—is reasonably but falsely believed to be genuine so is sufficient to coerce compliance. The 'threat' need not even be explicit. Imagine a woman mistakenly thinks the stranger who strikes up an acquaintance with her is a dangerous, escaped criminal. She complies with his requests in the false belief that failure to do so would provoke violence, though this is not so and is certainly not explicitly threatened.

When the harm threatened is sincerely, even if not truly, believed to be significant, proximate, and real, whether the threat is explicit or implicit, then the consent obtained is invalid. We may say that, in these circumstances, fear invalidates the consent. A point at this stage about the crime of rape is in order. The *actus reus* of rape, that is, the conduct which makes it a crime, is sexual intercourse without the consent of the woman. However, a traditional and influential definition of rape from the seventeenth century holds rape more particularly to be intercourse without consent 'by force, fear or fraud'. It might seem to follow from such a definition that only 'force, fear or fraud' can negate consent such that rape, unconsented sex, is sex obtained by 'force, fear or fraud'. Or it may be that consent can be negated in ways other than by 'force, fear or fraud', but that the crime of *rape* requires that the consent be negated by 'force, fear or fraud'. There might be other crimes besides rape in which consent is improperly secured and thus is invalid. In short one question concerns how we should define rape; another concerns when consent may be said to be invalid. I will return to the first in Chapter 9. The second merits attention now.

Clearly one can imagine the harms threatened varying in their seriousness, proximity, and reality, and, in proportion to such variation, our judgement of involuntariness would also vary. To repeat, there are degrees of voluntariness below that of the clear involuntariness of 'force and fear'. At what point should we fix the degree of involuntariness to which corresponds lack of consent? A useful guiding thought here is provided by the conclusion reached previously that what matters about consent, and what gives plausibility to the view that whatever is consensual is morally permissible, is that the giving of consent is the expression of a freely made choice. At what point then is the giving of consent no longer the expression of a freely made choice? The point is when a person's will is 'forced', 'overborne', or 'overcome'.[22] We can imagine cases in which no choice at all is made. Consider the woman who submits to the rapist in paralysed terror. No thought of whether she should or should not comply occurs. She is simply seized by a blind, overwhelming terror which compels her to do as she is ordered. She is 'forced' as the physically restrained and overcome woman is. In one case the forcing is effected through her mind, in the other through her body.

But imagine that the woman does entertain the thought of resisting the rapist. She is aware of the awfulness of the impending rape, as she is also of the reality and severity of the threats made to her, and of the opportunities to escape those threats. She calculates that compliance is the lesser of two evils. It may be said that whereas in the previous case the woman's ability to make any kind of choice was overwhelmed, in the present case a choice is made. There are alternatives open to the woman. Some might choose death rather than dishonour; she does not. If 'Hobson's choice' is, in effect, the 'choice' of only one course of action on offer, 'Hobbes's choice' is that of a course of action whose only alternative is grossly unattractive.[23]

Thomas Hobbes thought that an agreement secured under threat was, nevertheless, a willing agreement.

This seems wrong. What then makes the woman's 'choice' to have sex under threat an unfree one? The man issuing the threat may be described as deliberately structuring the context of the woman's choice so as to bring about the 'choice' he desires. He does this by proposing consequences for non-compliance with his demand that render it extremely unattractive. One way of expressing the degree of unattractiveness involved would be to say that compliance is thereby made *irresistible*.[24] This may be so but will mean that 'Hobbes's choice' is like that of the person who is psychologically overwhelmed by fear of the proposed outcome. A more natural way to express what transpires—and one that the law favours—is that the man leaves the woman with no *reasonable alternative* to compliance.

This still leaves us with problems. For instance, is what is reasonable or unreasonable as an alternative to be determined by reference to the agent's own particular beliefs and desires, or by some more general standard, that, say, of the normal rational person? A woman submits because she unreasonably but sincerely thinks the man is pointing a loaded finger at her. Or she submits to the threat of that which she has a quite exceptional but deeply felt fear, that, for instance, of being tickled. The law may be inclined to rely on the objective standard of the average or reasonable person. But it needs also to be sensitive to the particularities of context and character when these can be determined as appropriate to a case. Again the unreasonableness of the alternative threatened may be judged in various terms: as a function only of its awfulness in itself, of the awfulness of complying (assuming the threatened alternative is worse), of how much worse it is than what is demanded, and of how awful the situation as a whole—only either compliance or threatened consequences—is.[25]

Given these complications it may be impossible to specify any clear and agreed criteria whereby the point at which a choice that is less than fully voluntary possesses that degree of involuntariness which invalidates any consent given. Certainly it is most likely impossible that criminal law could be formulated in a manner which provides lawyers, judges, and juries with unambiguous, perspicuous guidelines for determining that point. At most courts will rely on a shared understanding of what it means for someone to be 'left with no choice', to have 'no alternative but to' comply, to be 'forced' into agreeing.

4

Real Consent

THE PREVIOUS CHAPTER CONCERNED itself with the questions of what is it about consensuality that makes consensual sex permissible, and what exactly is consensuality. This led to discussion of the legitimating role of consent and the definition of valid consent. The third question broached at the outset of the previous chapter was whether consensuality is enough, that is, whether the Principles of Consensuality and Non-consensuality provide necessary and sufficient conditions of moral permissibility. It is to this question that the present and the next chapters are devoted. Answering this question will involve discussion of, first, a number of situations which might appear consensual but are perhaps not; second, the role of third parties; third, the relative plausibility of the Principles of Consensuality and Non-consensuality; and, fourth, challenges to these principles. This chapter takes up the first topic.

When Is Consent Not Really Consent?

The previous chapter discussed the standard view that consent is valid if voluntary, informed, and given by someone capable of consenting. However, there are cases in which knowing, willing consent appears to be given by capable persons to some state of affairs, and yet there is room for doubt as to whether that state of affairs is morally tolerable. It may be that the appearance of knowing, valid, and capable consent is just that, an appearance, and that the standard view of valid consent combines with the Principles of Consensuality and Non-consensuality adequately to explain our doubts. However, it may be that these cases do not, on the standard view, count as ones in which the consent given is invalid, and yet our doubts still remain. In that case one way someone could express these doubts is by suggesting that the Principles of Consensuality and Non-consensuality are false; another is to propose a definition of valid consent which extends beyond the standard view. Whatever our eventual decision we should become clearer about consent, consensuality, and moral permissibility.

There are three kinds of case which raise the doubts in question. In all three it should be noted that it is not simply the fact that certain things are true of the circumstances in which an individual consents which is important. It is rather that certain facts obtain *and* play a role in explaining why the individual consents. The first kind of case is where there is a significant measure of inequality between the parties to the exchange. In the discussion of this kind of case I shall concentrate on economic inequality, leaving to Chapter 6 the vexed issue of gender inequality. The second sort of case is where the parties to the exchange occupy the respective roles defined by an institutionally or professionally defined relationship, such as that between doctor and patient, analyst and analysand, teacher and pupil, priest and parishioner. The third sort of case is one in which the individual who consents has a weakness, vulnerability, or psychological attribute such that they are highly disposed in some circumstances to consent to certain kinds of proposal.

Unequal Partner and Indecent Proposals

Richard, the fabulously wealthy billionaire, and the poor but honest Mary have consensual sex. Why might one think that the extreme disparity in their economic circumstances undermines that consensuality or, consent notwithstanding, casts doubt on the moral permissibility of their relationship? There are five reasons for thinking this.[1] The first is that Richard makes use of his extreme wealth to issue a credible threat of dire consequences lest Mary not have sex with him. His wealth can make such a threat both more realistic and its consequences more serious. Such a scenario is covered by the standard view, and any consent given is invalid.

Second, Richard offers Mary an obscenely large amount of money to sleep with him. The proposal is indecent for what it proposes and for the sum it names. But is Mary's agreement, if forthcoming, non-consensual? There would be agreement that Richard is making an offer. Like a threat an offer is a proposal which alters the context in which the other makes their choice with a view to making non-compliance unattractive. Assuming Mary does not find the idea of sex with Richard unimaginably repulsive or that the sum is large enough, Mary will feel that not sleeping with Richard compares poorly with doing so. Indeed it may compare so poorly as to leave Mary with no reasonable alternative but to go ahead and have sex with Richard. If, then, threats invalidate consent by leaving the person threatened with no reasonable alternative but to comply, do not some offers similarly invalidate consent? If Richard's offer is generous enough, will Mary's 'consent' be invalid?

There is disagreement among philosophers about whether offers can, like threats, 'coerce'. Some would prefer to speak of 'exploitative' offers. In addition there are features of offers, not shared by threats, which make them less morally unattractive. Threats propose harms or evils that would not otherwise befall the person threatened, whereas offers propose goods or the prevention of harms that, absent the offer, would otherwise not occur. Richard could secure Mary's sexual compliance by threatening to reduce her already poor situation, and that of all her family, to complete destitution. If Mary does not sleep with Richard under threat, she is ruined. If she refuses his offer, her situation is merely unchanged, whereas it would be immeasurably improved if she agreed to his proposal. Additionally offers expand a person's options, whereas threats do not. There are things that Mary will be able to do if she decides to sleep with Richard that would not have been open to her before he made his offer.

This is all true. But whether we describe a proposal as an offer, a threat, as coercive or exploitative, the issue at stake is whether a proposal invalidates the person's subsequent consent.[2] Whether Mary agrees to sex with Richard on pain of being reduced to penury or on the promise of immense reward, she is surely, in either case, left with no choice; she is given no reasonable alternative but to; she is 'forced' to agree. Why then should Richard not be guilty of rape in both cases? By way of an answer let me explore two suggestions which are due to Joel Feinberg. The first is that much depends on how it comes to be that there is inequality between Richard and Mary; the second has to do with the degree of involuntariness in such a case.

Feinberg is sympathetic to a distinction between the exploitation of a situation, already existing, and the deliberate creation of that situation with a view to making a coercive offer within it: 'When A deliberately creates the circumstances of vulnerability which he later exploits with a coercive offer, his coercion virtually always reduces the voluntariness of B's consent sufficiently to render it invalid. But when A merely exploits circumstances that he finds ready-made, then frequently, though not always, B's consent, so produced, remains valid'.[3] If Richard was responsible for Mary's poverty, so the argument seems to go, then Mary's consent to his offer of sex for money is probably invalid. If, however, Richard merely 'happens upon' poor Mary, then her agreement to the very same offer is probably valid. This is odd. The main issue is the voluntariness of a decision within some context. The question of who (other than the maker of the decision) may be held responsible for the bringing about of that context seems distinct from the main issue. Imagine that Richard's equally rich brother, Dick, effectively pimps for Richard by finding women whom he can reduce to straitened circumstances and then put in the path of Richard, who knows nothing of his brother's endeavours on his behalf. It seems implausible to suggest that Mary's consent to Richard's offer is valid if she is the victim of Dick and Richard but not if she is the victim solely of Richard.

If the reply is made that what matters is whether the situation within which a coercive offer can be made is the result of deliberate human agency, whether or not the agent is the maker of the offer, then the original distinction, between mere exploitation of a situation and coercion within it, is simply in danger of being lost. For all poverty can, on a plausible account, be attributed to the actions of human beings. Or at least it can be maintained that since the poverty of certain individuals is a foreseeable outcome of some set of alterable social and economic arrangements, it is the responsibility of those who could but do not change those arrangements.

Feinberg's thought might be that Mary's options are reduced by Richard's deliberate actions in impoverishing her, whereas her merely falling into poverty is like a fact of nature which does not constitute a limitation of her freedom. Thus, Mary's decision within a context of reduced freedom is to that extent less voluntary. But Feinberg himself is quick to insist that the extent of a person's freedom, in the sense of the number of options open to her, is distinct from the voluntariness of her choice of any one of those options. A can enlarge B's options but force B to choose only one of these by rendering all the others ineligible.[4] Or A can reduce the number of options open to B but make more of those that remain eligible than were in the larger set. In short, freedom to choose and voluntariness of choice can be distinguished.

We are left with the thought that, however Mary comes to be poor, Richard's offer of sex for money may be such as to leave her with no choice. Is Mary's consent to sex in these circumstances invalid, and is Richard guilty of rape? Feinberg's second suggestion is that the voluntariness of Mary's agreement is reduced sufficiently for Richard to be unsuccessful in suing for breach of contract if Mary takes the money and runs. However, it is not reduced so much as to make Richard guilty of rape if

Mary takes the money and stays. Mary's agreement to have sex with Richard is sufficiently involuntary to invalidate the contract but insufficiently involuntary to count as unconsented and thus as rape.[5] This seems a more plausible suggestion. We are, however, now left with the problem that just as there are degrees of involuntariness induced by threats of varying kinds, so too there are degrees of involuntariness induced by offers of varying kinds. We may be inclined to think that, on the whole, consent which results from offers is more voluntary than that which results from threats. But it is still the case that there should be some offers which overcome the will more effectively than some threats. Why then should not a certain kind of offer under certain circumstances figure as one of the factors that vitiate the victim's consent in the context of sexual offences?

We may be unwilling to extend the crime of rape to include, as one of the circumstances in which consent is not forthcoming, the making of a coercive offer. We may, nevertheless, also think that there should be a crime of procurement, specifying a range of financial inducements which are such as to make the procured person's consent insufficiently voluntary. However, our suspicion might be that such a law is paternalistic, designed principally to protect the victim from her own desires rather than, as is the case with rape, also penalise the offender. This suspicion derives from the thought that we understand (and wholeheartedly condone) the desires of one who consents from fear, but do not endorse (while understanding) the desires of someone who consents from an overwhelming wish for an improvement in her situation. Terror excuses where greed does not. This is not to deny that both may be irresistible motives to action; it is to find the first but not the second an estimable trait of character.

Greed is not at issue in the situation where there is a third reason for thinking Richard and Mary's unequal status sufficient to invalidate Mary's consent. This is where Mary is so poor, so destitute, and so starving as to have no choice but to agree to *anything* Richard proposes so long as it provides her with some measure of relief from her desperate situation. Richard does not have to be so fabulously rich as to make her an obscene offer. Nor does he need to demand sex. She would be willing to do anything for him. Inequality is not the issue here. It is not the fact that Richard and Mary enjoy vastly disparate lifestyles which explains her consent; it is rather that Mary has no lifestyle at all. It is her absolute and dreadful poverty which leaves her with no choice but to agree to whatever offers some improvement in her position. She agrees out of dire necessity, and may be said to no more consent than she would if agreeing with a gun to her head.

A fourth reason for being suspicious of the agreement between rich Richard and poor Mary may be expressed in terms of their unequal bargaining positions. If Richard and Mary were negotiating the price of a commodity, one would think Mary at a disadvantage on account of her being much poorer than Richard. Imagine that P is the fair price for the good Mary is selling to Richard. Mary's poverty makes her more willing to sell below P, and Richard's wealth renders him comparatively indifferent to the success or failure of the transaction. Richard can afford not to buy, while Mary for her part cannot afford not to sell. The difference between concluding some agreement on price and not doing so is greater for Mary than it is for Richard. And this difference in their positions will make it easier for Richard to strike a bargain that suits him. He does not have to do this, but he can if he chooses, whereas Mary cannot.

If Richard is a millionaire punter and Mary a poor prostitute, this difference in bargaining power might then be reflected in the price of any sex they agreed to have. The difference would not of itself show that the agreement to have, and pay for, the sex was involuntary and thus non-consensual on Mary's part. But what if there is no question of payment for sex? Then there is no 'price' of sex, or at least not one that is met by the resources of which Richard has so much more than Mary. When Mary considers whether or not to sleep with Richard, his wealth does not provide him with a bargaining counter (he does not offer to pay), nor does it give him an advantage in negotiation (no discussion of the terms of agreement is had). So long as the sex is free, it would seem that the differences in wealth give neither of the parties to it any evident bargaining power or superiority.

However, there is one last possibility, a fifth reason that Richard's and Mary's economic status may be relevant to the issue of her consent. This has to do with the effects of poverty on character. In cases of entrenched deprivation a person may accommodate herself to her disadvantaged position—that is, she may adjust her goals downward so as to deal with the severe disappointments that her life would otherwise bring. Poor Mary might, as a result of living the poor life, have become accustomed to accept much less than she otherwise would. A simple-minded utilitarianism would expect to see social and economic inequality directly reflected in a comparative measurement of people's desires and their realisation: Mary being less well off gets less out of life than Richard and is, in consequence, unhappier. But if Mary expects to get less out of life, she may be just as happy as Richard. In this manner the simple-minded utilitarianism is embarrassed.[6] This may be true, but it is not clearly relevant to the question of Mary's consent. Mary's poverty may make her less inclined to expect her life to go well, but it does not obviously incline her to say 'yes' to everything proposed to her. One's character may be such as, in general, to agree to what others, in general, would not. And this character may be a product of one's poor circumstances. But if that is one's character, then whatever the reason for its being that way, one is probably best judged as not fully competent to consent.

Poverty may inure a person to life's disappointments to such an extent that she can never say 'no' to anything. But her inability in this regard, not her poverty, is what vitiates her consent. For what matters is her lack of capacity, not its explanation. It seems then that the inequality between Mary and Richard does invalidate her consent if Mary is so poor as to have no real choice; it may do so if Richard's offer is so tempting as to leave her with no choice. But it does not of itself incapacitate Mary from making a choice. Nor does Mary's poorer bargaining position make her consent invalid, even if it may lead her to agree to less than she otherwise would.

Exploited Consent

Richard is Mary's doctor, analyst, priest, or teacher, and while he is occupying that role, Mary agrees to have sex with him. Is her consent valid? This question may be answered once the issue it seeks to focus attention upon is clearly identified and separated from corollary matters. It is evident, for instance, that a consensual relation between professional and client may, even if genuinely consensual, be morally impermissible. Sexual intimacy will probably seriously compromise the professional nature of the relationship, which requires impartiality, objectivity, and independence. It may also have adverse effects upon third parties. Other patients will distrust and perhaps refuse to share confidences with a doctor they know to be sexually involved with a patient. Pupils may no longer take seriously a teacher whom they regard as tainted by his affair with one of their group. And so on.

There are also a range of sexual behaviours which may occur in a work or professional context initiated by a superior and of which an inferior is an unwilling victim. Unwanted sexual attention may include attempts to coerce someone into a sexual relationship. This is sexual harassment and is appropriately covered by an effective independent complaints and discipline procedure.[7] It is also the case that a professional is in a position to issue credible threats, and even more insidiously to imply such threats, with a view to securing sexual compliance. A teacher may in the past have poorly marked a student who rejected his advances. A present student may reasonably believe that this is what he will do in her case if she refuses his request to have sex with him. If she cannot risk the consequences of academic failure, she may be said to be coerced into sexual agreement. In these circumstances the sex between professional and client is not consensual.

But what of consensual sex between professional and client which has no significant adverse consequences on anyone other than the two parties? Can it be said to be truly consensual? Most codes of ethics governing professional client relations expressly forbid or strongly advise against such sexual relations.[8] Is this so because such relations are outside the proper scope of a professional relationship or because they cannot, within such a relationship, be fully consensual? The worries expressed about such relations are either about the reasons they are entered into or the terms on which they are conducted. Let me explore each of these further.

The relationship between professional and client certainly displays an inequality of power and status. The professional is likely to occupy a social ranking and enjoy an esteem not possessed by his client. That may make him more attractive to his client, but it would do so even if she was not his client. Power may be an aphrodisiac to someone over whom that power is not exercised. What matters is the influence exercised within the relationship. Here what is relevant are such features as dependence, trust, vulnerability, and emotional intimacy. Now it is important to be clear whether these features obtain in virtue of the relationship as such or are true of the person who becomes a client. A pupil is beholden to a teacher for his superior knowledge; a patient depends upon a doctor's medical advice; a parishioner needs the priest's counsel. Outside office hours the patient, pupil, or parishioner is her own person and depends on no one. However, somebody may enter into a professional relationship because they are vulnerable and in need of the help which perhaps only the professional can supply. The analysand who seeks therapeutic treatment from the analyst is already to some extent damaged and vulnerable.

There is a final feature of the professional relationship which is relevant. That is, that it is normally conducted in ways that require trust and openness, emotional intimacy even. A patient, and certainly an analysand or counselled person, must open herself up, lay herself bare, share significant confidences with her doctor. A pupil must be prepared to reveal her knowledge and intellectual skills to her teacher, must accept that her capacities will be assessed in ways that may bear significantly on her self-esteem. So the professional relationship is itself one in which the client is dependent upon her professional, it is one in which the client herself may be vulnerable, and it is conducted in a manner which requires trust and openness. These various features can, and most certainly often do, combine to bring it about that a client will consent to a sexual proposal by her professional. Of the relationship between a family lawyer and his client, one judge has written perceptively: 'Those who undergo both marital breakdown and contested litigation in its wake are generally, if transiently, emotionally and psychologically disturbed. Being unstable they are vulnerable. A great deal of hope and faith is invested in their chosen advocate who becomes for a short phase in their lives protector and champion. The opportunity for the lawyer to abuse that dependent trust is obvious'.[9]

For his part the professional may manipulate the terms of his relationship with his client to make her sexual consent more likely. He may play on those features of dependence, trust, and vulnerability which characterise the relationship. He may do so knowingly and deliberately. There is evidence that professionals who conduct affairs with their clients are serial offenders, deliberately targeting those they can identify as having low self-esteem or as being especially vulnerable.[10] It is also true that the terms under which any relationship between professional and client is conducted are likely to be unfavourable to the client. This is not least because the professional, unlike the client, has control over how such a relationship, once entered into, is conducted. A student, for instance, is unlikely to be able to determine how long an affair with her lecturer lasts, how regular contact is, who initiates meetings, who knows about it, where it is conducted, what is ruled in or out as an appropriate expression of the relationship, and so on. And this lack of control may be attributed to the terms of the initial, professional relationship between herself and the lecturer in which it is he who determines its terms. The vast majority of students who enter into affairs with their lecturers suffer as a consequence and subsequently report their deep regret that they ever embarked upon such affairs.[11]

All of the above worries may be legitimately expressed, while the following is also true: Clients may knowingly and deliberately initiate sexual relationships with their professionals. They may do in an attempt to influence the terms of the general relationship, to secure better marks from their teacher, for instance. They may be fully aware of the dangers of any sexual relationship and proceed in that knowledge. Such relationships may endure beyond the period of professional dependence, and indeed may mature into long-lasting, loving partnerships. Yet the worries about the majority of such relationships, and the pattern they display, remain.

How is it best to understand these worries? The professional may be said to exploit his client.[12] The term 'exploit' is appropriate since it appeals to the core understanding of exploitation as one side taking unfair advantage of the other. A more formal representation of exploitation sees it as defining any situation in which one party does better, and the other worse, than both would do in some alternative set of circumstances. Further, the difference between actuality and the conceivable alternative can be specified in terms of differential access to some set of resources. For a Marxist, capitalist exploitation occurs because the capitalist, but not the proletariat, has effective control over the means of production.[13]

The professional who sleeps with his client secures her consent because she is his client. There are features of the relationship which make that consent more likely, indeed maybe such that, absent the relationship, there would be no consent. He knows this, or at least he is negligent in his professional duties if he is not aware of it. Most codes of ethics warn against sexual relations.[14] Some training of the professional, especially that of the analyst or counsellor, will specifically caution him against its likelihood.[15] He tends to benefit from the relationship to the extent that she suffers from it. The giving of the consent is thus due both to the professional relationship and to the asymmetrical advantage of one party within it. This is exploitation. However it may still be properly termed consensual.

There may be the exerting of undue influence—Richard may represent sex to Mary as an essential part of her therapeutic progress—and the client may be unduly vulnerable to suggestion—stricken by grief at the death of her husband, Mary is desperate for comfort and human warmth. At some point then one may judge that a sexual affair between professional and client not only is wholly improper, and completely outside the scope of the professional relationship, but also takes place only because the consent is exploited and invalid. That point is an extremely hard one to determine, and even a professional ethics or disciplinary committee may find it impossibly difficult to police the sexual behaviour of its profession's members. But some jurisdictions do regard the client's consent to the professional as invalid. The Australian Crimes Act, 1900, includes as one of 'the grounds upon which it may be established that consent is negated' ' the abuse by the other person of his position of authority over, or professional or other trust in relation to, the person'.[16] The Canadian Criminal Code determines that, for the purposes of the sexual assault offences, no consent is obtained where 'the accused induces the complainant to engage in the activity by abusing a position of trust, power or authority'.[17]

The 'abuse' of which both laws cited speak may consist in the very fact that sexual relations take place between professional and client. Or it may be interpreted to mean a particular exploitative misuse of the features which characterise the professional relationship. Some but not all affairs between professional and client are abusive. The latter interpretation requires the point which distinguishes the abuse from the non-abuse of the professional relationship to be determined. The former understanding may seem too strong. Are there not many teachers who have gone on from the affair to marry their pupils, and similarly doctors their patients, analysts their analysands? In reply it can be said the law does not seek to penalise genuine mutual sexual attraction. Rather, it regards the worries about sexual relationships within the context of professional dependence—what occurs later is a distinct matter—as sufficiently great to warrant proscription.

Vulnerability

The third kind of case in which it might seem that the standard view of valid consent gets it wrong is one in which a consenting party has a weakness, vulnerability, or psychological attribute such that, in certain circumstances, she is more disposed to consent to certain kinds of proposal. Imagine a householder who has an inordinate but unreasonable fear of floods. She is offered insurance against flood damage by a travelling salesman even though she lives many miles from any river or sea. She accepts only because of that fear and without having any good reason, the fear apart, to do so. Someone may love collecting porcelain vases and thus be disposed to buy such a vase if offered one. The flood-fearful householder is a different case. She can be properly described as having a weakness or vulnerability, one that is exceptional or abnormal, one from which she may be said to suffer. John Kleinig offers other examples: 'A sponger may exploit another's generosity, children may exploit the love of their parents, a man may exploit the gullibility of the public and politicians may exploit the fear of the citizenry'.[18] Kleinig insists that such cases are non-coercive but 'involve one party's playing on some character trait of the other for the purpose of securing some advantage'.[19] They are to be condemned both because the exploiter demeans the other and because the exploited party displays a weakness of character.

There may indeed be manipulated consent where one person deliberately distorts the conditions under which consent is being sought in order to make that consent more likely, either through a misrepresentation of the facts or an aggravation of those character traits predisposing to consent.[20] The sponger misdescribes his needs; the advertiser misrepresents his product; the government exaggerates the extent of the danger; the salesman lies about impending floods. The child seeks to augment a parent's natural affection for their offspring; the salesman encourages the householder to be fearful of floods. And so on.

However, even though the consent is to be explained in terms of the individual's weakness of character, there may be no exploitation of that weakness. The salesman may sell a policy in good faith, ignorant of (and with no reason to suspect) the householder's particular disposition. In the film *Some Like It Hot*, Marilyn Monroe's character confesses that she is a sucker for saxophone players. That is good news for both the exploitative and the blissfully ignorant instrumentalist. There also need not be exploitation since advantage may not accrue to the one who secures consent as a result of the other's weakness. Imagine that Richard wins the favours of Mary only because Mary is incapable of saying 'no' to anyone who reminds her of her favourite film star. Richard's belief that Mary is uniquely attracted to him is disappointed and his self-esteem damaged. There can be exploitation with or without manipulation. The salesman may merely seize upon and make use of what he knows to be the householder's predilection. He does so without any special effort to misrepresent the facts or augment her existing fear. On the other hand, he may do so and be described as both exploitative and manipulative.

The individual's weakness of character does not amount to a general or 'global' incapacity to consent. It is rather that in *this* situation such a person is likely to give their consent to *this* suggestion. With regard to other matters and in other situations her ability to give her consent is perfectly normal. Now it will probably be thought that the householder's consent to the flood damage insurance policy is not valid and that this is so even if the salesman is merely lucky in finding such a householder and does nothing to encourage her weakness of character. If this is so, our reasoning may simply be that an incapacity to consent sufficient to invalidate any consent given need not be global, where this means a complete incapacity to consent to anything whether permanent or temporary. It can be an incapacity in some specific regard and with a scope limited to specific matters. However, we may want to see whether the three kinds of case discussed this far give grounds for a general extension of the standard view of valid consent.

Is the Standard View of Consent Sufficient?

Is the standard view of consent able to deal with the three kinds of case considered thus far? We may judge that it can if the main terms of that account are construed appropriately. Thus Richard does 'coerce' Mary into sex if his offer is sufficiently attractive or her economic situation is sufficiently dire. Richard does, as a professional, exploit an incapacity validly to consent on his client Mary's part if she is sufficiently dependent upon him or sufficiently vulnerable in that professional relationship. Mary is incapable of consenting validly to certain of Richard's proposals if she possesses a particular weakness of character.

We may, however, feel that in stretching the terms of the standard view this way there is a double loss. First, there is a loss in the robustness of meaning and perspicuousness which attach to terms like 'forced' and 'incapable'. Can the rich Richard really be said to 'force' Mary into sex with him merely by making her a very attractive offer? Can Mary really be said to be 'incapable' of consenting to sex with Richard merely because she is his professional client? Second, the use of the standard terms may make us lose sight of what interestingly distinguishes an abuse of a professional relationship of trust and dependence from a paradigmatic case of coercion or incapacity. The extended discussion of exploited consent in this context showed it to have a particular and worrying character, one that is not happily captured if one simply talks in the terms of the standard view.

A way forward may be to list a set of conditions under which consent is negated, and include, as the criminal codes cited did, a condition such as the abuse of a professional relationship. This has an ad hoc feel to it and, further, leaves unanswered the question of what it is that makes them all equally conditions which invalidate consent. It was argued in the last chapter that consent plays its role in supplying a moral warrant to that which is consented to inasmuch as the giving of consent is the expression of a free and voluntary will. A guiding thought here might then be that in all the conditions under which consent is invalid the giving of that consent is not the expression of a free and voluntary will. How might we judge that to be so in the three kinds of case instanced?

There are two relevant facts about these cases. The first is that without the defining features of these cases—the economic inequality between the parties, the professional relationship, the weakness of character—the consent would not be forthcoming. The second is that these features are ones that, while explaining why the consent is given, are not ones one would normally expect someone to endorse as the reason for their consent. Outside any professional relationship the client would not regard the existence of that relationship as an acceptable reason that she would agree to have sex with someone. I am not willing that my consent should be given only because of something about the situation or myself that normally and otherwise I do not think should explain why my consent is given. The basic idea is that people must agree to the reasons that they agree to something; we must consent to the context in which, and by reason of which, consent is given. Some have argued that a person's will is free only if her will is effective and it is the will she wants to be effective—that is, if she wants to want what it is she wants to do and does.[21] One might similarly argue that consent is valid if it expresses the free and voluntary will of the person who consents, and that is so only if she would consent to the giving of her consent. The standard view captures some but not all of the conditions under which a person would not give that second-order consent. The three kinds of case extend beyond the standard view but are captured by this understanding of what it is for consent to express the free and voluntary will of a person.

However, for some this may represent too much of an extension. The standard view, it will be said, is acceptable as it stands because within its own limited terms it expresses a commonsense understanding of when consent is clearly not valid. A proper answer to this thought requires looking at the context within which a standard of valid consent operates, namely, the Principles of Consensuality and Non-consensuality. It is important that consent be valid insofar as its validity supplies a warrant for the behaviour to which consent is given. The issue is, perhaps, not just what makes consent valid or real. It is, rather, what makes consent valid *enough* for the behaviour to which consent is given to be legitimate.

◀ 5 ▶

Consensuality and Permissibility

THIS CHAPTER FINALLY ADDRESSES directly the question of the adequacy of the Principles of Consensuality and Non-consensuality. Is it enough for some sexual practice to be morally permissible that it is consensual? And is a practice which is not consensual thereby impermissible? I propose first to clarify the phrase in the two principles which refers to the interests of third parties. Then I turn to a challenge that could be made to the view that consensuality suffices for permissibility before attempting an overall assessment of the adequacy of the two principles. I will conclude with some remarks about the relationship between any account of what makes consent valid and the two principles.

What About Third Parties?

The Principle of Consensuality states that 'a practice, P, is morally permissible if all those who are parties to P are competent to consent, give their valid consent, and the interests of no other parties are significantly harmed'. I have examined how one should understand a competence to consent and the validity of consent. I will now explore the final phrase of the principle. What or who are the 'other parties', and how are their interests 'significantly harmed'? If Harry and Sue have consensual sex, then their activity, according to the principle, is permissible just so long as no other party's interests are harmed. This might be the case if, for instance, Frank, Sue's husband, is injured by her adultery; or if Frank, an unrelated stranger, unwillingly but unavoidably witnesses their publicly engaging in sexual intercourse; or if Frank is the child who, as the foetus in Sue's womb, acquired a damaging sexually transmitted disease when Sue had sexual relations with Harry. We need, however, to be clearer both about whose interests count and what counts as the harming of an interest. This can best be done if I consider three very different sexual practices.

Bestiality

If Sue has sex with 'Harry' and 'Harry' is a dog, can we explain the wrongness of Sue's behaviour, if it is wrong, in terms of the harms done to the interests of 'Harry'?[1] Assume that we do think bestiality is wrong, that it is not merely abhorrent, disgusting, or unworthy of a human but also morally impermissible. We might think this on the grounds that sexual congress across distinct species is unnatural. And it would certainly follow from the truth of this claim conjoined to the truth of the general view that whatever is sexually unnatural is immoral that bestiality is immoral. Legal thinking about bestiality may proceed from the assumption that its wrongness has nothing to do with any lack of consensuality and does lie in its unnaturalness. In one of the rare British cases of bestiality, *Regina* v. *Bourne* (1952),[2] the defendant sexually excited a dog and forced his wife to have sex with it. His appeal against conviction was based on the claim that he could not be guilty of aiding and abetting a crime since his wife's non-consent meant she committed no crime herself. The dog's willing or unwilling participation was apparently beside the point, and the Lord Chief Justice declared that 'the offence of buggery whether with man or beast does not depend upon consent; it depends on the act, and if an act of buggery is committed, the felony is committed'.

The general view that sex is wrong if and when it can be described as unnatural is inconsistent with the view which informs the two principles. This does not mean that this view is mistaken. But this book is concerned to explore the implications of the general view which is constituted by the two principles. It is therefore more instructive to find an account of bestiality's putative wrongness in terms which might be consistent with or suggested by these two principles. Let me suggest that our main reason for thinking bestiality wrong, along these lines, would be that the animal is improperly used. However, the improper use cannot consist in the fact that the animal does not consent to participation in the sexual practice. An animal is not competent to consent or dissent. In this regard the animal's status is the same as that of the young child, or the comatose adult, or the seriously mentally ill person who is used as a person's sexual 'partner'. As with these other instances any evidence of pleasure or displeasure experienced could not be taken as displaying consent or dissent. In the absence of any capacity to give or withhold consent such behavioural signs cannot be taken as ways in which consent is given or withheld.

The impropriety of sexually using an animal is, then, most plausibly explained as harming its interests. An animal has interests to the extent that it can be said to have whatever makes up its well-being, which prospers or suffers in the measure that these elements prosper or suffer.[3] Let us in consequence say that the well-being of an animal which is sexually used is lessened or denied. It is arguable that an animal does not *sexually* suffer in an act of bestiality, that is, suffer a harm which may be thought of as specifically and irreducibly explicable in terms of the animal's sexuality. It does not suffer sexually in the way that a human victim of rape does. For that reason it may be said that the wrong of bestiality which is done when the animal suffers is captured within any general proscription against animal cruelty.[4]

However, the further question is whether the wrong of sexually using an animal lies simply in the using. One might think that a human who uses anything in nature for his own purposes and without regard to how he leaves nature in doing this is guilty of something like impiety. His behaviour displays a brutal and self-interested mastery of what can be mastered, but it is an overcoming of nature that is overweening; it is disrespectful of the balance of relations between human beings and their surroundings that should exist. Yet if this is wrongdoing, it is not necessarily the doing of a wrong to nature. Using an animal need not of itself be a wronging of the animal. It would be such a wrong according to some version of the familiar Kantian principle, discussed in Chapter 3, which demands that one treat the other as an end and not merely as a means. A human who engages in bestiality may treat the animal solely as an instrument for his own sexual gratification. Of course he need not. He may be attentive to the animal's sexual pleasure. Let us assume that he does treat the animal merely as a means. Is the animal something that can be seen as not merely having interests but also as being an agent or end which merits being treated as such? It is entirely possible to think it wrong to cause unnecessary pain to animals but believe that only humans (and creatures with the same morally relevant properties of agency, rationality, and self-consciousness) can claim the right to be treated as an end.[5] That an animal has a moral status in virtue of having interests that should not be harmed does not mean that it has the status of a moral agent enjoyed by humans.

Raymond Belliotti argues that 'the reason that it is generally considered morally wrong to use a being with moral status as a mere means for another's ends is that such action invariably wrongs the used party by setting back his or her interests'.[6] He concludes that the wrongness of bestiality as a use of the animal for human gratification depends on whether or not the animal's interests are in fact set back. This seems mistaken. The wrong of treating another as a means is distinct from that of setting back the other's interests, even if it is the case that treating another as a mere means invariably involves setting back the other's interests. Indeed Kant's principle identifies a wrong in the very act of so treating another irrespective of its consequences for the other. We may conclude then that animals as much as humans may well have interests which must be taken into account when we are considering the permissibility of sexual practices, but that they cannot, as humans can, lay claim not to be treated as mere means.

Necrophilia

If Harry has sex with Sue and Sue is dead, can we explain the wrongness of Harry's behaviour, if it is wrong, in terms of the harms done to the interests of Sue? Again, someone can offer a moral condemnation of necrophilia in terms of its unnaturalness. It is also possible to appeal to the indirect wrongness of necrophilia through its effects on relatives and friends of the deceased and, more generally, in its gross affront to the sensibilities of society. However, the interesting possibility is that necrophilia is wrong because it directly harms the interests of the dead person. That possibility is secured if we allow that a person's interests outlast his biological existence and that harm can be done to these interests even after the person's death. I have interests in what happens to me after I die which can be harmed or promoted. It is not the corpse's interests which are harmed or promoted. Rather, it is those of the person who becomes the corpse.[7]

In this way Sue's interests are harmed by Harry's necrophiliac behaviour even though Sue is no longer around to be aware of such harm, or indeed no longer exists as a subject of any experiences at all. What, however, if Sue had consented in advance of dying to her necrophiliac use by Harry? She might have done so, for instance, by including an appropriate clause in her will. It has been argued that if whatever is consensual is permissible, other things being equal, then Harry's sexual use of Sue should be morally tolerated.[8] Strictly speaking of course Sue is not a party to the sexual practice in question, and her consent pre-dates its occurrence. This might be thought to make the operation of the Principle of Consensuality otiose. However, we could understand Sue to be a party in the sense, already argued for, that her ante-mortem interests are at stake in the treatment of her corpse.

We might further argue that it is appropriate to modify the principle to read 'give or gave their consent'. After all one can imagine a party to a sado-masochistic encounter who will be unable, during that encounter, to express his wishes, giving carefully formulated prior consent to what he is prepared to allow subsequently. Nevertheless, caution is in order. A person's pre-consent to certain uses of their corpse cannot be revoked after their death. It would be all the more important, therefore, to ensure that any expression of consent to post-mortem use of their body was considered, made in full knowledge of its implications, and was indeed, and in every sense of the word, their final word on the subject. Such qualifications having been duly noted, it may be possible to think that both a person's interests and the effective scope of their consent can survive their death.

Exhibitionism and Public Indecency

If Harry has sex with Sue in a public place and in doing so they are unavoidably witnessed by Frank, can we explain the wrongness of Harry and Sue's behaviour, if it is wrong, in terms of the harms done to the interests of Frank? Or if Harry is an exhibitionist, can we explain the wrongness of his behaviour, if it is wrong, in terms of harms done to the interests of Sue, who cannot help but see him? In both cases the most obvious and familiar way to understand the ground for thinking that something wrong is done is that offence is caused to Frank and Sue, respectively. This offence consists in an unpleasant state of mind whose cause can be attributed to the other's behaviour.

Joel Feinberg believes it evident that offence, however significant, is both less serious than and different in kind from harm. At the same time he acknowledges that the prevention of serious offence is a good reason for the prohibition of some act or practice.[9] His reasoning is sound, and that leaves the Principle of Consensuality in need of further modification. It must be added that a practice is permissible if it neither significantly harms the interests of other parties nor occasions them serious offence. Now, however, the question is how serious must the offence given be to render something impermissible.

Feinberg rightly argues that the seriousness of offence, which can be gauged in terms of its magnitude, unavoidability, and whether it is consented to, must be balanced against the importance, both to the individual and society; the unavoidability; and the underlying motivation of the offending conduct.[10] However, Feinberg acknowledges the problem that is raised by the fact that the same conduct can occasion varying degrees of offence. Offensiveness can vary within the same society between persons, and also between different societies. Imagine then that George, unlike Frank, is not offended by the public sexual display of Sue and Harry. Or that François is not shocked by what Frank and George find offensive. More troubling still, imagine that Sue is offended merely by knowing that Frank and Harry, as a homosexual couple, have consensual sex in private and unseen.

Feinberg's solution consists in discounting 'abnormal susceptibilities' to offence at the level of the individual, while simply recognising the facts of inter-cultural variation and intra-cultural change in sensibility at the level of whole societies.[11] This solution is a pragmatic one, but it must recognise that everything now turns on where one starts from. What is 'abnormal' may be statistically rare within a society whose own general outlook and practices are 'abnormal' by comparison with other societies or which may have changed in such a way as to render what was once abnormal all too normal.

Perhaps the standards of normality could be evaluated. What matters is not whether one is offended but whether one ought to be offended. In a piece on privacy Richard Wasserstrom wonders whether that significant feature of our culture whereby we suffer pains (of embarrassment, for instance) at the disclosure of intimate facts about ourselves is a desirable feature of a culture. He considers the 'counter-cultural' argument that sees as healthier and happier a culture whose members are open and unembarrassed about their performance of those actions which our culture considers properly private. He reaches no conclusions but allows that the 'counter-cultural' claim could be considered merited or otherwise in terms of the value of certain kinds of interpersonal relationships, the necessity of privacy, and the way in which we can be with others in a shared world.[12]

Any attempted evaluation of that set of circumstances which explains why offence is suffered by some group of individuals is bound to be contentious. However, the fact that it can be attempted suggests that we may want to do more than, as Feinberg does, simply acknowledge the facts of the case as they are presently constituted. In saying that a practice which causes significant offence to others is for that reason impermissible, we may still leave it as an open question whether we might nevertheless find reasons—having to do with the desirability of the cultural context within which such offence is normally caused—to discount that offence or dispute its significance.

Is It Wrong to Use Someone Even with Their Consent?

At the outset of Chapter 3 I indicated that I would not attempt a full-blown defence of the general view that whatever transpires sexually between consenting adults is permissible. My concern has to been to explore this view from within as it were—what it means to describe some activity as consensual, why it has plausibility to think that whatever is consensual is permissible, and whether on its own terms consensuality really is enough for permissibility. That means that I shall not consider a cluster of views which appraise the moral permissibility of sexual conduct in terms other than consensuality. Let me briefly indicate what these views might be.

There is the familiar view—already cited in the discussion of bestiality and necrophilia—that a sexual activity is morally permissible only to the extent that it is 'natural'.[13] There is the paternalist view that activities harmful to the agent are wrong even if the agent knowingly and willingly engages in them.[14] There is the view, which might be termed 'social moralism', which holds that private consensual acts by individuals can have wider and deleterious social effects, especially when those acts violate the shared norms of the society to which the individuals belong.[15] In noting but not further discussing these views, I do not, to repeat a point made earlier, discount their importance or possible value. There is, moreover, a more direct challenge which strikes at the heart of the view that consensuality delivers permissibility. In Chapter 3 I considered and rejected the idea that this view derives its warrant from some version of the Kantian principle that individuals are ends and not mere means. I said that the Principle of Consensuality regards two persons' consensual sex as permissible even if one or both of them use the other merely as a means to their own ends. Is this really acceptable?

Consider the following scenario. Harry is a rock star, Sue an adoring fan. After a concert given by Harry, Sue manages to gain entry to the post-show party, where she explicitly offers herself sexually to Harry. Harry and Sue sleep together. It is a one-night stand, and the sex is perfunctory and unpleasant to Sue. In the morning Harry leaves with barely an acknowledgement to Sue of what has happened, and they never meet again. Most of us will find the events depicted in this story morally distasteful, and some perhaps will think that Sue has reason morally to complain about what has transpired. It is likely that expression will be given to this distaste or to Sue's complaint in some such phrase as 'Harry merely used Sue'. Let us try to be clear what this consists in and why, if at all, it constitutes a wrongful action on the part of Harry. We can best do this by carefully separating the elements that can, and often do, go together in a case of one person wrongfully using another.

Manipulation

Had Harry 'played upon' Sue's adoration or manipulated her into agreeing to sleep with him, we might, it seems, have reason to condemn his behaviour. He could have done so by initiating the encounter, by 'playing up' to the role of rock star, by singling her out for special attention, and by leading her to believe that her devotion as a fan could and should find its proper expression only in sexual compliance. Manipulation need not involve deception, and it may secure consent that is properly described as voluntary. Feinberg speaks of consent 'won by seductive luring, beguiling, tempting, bribing, coaxing, imploring, whimpering, flattering, and the like, short of deceptive innuendo, threats, or coercive offers (which diminish or nullify voluntariness)'.[16]

What exactly we should understand by manipulation is unclear. It stands between coercion, which is clearly unacceptable, and persuasion, which is clearly acceptable. We examined coercion in Chapter 3. Persuasion is the proffering of reasons, sincerely believed to be good ones, to another with the intention that these, if accepted by the other, should lead her to act upon them. I manipulate you if I make use of some part of your motivational make-up in some set of circumstances with the view of getting you to do something I want you to do but you might not have wanted initially to do. That trait or desire or motivational feature need not be a weakness. I can play upon your generosity or any other virtue you possess. Manipulation need not be to one's advantage. I could manipulate you into doing what benefits you, or another, or simply to prove that it can be done.

Manipulation of a tool or instrument is commended. Playing on a violin to produce sweet sounds ('coaxing' such sounds out of the violin) is a lauded skill. Why condemn such skills in the manipulator of persons? The skill of the accomplished seducer, who learns in each case what feature of the other can be played upon to yield consent, may be grudgingly admired, but he will hardly be respected or morally praised. We think this for two reasons. First, the seducer cannot be honest and his intentions transparent to the other without defeating his purposes. When the seducer praises the other's beauty (and he may sincerely believe the other to be beautiful), he intends that praise to serve his seductive purposes. The 'victim' of seduction is not misled as to his beliefs (he honestly thinks her beautiful), but she is misled as to why he tells her that she is beautiful. Second, the manipulator treats the other as an instrument to be played. He does not respect her character for itself, as an end, but only as that which can be acted upon to fulfil his purposes. He treats her, or some part of her, as a means to his end. It seems further that it is the second feature of manipulation which explains the first. For he cannot successfully seduce the woman who is fully aware of the seductive intent of his praise, attentiveness, and whatever.[17]

Exploitation

Harry, the rock star, did not deceive or manipulate Sue. She gave her consent to the sex, and she initiated the encounter. Is Sue harmed by the sex? She may well feel disappointed and regretful on the morrow, wishing that she had never set out to sleep with Harry. She may no longer be a fan, and she may now see her previous adoration as a sad failing on her part. She may hurt, but she cannot claim to have been injured. Yet she may claim to feel cheated, not in the sense that she was lied to but rather in the sense that she has been exploited.

Many tie into their understanding of exploitation in relationships what has previously been discussed as manipulation. The core idea of exploitation, as was explained in Chapter 4, is that one party gains from his relationship to the other more than he otherwise would in some suitably specified baseline set of circumstances. What most often seems to distinguish this baseline from the situation in which exploitation is possible is the absence of some weakness or vulnerability on the part of the exploited person. In this sense Harry exploits Sue's devotion as a fan to gain her consent. But Harry does not, in the imagined scenario, 'play on' this characteristic to secure the consent. His good fortune is to be the rock star she happens to adore. Were he not the star, he would not benefit in this way.

But is Harry wrong to exploit Sue, that is, to enjoy benefits that he would not otherwise do? He would, arguably, be wrong if Susan would be harmed by sleeping with him. This is because Harry should not be the instrument of another's harming herself for his benefit, her consent notwithstanding.[18] He would do wrong if, for instance, he slept with her knowing, as she did, that she thereby voluntarily risked getting pregnant or contracting a sexually transmitted disease.

If no harms befall Sue, is Harry still wrong to gain in this way? There is surely a sense of exploitation which does not automatically imply moral condemnation. George exploits his extraordinary good looks, charm, intelligence, and sensitivity to the needs of others to win the favours of women who are disposed to be won over by just these characteristics. George gains from his possession of these features what he would not gain were he to lack them. George did not come into possession of these features in any morally inappropriate way. But then neither did Harry immorally succeed to his status as adored rock star. So what is wrong with George and Harry both exploiting, that is, simply making use of, their good fortune?

Yet, as things turn out, Harry does get more out of the encounter than Sue. His sexual pleasure is obtained at the expense of Sue, who gains little or nothing from her night with Harry. Imagine that I sell you something which gives you far less pleasure than you had expected. Is this unfair and do I wrong you? I do if I have misrepresented what I am selling you, or if I sell it to you at a price which is greater than one you should have paid. But if it just so happens, and not in consequence of any improper influencing of the sale, that you are disappointed by what you knowingly and willingly purchase, then you cannot complain of unfairness.

It is surely true that most of us have freely entered into sexual relationships and activities which did not live up to our expectations or wishes. It was not as good for us as it was for the other. This cannot be described as unfair since there seems no principle of justice which prescribes a fair distribution of sexual pleasures to the participants in a consensual activity. Sex is a mutual giving of each to the other. It is not required that the giving be equally proportioned. We commend generosity and reciprocity in sexual partners, but we cannot be said to think that such generosity and reciprocity are obligatory.

A principle of fairness which might operate in this context is one which prescribes that each party enter the sexual relationship willingly and knowingly. In this way no partner is disadvantaged in advance of the relationship's occurrence. The Principle of Consensuality seeks to give expression to this prescription. This principle allows that things could subsequently turn out unfavourably for one party or less favourably for it than for the other. Such an outcome is allowed for in just the way that a sporting contest which results in a heavy defeat for one side is nevertheless fair if both sides entered the contest willingly and in a proper understanding of what game was to be played. The fair result of a contest in this sense of fairness is not a tie but one, whatever it might be, which follows from the voluntary and knowing participation of its parties.

Using Another

Yet the thought persists that Harry is doing something morally distasteful. He knows that he will obtain sexual pleasure from sleeping with Sue, and he is indifferent to the fact that she will probably receive none. He is careless with Sue in the sense that he does not care about her. This is what is meant by 'using' another, treating her as a means to one's own ends. Harry most certainly does treat Sue merely as a means to his own sexual gratification. He does not attend to her as a sexual end, that is, as someone who can herself be gratified. Is Harry wrong to behave in this way?

It does seem that there is a wrong in using someone which is not reducible to deceiving or hurting them.[19] Nor is the wrong of using another explicable in terms of, or even necessarily associated with, the unfairness of some bilateral exchange.[20] Does it follow that in each and every instance of some relationship with another it would be wrong to use the other? Bernard Baumrin has argued that 'the voluntary choices by X and Y to engage in a sexual interaction creates in both X and Y new positive duties and rights, and failure by either to do that which fulfils the former violates the latter and is immoral'.[21] Baumrin believes that the central positive duty created in this manner is one to treat the other as a nonmeans. Baumrin is surely right to maintain that no plausible moral theory could show that using the other sexually exclusively as a means is justified. It does not follow that it is impermissible to do so, and that it is obligatory to treat the other sexually as an end. It would do so if both parties contracted, explicitly or implicitly, to enter into a sexual relation with the intention of so behaving. Few voluntary sexual encounters have this character.

Might we think that all sexual encounters should be regulated by what we could call the 'mutual ends' ideal wherein each partner strives equally hard to treat the other as more than a mere means to his or her own ends? Surely we can construct a spectrum of encounters. At one end is the ideal of two loving, reciprocally responsive, and attentive individuals. We admire such a relationship. We may also envy it, wistfully remember it, regret its impossibility for us, aspire to it. But we surely do not morally condemn each and every relationship which falls short of the ideal. There are sexual encounters wherein each partner wilfully seeks only to realise his own ends, leaving the other to realise his as he can. One may know that the other will get something out of the encounter without, for one's own part, thinking of the other as anything more than a means. A client pays a prostitute for sex indifferent to her sexual desires. She, for her part, sells her services to him only for money. She is a mere means to his sexual gratification. He is a mere means to her enrichment. Imagine that Sue is a seasoned 'groupie'. She collects rock stars and can now add Harry to her list. He gets a night's pleasure; she gets a further trophy. Or, finally, consider the self-confessedly casual and promiscuous sexual interactions of gays in the 1970s, best exemplified in the 'bathhouses' of San Francisco. Why is it not appropriate to think of gays who behaved in this way as pursuing their own pleasures relentlessly, riotously, and recklessly, without any conscious concern for the other as anything more than a mere means?

We can characterise sexual encounters towards the other extreme of the spectrum to that of the 'mutual ends' ideal as casual, cheap, unloving, cold, empty, impoverished, shallow, and many other similar adjectives. To say of such sex that it is 'bad' for this reason is not to say that it is morally impermissible anymore than 'bad' sex in the sense of unpleasant sex is proscribed. Sex can be evaluated, and thus be described as 'bad', in non-moral ways. Yet it remains true, as Thomas Nagel observes, that 'bad sex is generally better than none at all'.[22]

It is surely also true that the requirement that one always treat the other in every sexual encounter as more than a mere means, that one never use the other, is impossibly stringent.[23] Perhaps, even so, scale matters. Harry the rock star who sleeps only with adoring fans, selfishly making use of their adoration for his own sexual gratification, is an ignoble figure. But he may ultimately be pitied more than he is condemned. Sue the eternal groupie who sleeps only with rock stars and merely to tick off names is also more to be pitied than her 'conquests' are to be accused of moral wrong. This is not to say that we should not be alert to the dangers of coercion, manipulation, deception, exploitation, and abuse of power in any sexual relationship which falls seriously short of the 'mutual ends' ideal. But in the absence of these defects, we are left with failures of love and respect.[24] Sexual relationships which fail in this regard are less than perfect. They are not impermissible. And to stipulate that all relationships should always aspire to meet the 'mutual ends' ideal is impossibly demanding. We inhabit and negotiate an imperfect world in the awareness of its defects. Our encounters within it can surprise, disappoint, but also frequently please us. Idealising philosophers should not seek to prevent us from leaving the house by demanding that every journey taken outside should be without perils, setbacks, and the occasional failure to reach one's destination.

Is Consensuality Enough?

The view that a sexual practice is permissible if its parties give their valid consent and no others are harmed has plausibility. It does so provided that we acknowledge that consent can be given in advance of the practice, and that others can be harmed by being seriously offended. It does so also provided that we can give a perspicuous account of what is meant by 'valid consent'.

The Principle of Non-consensuality gives expression to the view that something is permissible *only if* consent is given. Without consent, says this principle, a practice is impermissible. This principle is implausible for the reasons given in Chapter 2, where it was argued that general principles of permissibility through consent should be sensitive to the particular nature of any sexual relationship. Some relationships are such that it would be wrong to presume that consent is needed. In others it may be safe to assume that consent is given. In general there are activities and practices whose moral permissibility is not in question. They do not, as it were, need the giving of consent to be permitted.

A more plausible principle is that of Dissent: 'A practice, P, is morally impermissible if at least one of those who are parties to P, and who are competent to consent, does or did dissent, even if the interests of no other parties are significantly harmed, nor are these others occasioned serious offence'. This principle expresses the idea that what makes something impermissible is not that someone simply fails to consent to it but that they actually withdraw consent or positively refuse to give it. Is then a sexual practice only impermissible if consent is withdrawn? Answering this question gives us a proper sense of the relationship between consensuality and permissibility.

All those who urge an account of sexual morality which rests on something other than consensuality will insist that there are some sexual practices, to which the parties involved consent or do not dissent and which do not affect third parties, which are nevertheless impermissible. They are 'unnatural' or seriously harmful to the parties or violate an allegedly shared 'social morality'. But if consensuality is regarded as the sole proper basis of permissibility, then these accounts will be rejected. The absence of dissent from some practice where it could validly be expressed will be enough to show that the practice is permissible. In short, the popular view—that the only rule in the sex game is consent—is formally expressed in the claim that, provided third parties are not adversely affected, the giving of consent is sufficient but not necessary for permissibility, whereas dissent, the positive refusal to consent, is both necessary and sufficient for impermissibility.

However, the discussions of the last three chapters have revealed areas of concern. These have arisen from discussion of cases where it might be thought that consent is not 'really' valid, and also cases where the presence of consent is nevertheless accompanied by serious failures of love and respect within the relationship. The first sort of case was discussed in the previous chapter, the second sort of case earlier in this chapter. Strains show in what we can understand by both consent and permissibility. Worrying about the permissibility of Sue's sexual relationship with Harry where Harry is Sue's doctor, priest, or teacher might lead us to doubt whether Sue's consent to this relationship can really be valid, even though it will probably be said to be so on a familiar, standard account of valid consent. Recognising that Harry's unloving sexual gratification at the expense of Sue is nevertheless consensual on the parts of both Sue and Harry might lead us to worry whether we have properly and completely evaluated that relationship in terms of its permissibility, even though the notion of moral permissibility is a familiar, standard one.

Our intuitions are by no means clear here. Perhaps we can do no more than try to give a rough shape to our worries. If these assume sufficient weight to cast serious doubt on the overall plausibility of the popular view, then our gaze should turn to the other available accounts of sexual morality. If we remain broadly convinced of the plausibility of the popular view, then we can do two things. First, we might remind ourselves of the dangers of any overly moralised account of some human activity. That something is morally permissible does not mean that it has been exhaustively evaluated; there are non-moral criteria by which it might be appraised. That something is morally permissible is not by any means the only or even perhaps the first thing that needs to be said about it. There are activities, and features of activities, for which moral permission does not need to be sought, nor does the very question of seeking it properly arise.[25]

Second, we might consider the relationship between the principles of consensuality and the definition of valid consent. The point of being clear as to what validates consent is that, within the context of these principles, such consent has a legitimating role. Valid consent renders permissible what might otherwise be impermissible. It is reasonable then to think that consent must be *valid enough* to provide such a warrant. One might think of the relationship between the validity of consent and the permissibility of whatever is consensual in terms of the model of 'reflective equilibrium'. This is the method by which moral principles and moral judgements are both adjusted to yield an acceptable 'fit'.[26] Similarly one could adjust both what is considered permissible and what shall count as valid consent until there is a 'fit' between the Principle of Consensuality and the definition of valid consent.

Alternatively, one might retain a standard understanding of what invalidates consent—ignorance, coercion, and incompetence—and argue that there are some valid but valueless forms of consent. In other words one believes, for example, that the consent of a patient to have sex with her doctor is just as valid as that of a paradigmatic case of valid consent, since it is the willing and knowing consent of someone able to give or withhold her consent. Yet one also judges that the consent of the patient is devalued by the existence of the relationship between her and the doctor. Its validity is not or may not be enough to legitimate the sexual relationship between them. Such a proposal leaves it open where the line is to be drawn between valid but valueless consent and validating consent. And in doing so, the proposal limits the scope of the Principle of Consensuality without making the terms of the reduced limit clear. Nevertheless, the proposal has the merit of refusing to regard the devalued consent of someone as not being the willing and knowing consent of someone able to give her consent. The proposal says that it is consent for all of that.

Let me summarise the conclusions of a chapter which has addressed a number of different issues. Two principles constitute the general view about the moral permissibility of consensual sexual activity. The Principle of Consensuality holds that 'a practice, P, is morally permissible if all those who are parties to P are competent to consent, give or gave their valid consent, and the practice neither significantly harms the interests of other parties nor occasions them serious offence'. The Principle of Dissent maintains that 'a practice, P, is morally impermissible if at least one of those who are parties to P, and who are competent to consent, does or did dissent, even if the interests of no other parties are significantly harmed, nor are these others occasioned serious offence'.

The 'other parties' mentioned in these two principles may be considered to include animals and dead persons. In considering whether parties have been occasioned serious offence, we should discount 'abnormal sensibilities', but also remain sensitive to cultural differences and to the possibility of evaluating the underlying attitudes that inform any particular sensibility. The Principle of Consensuality tolerates one person sexually using another. This need not involve that person deceiving, manipulating, or exploiting the other. Insisting that people do not consensually sexually use each other seems to be unrealistically stringent.

Nevertheless, a concern that the Principle of Consensuality does tolerate the sexual use of others can now be added to the worries explored in Chapter 4 about the proper scope of valid consent. In recognition of these two sorts of worry we might do a number of things. We might abandon the general view which the two principles express in favour of some other account of sexual morality. We could accept that the Principle of Consensuality provides a necessary but not a sufficient condition of moral acceptability, acknowledging that there are consensual but impermissible sexual activities. The general view, on this option, would need supplementing with other moral notions. We might insist that the general view remain the correct one but extend our understanding of what should count as valid consent. We might insist that the general view remain the correct one but add that there are appropriate non-moral criteria for evaluating the sexual activities which that view tolerates.

I shall leave these broadly sketched suggestions to one side and without further comment, for a major challenge to the general view has still not been dealt with. This is the challenge, associated with feminism, which consists in the claim that under present conditions women as a group do not and cannot ever give their genuine consent to any sexual relationship with men. This is the subject of the next chapter.

6

Gendered Consent

Never is it asked whether, under conditions of male supremacy, the notion of 'consent' has any meaning.

—*Catharine MacKinnon*, Sexual Harassment of Working Women

THE QUESTION JUST POSED must be answered if the preceding analysis of this book is not to be largely beside the point. The question's author, Catharine MacKinnon, offers an influential account of the meaning of 'consent' under conditions of male supremacy which in fact purports to show that the preceding analysis does miss the point. For her account argues that when, as is the case, relationships between men and women are constituted under conditions of domination and subordination, a woman's consent within these relationships—and, in particular, her consent to sex with a man—is improperly described as consensual. MacKinnon's work is particularly influential, but a version of the claim can also be found in work by Carole Pateman.[1] This chapter critically evaluates that general claim.

This chapter does not presume that MacKinnon's is the only feminist writing that bears on the issue of sexual consent. It is not. But it is the most stark, the most striking, and the most direct critique of a view about the validity of sexual consent which is central to the arguments of this book. Nor does this chapter assume that there is not a wealth of feminist work about sex, sexuality, and the relations between the genders. There is. But this chapter is within a book specifically directed to an examination of sexual *consent* and not of sex or sexuality in general.

Before proceeding further, let me first deal with a separate point which concerns the standard the law employs to allow the inference to be drawn that a woman's consent has been given. A familiar criticism of the standard of consent which has been used in the crime of rape is that it permits submission to, or acquiescence in, sexual activity to be understood as consensual participation. Consent is construed as the contrary of dissent, which, in turn, is taken to be evidenced by clear signs of refusal, such as physical resistance. A woman who submits, silently and passively but unwillingly to a sexual assault does so consensually on this criticised standard of consent.

The use of the standard may derive from the assumption that rape is sex effected 'against the will' of the woman, and that this requires that there be evidence of that will being overcome—evidence both of force being used by the man and of resistance to that use of force by its victim. It is of course proper to insist that it is lack of consent which defines the crime of rape, and that, further, consent may both be negated without the use of force and be absent despite the lack of any explicit signs of dissent. Silent submission is not consent. Catharine MacKinnon rightly, and memorably, remarks that the criticised standard of consent is such that a dead woman may be said to give her consent.[2] Similarly Carole Pateman maintains that genuine consent is to be distinguished from 'habitual acquiescence, assent, silent dissent, submission or even enforced submission'.[3]

A general point is broached by the criticism of this particular standard. This is that these kinds of standards, and evidential rules in general, which operate within the context of the law governing relationships between the genders, are constituted from a male understanding of what is appropriate. In consequence they deny a woman's understanding of what is proper and will operate to the detriment of women. In similar terms it could be maintained that the 'reasonableness' of a man's belief that a woman did consent to sex with him is understood by the law in male terms—what it is reasonable for a man to believe about a woman's behaviour and sexuality. Since establishment of the man's possession of a 'reasonable' belief in consent is sufficient to acquit him of the charge of rape, the law which employs such a standard of 'reasonableness' cannot but fail equitably to legislate the relations between men and women.

These criticisms may be well founded. But they concern the operation of the law, standards of evidence, rules of interpretation, and so on, which are open to change. There are signs, for instance, that the criticised standard of consent is no longer being used. In the British case of *Regina* v. *Olugboja* (1981) the Court of Appeal dismissed the claim that there can only be an absence of consent if the victim's mind had been overborne by fear of death or duress. The judges declared that 'there is a difference between consent and submission; every consent involves a submission, but it by no means follows that a mere submission involves consent'.[4] The jury should merely determine whether in a particular instance the victim had or had not consented.

But these kind of changes—actual and possible—are beside the point. Even if the law was changed so as to operate with a standard of consent which was, in the argued sense, fair to both the man's and the woman's understanding of what it is to give consent, there would still be the outstanding charge—that a woman's consent, however it is given, does not count because it cannot be genuine. It is this charge which needs to be evaluated. The charge may be understood as constituted by three distinct claims, which can be asserted conjointly but which should be appraised separately. The three claims summarily presented are as follows. First, significant, structured gender inequality causes any individual relationship between a man and a woman to have features such that it is impossible for a woman really and truly to give her consent. Second, the nature of sexuality is such that a woman cannot really and truly be said to consent to a sexual relationship. Third, inasmuch as heterosexual relationships between men and women are enforced and alternative forms of relationship for women are precluded, a woman does not really and truly consent to any particular relationship with a man.

The first thing that should be said about the form of all three claims is that if they are intended to be universal in scope, they are very strong claims indeed. The universal claim is that every woman in every instance of a sexual relationship with a man does not really consent to that relationship. If the universality of that claim is said to follow from some characterisation of what it is to be a woman, then the further charge of 'essentialism' will be lodged. It will be lodged whether the source of the essence is alleged to lie in woman's biology or in her constituted gender identity. Essentialism in feminist theory is and has been criticised by feminists. Its particular failings in the context of a critique of consent have also been exposed.[5] MacKinnon has been charged with an essentialism which is inconsistent with that methodology which she takes to define feminism. The methodology is constituted by a reliance on the experiences and voices of woman. But such a methodology can at most only ground a 'weak essentialism', that is, warranted generalisations about the actual condition of women as they report it in their particular societies.[6]

A defeasible generalised claim of this kind is vulnerable to obvious counter-instances. It can be maintained in its general form only by denial of the authenticity of any sincere report from a single woman which contradicts it. When women claim to have consensual sexual relations with men, they must be disbelieved. We will return to this point, which we might call 'the denial of individual consent'. Further, the general claim can be maintained in its simple form only by a denial of the relevance of differences among women. That women are of different racial, national, cultural, and economic backgrounds is not pertinent to the veracity of the central claim.[7] All that matters is that they are women, and this is thought sufficient to explain the invalidity of the consent they give. Again we will return to the point, which we might call 'the failure of false uniformity'.

Gender Inequality

What then of the first claim—that significant, structured gender inequality causes any individual relationship between a man and a woman to have features such that it is impossible for a woman really and truly to give her consent? Carole Pateman argues that insofar as relations between men and women are not those of equals, as they are not, it is improper to speak of consent. She describes 'the failure in liberal-democratic theory and practice to distinguish free commitment and agreement by equals from domination, subordination and inequality' and clearly intends this general point to have application to the sexual relations between men and women.[8]

It is important to be clear in what respect men and women are not equals. It cannot simply be that women and men are not socio-economic equals. Of course, they may not be, and, for reasons discussed in Chapter 4, the woman who is considerably poorer than the man may not give her 'real' consent to his sexual proposals. However, if that were the nature of the claim, then it would not be a claim specifically about *gender* inequality. It would be a claim about the implications of socio-economic inequality in general and applicable to the relationships between men and women only in those cases where men and women occupy the positions of rich and poor, respectively. Further, it would be a claim that also applied to relations between the members of different races, nations, religions, even generations, so long as there was a correlation between membership of these groups and differential socio-economic status. Further, it would follow from the truth of the general claim that a very poor man does not give *his* 'real' consent to the sexual proposal of a very rich woman.

Clearly there is no simple and invariant correlation of the required kind between gender and socio-economic position, even if it is true that, for instance, on average women are worse off then men. That men as a group fare better than women as a group does not mean that this individual man must fare better than this individual woman. Gender inequality must be understood as an inequality between men and women as such and independently of their socio-economic status as a group or as particular individuals. Differential socio-economic status, if it does exist, might then be viewed as an expression of or result of this more fundamental gender inequality. But, for instance, a relationship between a man and a woman would not, on this account, be one of equals even if the two individuals were, as a matter of fact, of equal socio-economic rank.

Construed as this kind of a claim the view that gender inequality is sufficient to negate a woman's consent in all instances appears implausibly strong. For the inequality of simple gender must be so pronounced as to outweigh any countervailing inequality in dimensions other than gender. A rich woman does not really consent when she enters into a relationship with a poor man because the power or influence of her greater wealth is trumped by the greater weakness of her sex. This is also so when a white woman relates to a black man, or a female member of the ruling class relates to a male member of the ruled class.

The various possible dimensions of inequality in power and status— along racial, socio-economic, and gender lines—may be both constituted and expressed in different ways. It is also implausible to think that the various dimensions are additive in some simple way, such that a rich, white man has an overall power that is merely a sum of the power attributable to his wealth, race, and gender. The various dimensions of power will overlap and interact in a complex fashion. It is highly unlikely that there will be a concrete case of gender inequality alone between a man, *simpliciter,* and a woman, *simpliciter.* However, the point under consideration here is what the dimension of gender inequality is when it is abstracted from, and recognised not to be reducible to, these other dimensions.

Consider the most plausible explanation of such gender inequality that is consistent with feminism. This is that women are socialised to be the subordinates of men.[9] Pateman writes of the pattern of sexual relationships that 'the "naturally" superior, active and sexually aggressive male makes an initiative, or offers a contract, to which a "naturally" subordinate, passive woman "consents"'.[10] Pateman's use of scare quotes around the two occurrences of 'naturally' is intended to convey her disavowal of any view that such subordination is grounded in the nature of the sexes. It is rather the result of a pattern of socialisation and acculturation. When a woman consents to sex with a man, she does not 'really' give her consent because, irrespective of all the other respects in which she may have greater rank, wealth, power, and status than this man, she is, as all socialised women must be, his passive subordinate.

The weakness of this claim is directly proportionate to its universal form. For the claim is that all women must be the victims of gender inequality. They must be so whatever other social factors operate to determine their particular identity. They must be such victims whatever their own experiences and sincere reports of non-passivity and 'real consent'. A woman may feel herself to be the equal of a man and consider that she does enter freely into a relationship with him, but her status as his gender subordinate gainsays her own consciousness of equality and freedom. Finally such an account cannot explain the successful resistance of women to their socialised status. Women who refuse relationships with men are not passive subordinates. Nor are those who seek to expose the non-naturalness of such a gender identity. Yet a process whereby gender inequality is maintained, supposedly sufficient to negate the apparently willing consent of all women, cannot at the same time be such as to allow for resistance to and dissent from that process by some of its supposed victims.

The Erotization of Dominance and Submission

The claim that women are the socialised subordinates of men must be intended to describe the pattern of all relationship between the genders. However, it is conceivable that, independent of any general inequality, the nature of sexuality is such that, in a specifically sexual relationship between a man and a woman, the woman does not really give her consent. This is argued by MacKinnon when she describes heterosexuality as the 'erotization of dominance and submission'.[11] *All* heterosexual encounters are constituted by and in the man's sexual subordination and forced violation of the woman. This is true whether or not the woman gives her consent. For this reason MacKinnon, notoriously, argues that there is little real difference between coerced sex, rape, and normal, consensual intercourse. 'The problem remains what it has always been: telling the difference. . . . The uncoerced context for sexual expression becomes as elusive as the physical acts come to feel indistinguishable. . . . Perhaps the wrong of rape has proven so difficult to articulate because the unquestionable starting point has been that rape is definable as distinct from intercourse, when for women it is difficult to distinguish them under conditions of male dominance'.[12]

It is important to distinguish two versions of this claim. One is that heterosexual intercourse in inherently a violation by the man of the woman. This claim can be supported by a description of such intercourse in language which illuminates its allegedly violative character. MacKinnon cites the work of her collaborator Andrea Dworkin, who writes in this fashion. Consider the following extracts: 'In practice, fucking is an act of possession—simultaneously an act of ownership, taking, force; it is conquering; it expresses in intimacy power over and against, body to body, person to thing. "The sex act" means penile intromission followed by penile thrusting, or fucking'.[13] 'Intercourse is commonly written about as a form of possession or an act of possession in which, during which, because of which, a man inhabits a woman, physically covering her and overwhelming her and at the same time penetrating her; and this physical relation to her—over her and inside her—is his possession of her. He has her, or, when he is done, he has had her. By thrusting into her, he takes her over.'[14] 'He has to push in past boundaries. . . . The thrusting is persistent invasion. She is opened up, split down the centre. She is occupied—physically, internally, in her privacy'.[15]

Dworkin, and MacKinnon by her approving citation of Dworkin, characterise heterosexual intercourse as 'possession', 'occupation', 'conquest', and 'invasion'. These terms have clear evaluative connotations, but, of course, the crucial question is whether one is entitled to describe an action in such evaluative terms when a neutral description would be adequate to a specification of the action in question. 'Hitler invaded Poland' says more than merely 'Hitler entered Poland'. It says that Hitler's entry of Poland was wrongful, and wrongful in this instance because the entry was unconsented by Poland. The mere fact of entry is not in itself wrongful. The thousands of tourists who annually enter Poland from neighbouring countries do not do so wrongfully and are not described as invaders. To state or imply that heterosexual intercourse is an 'invasion' by the man of the woman is a misleading re-description of the action inasmuch as it begs the question of its wrongfulness. In particular if—as seems the most plausible reading—the wrongfulness of any 'occupation' lies in its being dissented to by the occupied party, then the description of heterosexual sex as an 'occupation' presumes that all heterosexual sex is unconsensual simply in virtue of being heterosexual sex,[16] and whether or nor its parties take themselves to be consenting. At this point the claim then runs foul of the 'denial of individual consent' point.

But perhaps Dworkin's language should be taken as rhetorical and non-evaluative. Consider the use of the words 'forceful' and 'violent' in certain contexts. To say of a person's manner of speech or argument that it was 'forceful' ('He put his point forcefully') or 'violent' ('He argued violently against her view') may simply amount to a description of the manner of its accomplishment without any implication of its being done wrongfully. The person did not employ force or violence against anyone when he spoke this way. Similarly Dworkin might be taken as using the colourful rhetoric of military description to illuminate the manner in which heterosexual sex is accomplished without implying any moral condemnation of that activity.[17] This is a possible interpretation, but it is unlikely given the overall tone of her writing. Moreover, to so interpret her would be to make her comments largely beside the point. We might wonder why people should choose to engage or derive pleasure from an activity so characterised. But we would not be automatically led to think that they could not possibly be consenting to it.

This takes us to the second way of understanding the claim that heterosexual sex is 'eroticized dominance and submission'. This is a claim about the way in which heterosexuality is constituted in our culture. It is not a claim about the very nature of sex, sex *simpliciter,* sex as such. It is a claim about sex as it is for us now under these specific social conditions. This appears to be MacKinnon's claim. She insistently and consistently resists any description of sex and sexuality as having an invariant, natural, or biological character. Heterosexuality is a 'construct', an 'institution', a 'creation'; it is 'culturally defined'. It is culturally specific insofar as it is such a creation. It is invariant only inasmuch as male supremacy is universal. Crucially, MacKinnon further believes that sexuality, so constituted, is what determines the identity of women and the nature of their general relationships to men: 'Sexuality is that social process which creates, organizes, expresses, and directs desire, creating the social beings we know as women and men, as their relations create society'.[18] 'Sex as gender and sex as sexuality are thus defined in terms of each other, but it is sexuality that determines gender, not the other way round'.[19] This yields the following picture: Sexuality is itself constituted (by male dominance and female submission) and itself constitutes the social relations (of male dominance and female submission). 'Sexuality becomes, in this view, social and relational, constructing and constructed of power'.[20]

What can be said in response to this picture? First, the now familiar point of 'false uniformity' can be made. Sexuality is constructed in an absolutely uniform manner; it knows no significant differences.[21] Second, it is resolutely reductionist inasmuch as sexuality alone, and to the exclusion of social and economic factors, explains women's subordination to men. Third, the value of the picture to elucidate our situation is open to challenge. Male power is both explanatory of and explained by the constitutive character of heterosexuality. Sexuality is, as MacKinnon says, both 'constructing and constructed of' that power. There can be, it seems, no independent characterisation of that power outside its effects. Nor can be there any explanation of how it comes to be set in its place of unparalleled, and apparently steadfast, dominance.

Fourth, and most pertinently given present concerns, it is hard to see what counts as support for the picture. MacKinnon appears to be drawn in two directions, reflecting a tension between her commitments to feminist methodology and practice and the conclusions of her particular feminist theory. In characterising heterosexuality as 'eroticized dominance and submission', MacKinnon appeals to the experience of women. In particular she cites the evidence of rape, battery, pornography, sexual harassment, and so on. The point of doing so is to suggest that these experiences are especially revealing of how sex in general is for women under conditions of male supremacy. The act of rape is somehow paradigmatic. Or, again, the pornographic representation of sex is merely a particularly revealing picture of what men, in general, desire in and from women. Thus, women's reports of sex 'look a lot' like victims' reports of sex, as these in turn 'look a lot' like what pornography says is sex.[22] Of course the qualifying use of 'a lot' is important. If rape and normal sex were completely indistinguishable, it would follow that the victims of rape could not tell that they had been raped. Or every report of 'normal' sex would have to be an allegation of possible rape. That would be a reductio ad absurdum of such a strong construal of the claim, and it would surely be sufficient to discredit it.

Feminism rescues from obscurity and silence the testimony of women, their reported experiences of violence, subordination, and abuse at the hands of men. To read or hear such testimony is to be given a powerful reminder of the depredations of abusive male power. Against the denials or suppression by men of it, feminism appeals to such testimony as support for its exposure of male oppression. Crucially, however, the testimony of women cannot invoke the very distinctions which MacKinnon alleges are false and ideologically male ones. MacKinnon's claim is that women cannot tell the difference between rape ('abnormal') sex and 'normal' sex. The language is explicitly phenomenological and epistemological. It is about what women say, report, feel, and believe to be the case. Note, then, from the quotation given earlier, suggesting that rape and normal sex cannot be distinguished, the use of the following phrases: 'telling the difference', 'come to feel indistinguishable', 'for women it is difficult to distinguish them'.

However, it is clear that very many women report their unequivocal awareness that rape is *not* normal sex, and very, very many women report their awareness than normal sex is most definitely not rape. This much seems empirically incontestable. It is open to MacKinnon to make two moves. First, MacKinnon can discount the testimony of those women who assert the evident distinctness of normal sex, or accord a particular weight to the testimony of those who avow that rape and normal sex cannot be separated. The problem then is to provide an independent justification of such a differentiation, one, moreover, which gives a presumptive weight to the reports of what is likely to be a minority of women. Thus critics of MacKinnon have often called attention to her inconsistency in privileging some women's experiences while apparently denying the veracity of other women's. She believes those who speak of abuse by men but disbelieves those who report enjoyment and consent with men.[23] The further critical point to be made is that MacKinnon unwarrantably prefers to draw her testimony from the sphere of sexual peril, not pleasure, and that it is women as victims who figure most prominently in her analysis.

The other move MacKinnon can make is simply to assert that heterosexuality is of a certain character, whatever women might say. That of course is to discount the testimony of women upon whose foundation feminism rests. Moreover, it is hard to see what could provide a warrant for a simple, bald assertion of this kind. Dworkin's re-descriptive approach might be used, but this has already been subjected to criticism. Other argumentative forms, such as that which asserts the shared sexual character of rape and normal sex ('Like heterosexuality, the crime of rape centres on penetration'[24]), are obviously fallacious. The employment of such devices comes dangerously close to sophism.

There is one way in which the assertion—that heterosexuality *is* the erotization of dominance and submission—can be maintained at the same time as the reported experience of women need not be accorded undisputed evidentiary significance. This is to argue that women experience their sexuality within the context of the exercise of male power, and that this exercise of power is sufficient to shape that experience in certain ways. The experience of women has been 'circumscribed and defined' by the 'construct' of sexuality,[25] which the theory maintains is the construction of male power. For MacKinnon 'men *create* the world from their own point of view, which then becomes the truth to be described. . . . *Power to create the world from one's point of view is power in its male form'*.[26] The more successful men are in shaping the way the world is experienced, the less independent warrant women's experience of that world has as an alternative or challenge to the male point of view.

Now MacKinnon is inclined to think that men are very successful in this project. Male dominance is 'metaphysically near perfect. Its point of view is the standard for point-of-viewlessness, its particularity the meaning of universality'.[27] Her claim, if true, has paradoxical consequences. The exposure of male power is due to the testimony and experience of women who contest it. But such contestation is subverted, indeed dissolved, by the very success of that male power. Male power makes impossible its own critique in the form of feminism.[28] Indeed MacKinnon is quoted by one critic as describing female power as 'a contradiction in terms'.[29] The emancipatory project of feminism is simply gainsaid by the implications of its own theoretical conclusions.[30] More pertinently the attempt to provide a critique of every woman's consent as merely 'eroticized submission' would seem to be without foundation. The testimony of women upon which it might rest is inconsistent, and there is no way, which does not beg crucial questions, of thinking that some forms of testimony should be believed and others denied. If the critique of all women's consent does not rest upon any testimony, then it is hard to see what grounds the assertion, especially as the very reasons for making the assertion deprive that assertion of any warrant.

Compulsory Heterosexuality

The third claim within the feminist critique of consent under consideration is that, inasmuch as heterosexual relationships between men and woman are enforced and alternative forms of relationship for woman are precluded, a woman does not really and truly consent to any particular relationship with a man. Consider the parallel example of marriage. In some societies women must marry if they are to have any reasonable expectations of securing the means of subsistence. Women are not permitted to, or it is made impossible for them in other ways to, lead an economically independent life. Their future health and well-being are inseparable from those of the husband they must find. It may of course be true of any particular woman within such a society that she can choose her husband. She may not have many potential husbands from which to choose. She may 'choose' only in the sense that she is herself chosen and accepts or declines the offer made. Nevertheless, it need not be the case that she is compelled to marry some one particular man or that each particular marriage is arranged. However, what matters is that, whether or not she can and does choose whom to marry, she does not have any choice over whether to marry at all.

It could then be said, to return to the main claim, that women may choose their particular male sexual partners but do not choose whether or not to be heterosexual. To that extent their 'consent' as individuals occurs within a context of compelled heterosexuality and cannot be properly described as freely given.[31] Adrienne Rich describes heterosexuality as 'something that has had to be imposed, managed, organized, propagandized, and maintained by force'.[32] Christine Overing describes the 'institution of heterosexuality' as 'the systematised set of social standards, customs, and expected practices which both regulate and restrict romantic relationships between persons of different sex in late twentieth-century Western culture'.[33]

In the face of the very many women who regularly claim freely to have and to enjoy heterosexual relations with men, the claim that women are compelled to be heterosexual looks implausible. It would be plausible only if the following could be provided: first, sufficient evidence of systematic compulsion and, second, reasons to think that, in the absence of such compulsion, women would not make a choice of heterosexuality. Neither is likely to be forthcoming. Let me take each in turn. In the first place, it is important to point out that evidence for the compelling of women into heterosexuality could also, and probably with more reason, be cited as evidence of compulsion into certain forms or expressions of heterosexuality. Indeed it is surely more likely that pressures—social, economic, political, and legal—should be and are brought to bear on women not that they be heterosexual as such but that they be heterosexual in particular ways or within specific limits. For instance, women, if they are the subject of compulsion, are forced to be sexually initiated only within marriage, to be sexually monogamous, to have procreative sex, to be sexually passive, and so on. In short, evidence of compulsion into heterosexuality may also, and more likely, be evidence of a compulsory *regulation* of heterosexuality.

There is a further and more decisive point to be made. This is that such enforced restriction and regulation tell against, rather than in favour of, the claim that heterosexuality as such needs to be compelled. If women have to be forced to be monogamous and passive, it is surely reasonable to infer that, in the absence of such compulsion, they might be polygamous and active. They need not be non-heterosexual. Rather, they might well be heterosexual in ways embarrassing to the interests of men.

Notwithstanding this point, the evidence of literal physical compulsion is not itself compelling. Such evidence as is cited (child brides, capital punishment for heterodox sexuality, the harem, marital rape) is restricted in scope of its application—culturally, historically, and intra-societally—and insufficient to show that all women everywhere are forced to be heterosexual. Of course the claim of compulsion looks most convincing if it is characterised as not explicit. Rich says that heterosexuality 'has been forcibly and subliminally imposed on women'.[34] 'Subliminally' does the work in the argument that 'forcibly' cannot. Yet we can really only understand subliminal compulsion as systematic socialisation, and, even then, the use of the word 'compulsion' is strained. If we accept such a usage for the sake of the argument, it is necessary to ask, What would show that there is such systematic socialisation, in a pejorative sense, rather than, for instance, a simple and innocent transmission of basic values and beliefs across generations? Part of the answer to this lies in our being clear about what would be the case in the absence of any purported socialisation. I will return to this in due course.

However, part of the answer also lies in our being clear about what is supposed to be doing the work of socialising. To talk, for instance, merely of the 'idealisation of heterosexual romance in art, literature, media, advertising, etc.' seems inadequate.[35] Could *that*, however pervasive, be systematic enough to count as 'subliminal compulsion'? It should also be obvious that the exclusion of alternatives to heterosexuality—lesbianism, bisexuality, and celibacy—by forcible repression and stigmatisation should not be necessary if systematic socialisation had done its job. It should further be evident that neither compulsion nor the exclusion of alternatives is fulfilling this combined task if significant numbers of women are not heterosexual—which is the case.

It might be still be argued that the 'preference' of the majority of women who are heterosexual is only an adaptation to the seeming impossibility of choosing otherwise, the apparent inevitability of being only heterosexual. Women might not feel compelled to so choose, and indeed things need not be so arranged as to compel them. Nevertheless, when they choose as they do, it is because they have somehow come to feel themselves unable to choose otherwise. This is because things are arranged so that it is thought by them that only certain ways of life can be pursued or are how it must be for them. The

phenomenon of adaptive preferences is important, and its proper acknowledgement serves to check too ready an acceptance of the validity of uncoerced choices.[36] Yet it is important to add that a person's preferences can be
adapted to the circumstances of her choice and remain rational. They need
not be untrue to her deep-lying or real desires, or harmful to her. Moreover,
that she has come to acquire the preferences in this way need not be inconsistent with her having a general competence to evaluate and think about her
preferences. For these reasons it would be improper to conclude that adaptive preferences should not be respected. The consent to some activity which
springs from such a preference should not be discounted.[37]

In the absence of such alleged compulsion to be heterosexual, would
women be heterosexual anyway? A positive answer seems compelling. To
think that, whatever the social form, women (and men) are, in the main
and on the whole, heterosexual is not to think heterosexuality 'innate',
'natural', or 'normal' (in its evaluative sense). It is merely to make a very
reasonable, if defeasible, presumption which draws inductively on evidence
from history, anthropology, and sociology as well as psychology and physi-
ology. Making this presumption is consistent with a refusal to stigmatise
non-heterosexual activity and with a belief that any compulsion into particular consensual and non-harmful ways of life is reprehensible. The fact is
that very many women, made fully aware both of the alternatives to heterosexuality and of the charge that their heterosexuality is compelled, continue
to be heterosexual. To insist that such women are compelled 'subliminally'
to choose as they do would seem, at the end of the day, to be a case of, ob-
stinately and prejudicially, discounting choices that one cannot, for one's
own part, share or endorse.

Consent does have a meaning for women. They can and do consent to
heterosexual relationships with men. That does not mean that women and
men always understand consent to these relationships in the same ways, or
that women are immune from various pressures to constrain and regulate
these relationships, or that such constraints operate to the prejudice of
women and to the benefit of men, or that the existence of such constraints
cannot be explained in terms of a disparity of power between men and
women, or that heterosexuality is or should be the only possible sexual
choice for women, individually and as a gender. However, to understand
these qualifications in a way that denies that women ever do validly consent
to sex with men is mistaken. It also, ironically, represents a refusal to take
seriously what women themselves take seriously: their own giving and
withholding of consent.

◀ 7 ▶

The Limits of Consensuality I: Incest, Prostitution, and Sado-masochism

THIS CHAPTER AND THE NEXT TWO examine a number of areas in which the Principles of Consensuality and Dissent clearly apply but where the application of these principles does not, somehow, seem enough. The areas of interest are incest, prostitution, sado-masochism, rape, and the sexual activity of those below the age of consent. In the first three of these areas there are features of the activity specified which, notwithstanding the giving of valid consent, lead us to doubt the permissibility of the activity. In the case of incest it is the matter of who the consenting sex is between, in the case of prostitution it is that the consenting sex is bought and sold, and in the case of sado-masochism it is that the consenting sex is harmful. The worry is that the Principle of Consensuality remains inadequate to a proper evaluation of the sexual activity in question. These are thus cases in which the putative robustness of the Principle of Consensuality is usefully displayed.

The second two cases, which will be the subject of the next two chapters, have features which go beyond the terms of the Principles of Consensuality and Dissent. In the case of the crime of rape there are issues to be broached about the conduct of trials, rules of evidence, and proceedings, as well as about different expectations of reasonable conduct. In the case of the age of consent the nature of childhood and the sexuality proper to it needs to be put on the agenda for discussion. The worry here is that the Principles of Consensuality and Dissent do not provide a comprehensive moral evaluation of all the aspects of these cases. They are thus ones in which the alleged fullness or richness of these principles might be considered.

It is worth repeating that this book does not offer a full-blown defence of the principles against competing moral principles of sexual conduct. It is rather concerned, admittedly from within a broad acceptance of these principles, with making good sense of how these principles might regulate sexual activity: what exactly is consensual activity, why the notion that whatever is consensual is permissible has plausibility, and whether consensuality on its own terms really is enough for permissibility. Each of the five problem areas raises doubts, each in its own way, about the sufficiency of the Principles of Consensuality and Dissent. They will be considered then in the light of the challenge they pose to these principles.

There is a further point which now needs to be made. The problem cases under consideration are appropriate possible subjects of criminal law. Reference will be made, as it has been made in earlier chapters, to particular criminal cases and to legal statutes. The general view considered in this book is a view about what is morally permissible, and not about what should be legally tolerated. It does not follow from its being true that some activity is morally impermissible that it should be illegal. It would not always be appropriate—because, for instance, it would be counterproductive or a misuse of the law—to criminalise an activity or practice which, it could be agreed, was immoral.

Let us agree that some activity is judged not to be permissible by the Principles of Consensuality and Dissent. What would be needed to show, further, that this activity should also be made illegal? There is no simple answer to this question. Any answer would need to take account of the harm occasioned by the activity, the degree of dissent to the activity, the function of the law as an instrument of behavioural change, the prevalence of the activity, and so on. No general answer is given here, although when I discuss some individual cases, I make suggestions about the proper scope of the law. To repeat, this book is about the moral permissibility of consensual sexual activity. And it certainly does follow from the fact that some activity is morally permissible that it should not be a crime.

Incest

Incest is a form of sexual activity characterised in terms of the nature of the relations which obtain between the parties to it. It is normally held to be objectionable in virtue of its being sex between persons so related. The relations in question are familial. The familial relations may be co-extensive with or determined by biological or blood relations. But they need not be, and in many instances they have not been exclusively understood in this way. The 1761 English Book of Common Prayer, for instance, contains a 'table of kindred and affinity, wherein whosoever are related, are forbidden in Scripture, and our Laws, to marry together'. Almost half of the prohibited unions are with genetically unrelated persons, principally and most obviously those relations acquired through marriage.[1] It is of course also true, and often noted, that different societies may delineate the scope of prohibited familial intimacy in different ways. Who may and may not be 'kissing cousins' varies across cultures.

The social condemnation of incest is also said to be socially invariant, even though in some societies there has been systematic and wilful violation of the supposed prohibition. The Ptolemaic dynasty in Egypt is an obvious example. Such exceptions duly noted, it may be asked, Wherein lies the rationale for such general condemnation? A simple, if ultimately unsatisfactory, answer is provided by the Principles of Consensuality and Dissent. Raymond Belliotti, for instance, maintains that 'at the core of incest's immorality is non-consensuality. . . . The act typically involves rape'.[2] In particular Belliotti thinks that the typical incestuous act is the sexual abuse of a child by a parent, normally male.

It is true, statistically at least, that the typical incestuous act is parent-child. Further, *any* abusive adult-child sexual relationship is wrong because it is non-consensual. Or rather in such a case less than 'real' consent is obtained only through the abuse of those features of trust, dependence, power, and authority which generally serve to define the relationship between adult and child. This might suggest that the wrong of incest is an instance of a more general wrong, that of abusing relations of authority to obtain sexual consent.[3] The abuse by a teacher of his pupil would be a further instance of this wrong. The degree of trust, dependence. affection, and identification will be that much greater in the case of the parent and child. But that just constitutes incest as a much greater, not an essentially different, kind of wrong.[4]

However, two comments are in order. The first is that it would be mistaken to think that incestuous adult-adult relations, whether between grown child and parent, or between grown siblings, escape these terms of condemnation. This is because the incest in question may have been initiated at an earlier time and may merely reproduce the relationship of abusive domination which was established from the outset. Such considerations also make it dangerous to suggest a simple division between grossly unacceptable parent-child incest and possibly acceptable sibling incest. The latter may also arise from an abuse of superior power and authority. Indeed the evidence of older brother–younger sister incest confirms this to be very often the case.

The second set of comments runs in a very different direction to the first. It departs from the thought, which will be had by many, that such a reductionist account of the wrongness of incest is unsatisfactory. It is reductionist inasmuch as it offers a translation of the immorality of incest, without remainder, into the general terms of the immorality of non-consensual sex where the absence of consent is attributable to the abuse of a certain kind of relationship. The account will be thought unsatisfactory on the following grounds. Incest, it will be said, is wrong for reasons which go beyond, and indeed may be entirely different in kind, from those offered in the reductionist account.

Now some of these reasons might be captured by the provision within the Principle of Consensuality which exempts practices harmful to third parties. Two kinds of harm are relevant here, those to possible future offspring of an incestuous union and those to the family. Let me take each in turn. A familiar argument against incest is that it carries significant eugenic risks, namely, an increased possibility of genetic deformities. To say that the general perception of incest as immoral is to be explained in terms of these risks holds little water. Such a perception obtains in the absence of any consciousness of such risks.[5] Notwithstanding ignorance of these alleged dangers, it is sufficient to make the following three points. First, where the proscribed familial relations do not coincide with any biological relations, the risks can be no greater than they would be in any normal, sanctioned sexual relationship. Second, the risks are now generally agreed to be exaggerated and, insofar as they are serious, to require prolonged interbreeding.[6] Third, steps can be taken significantly to minimise the dysgenic outcomes of incest, most obviously by preventing pregnancy. That there may still be a risk of some harms to future persons cannot supply a convincing reason for thinking incestuous sex so much worse than many instances of non-incestuous sex.

The damage incest allegedly does to the family can be appreciated only by our seeing the family as having both intrinsic and instrumental worth for its members. The family supplies to its members a valued sense of identity, belonging, together with unconditional love and support. Or at least an idealised family, to which many, if not all, actual families approximate, does so. At the same time the family serves as that institution whereby individuals are socialised and educated into the possession of those capacities, aptitudes, and outlooks required of a citizen and functioning member of a society. It is normally thought not only that does the family fill this role well, but also that no other agent of socialisation could do so as effectively and without unacceptable costs.

Given that the family does have this value incest is to be deprecated for subverting it. Incest does so in a number of ways. It induces conflict and instability in familial relations; it breaks down the relationship of trust that must exist between adult and child if the former's socialisation of the latter is to be effective; it denies the child the opportunity to develop into independent maturity within a context of bounded intimacy and affective identification with significant others; it subverts the terms of the boundary between family and outside word which must exist if the eventual adult is to pass from the family into the larger social world and enter into exogamous relationships. And so on. Such arguments, which may appeal to Freudian understandings of psycho-sexual development and anthropological theories of society and kinship, are familiar enough.

The problems with regarding such alleged harms as supplying a sufficient condemnation of incest are twofold. First, it is possible to conceive of practices or sets of circumstances which do the same sorts and amounts of damage to the family but which do not appear to be subject to the same degree of extreme moral criticism. Consider, for example, intra-familial violence, parental subscription to very rigid or fundamental religious views, extreme poverty, ready toleration of and participation in criminality, excessive parental coldness or emotional indifference, and so on. It may still be insisted that incest is just so much worse in its consequences. But that looks implausible. Or at least it is unlikely that incest can be so much worse in its effects as to explain the view of it as totally different in moral kind from these other cases.

Second, we are left with the cases of siblings separated at or shortly after birth who, on being reunited, experience overpowering feelings of mutual attraction which may lead them into sexual intimacy. Such cases (and there are very occasional cases of parent-child incest along the same lines) are rare but well documented. It does not seem that any straightforward appeal to the damage that these incestuous relationships will or might do to the institution of the family is open to those who insist that, nevertheless, they remain deeply immoral.

In summary, the fact is that the alleged moral awfulness of incest in all of its possible instances cannot be captured within the terms of third-party harms, either to future offspring or to family and society. What is there left to say? Defenders of the Principles of Consensuality and Dissent will insist that a distinction is to be drawn between permissible and impermissible instances of incest according to the terms of these principles. To those who maintain that incest in any form is a natural evil (*horror naturalis*) which is rightly abhorrent to all humans, it will be responded that our abhorrence of incest is a product only of custom, law, and convention.[7] There are, it will be said, no irreducible natural wrongs. There is only whatever the principles of morality, which are open to the critical validation of rational human thought, may determine to be wrong.

Yet a doubt remains. After all it is a taboo that seems to be in question. It is not merely that the prohibition on incest is exceptionless and weighty. For humans can recognise that an action falls under such a prohibition and desist from performing it. That some action is subject to a taboo means that the very idea of doing it should fill the person with unreflective horror. I do not so much recognise that I am expressly forbidden to do this thing as feel seized with overwhelming repugnance at the mere thought of doing so. It may be that incest is the subject of such a taboo because of deep-seated biological and socio-psychological imperatives which do not answer neatly and easily to the requirements of conventional moral justification. What it is to be a human and live a human life with others of our species may require of us that some behaviours lie beyond the boundary of the acceptable, of even what can be contemplated dispassionately.[8]

If doubts do persist about the permissibility of consensual incest that harms no one, then they may be satisfactorily expressed in these kinds of terms. This is not the place to debate the merits of such an understanding of naturally wrongful sex. Its merits, such as they are, illuminate in a particularly clear way the limits of that view of the sexually tolerable which is under discussion, that is, the one in which the permissible is exhaustively defined by the consensual.

Prostitution

Prostitution is the sale of sex. Does that fact make it morally objectionable? Prostitution may well meet the terms of permissibility set by the Principles of Consensuality and Dissent—both parties to the sale enter into a consensual agreement which causes no significant third-party harms—and yet doubts may remain about its permissibility. How should we express these doubts? In the first place it seems clear from writing on the subject that there is no clear, agreed definition of prostitution which begs no important questions. Both men and women can be prostitutes; both men and women can offer homosexual or heterosexual sexual services. Many write as if only women are prostitutes. This may reflect an important fact about the actual proportions of each gender involved in prostitution. But such an assumption can also disguise (or openly express) a view that whatever is morally suspect about prostitution is due in large, or sole, part to the sale by women, not men, of sex. It is as well to be clear when and why such an assumption is being made.

The economic and social status of prostitutes can vary across cultures and historical periods. Within one and the same society the class of prostitutes might include a wealthy courtesan servicing only one client as well as individuals forced by economic necessity to sell sex indiscriminately under difficult, dangerous, and unpleasant conditions. The prostitute can work the street or inhabit the penthouse. Assumptions that prostitutes 'are an inferior sub-class of the human race' can and do inform the discussions of the subject.[9] Such assumptions support the view that prostitution is an especially degrading profession, or that what is sold is degraded sexuality. But of course prostitutes can have, and have had, an entirely different status. Prostitution is, as Joseph Kupfer points out, a practice like many others 'whose moral standing is context-sensitive, depending on a culture's values and beliefs'.[10]

Some have argued that promiscuity or indiscriminateness is also a defining characteristic of prostitution.[11] And there is good reason to think that someone who is interested in selling something as their means of subsistence will tend to sell as much of that thing as she can to whomever will buy it. Yet any salesperson can choose to limit what and to whom she sells, and it is no different with prostitution. We have already instanced the courtesan with the single client. Even those prostitutes who work the street will explicitly limit the scope of the services they offer and the clients to whom they will offer such services. That prostitution should be thought of as minimally defined in terms of the sale of sex is important for this reason. Indiscriminate or promiscuous sexual activity may be considered distasteful—for separating sex from a necessary context of intimacy or love, or whatever. However, such a charge cannot be specifically directed at prostitution. Indeed it would be inaccurate to think prostitution, if it is objectionable, is so for this reason.

Might prostitution—as such or in some forms of the practice—nevertheless violate the Principle of Consensuality? Let me consider first the question of third-party harms. There are familiar criticisms of prostitution which do appeal to such effects, though most philosophical discussions, whether on the whole sympathetic or unsympathetic to prostitution, are fairly quick to dismiss the alleged moral significance of these effects. One such effect is the offensiveness of prostitution to those who have no wish to, but cannot reasonably avoid seeing or being caught up in its conduct. The avoidance of such harms can effectively be secured by appropriate regulative restrictions on prostitution such as, most notably, constraints on soliciting, the licensing of brothels and massage parlours, and the specification of 'zones of tolerance' removed from residential areas within which prostitutes can ply their trade.

Further alleged third-party harms include the spread of disease, the provision of a source of profit and influence for criminal groups that traffic in other illegal activities, and the undermining of valuable social institutions such as the family. To the charge that each of these alleged harms is caused by prostitution there is a persuasive reply. Prostitution is no more responsible for the spread of sexually transmitted diseases than is promiscuous sexual interaction in general. Moreover, prostitutes have strong self-interested reasons for taking precautions against the transmission of disease, and evidence suggests they are both aware of and prudent in regard to such risks. It is the very illegality of prostitution which attracts criminal elements who seek to control it and who associate its conduct with other criminal activity. Where prostitution is legal and well regulated such criminal associations are largely absent.

The damage which it is alleged prostitution does to the stability of marital and familial relations is of two kinds. There is a direct harm, which consists in the fact that the prostitute's client breaks the vows of fidelity and sexual exclusivity which may be thought to constitute the proper terms of the marriage. In this respect prostitution does not differ from adultery. Moreover, there is anecdotal evidence to suggest that the use by married men of prostitutes differs in a clear way from their conduct of adulterous liaisons, and in such a way as to indict the latter as far more damaging to the marriage than the former. Prostitution may also be thought indirectly to damage marriage and the family by effecting a divorce between sex and loving intimacy, whose necessary connection lies at the foundation of these institutions.[12] In this respect prostitution differs little from any indiscriminate or promiscuous sexual activity. Moreover, the fact that prostitution is the explicit sale of unloving sex may serve to mark the distinction between this kind of sex and the valued sexual intimacy which cannot be bought or sold.

Is prostitution truly consensual? There seems little doubt that clients or punters normally freely choose to buy the services of a prostitute. Are prostitutes free agents? There are two sorts of relevant worry. One is about the freedom of any choice to become a prostitute; the other is about the freedom of choice one may have as a prostitute. Prostitutes may enter prostitution from dire economic necessity. Others may have backgrounds of abuse and deprivation which make their choice of prostitution considerably less free than might be wished from that of a mature, rational economic agent. Prostitutes may be forced by their pimps into sexual activities in which they otherwise would not engage. Some may find themselves trapped within a vicious cycle of prostitution. This is true, for instance, of those who take drugs to relieve the misery of their lives and find themselves having to sell sex to buy the drugs. Some or all of these factors may coalesce in particular cases. Where this is so there are good reasons to worry about the voluntariness of a prostitute's consent.

However, these features are contingent aspects of prostitution as it is practised in certain contexts. They do not show prostitution as such to be non-voluntary. Moreover, it is worth pointing out that many prostitutes will stress the voluntariness of their entry into the profession, and indeed may assert its clear preferability to some other far less desirable forms of paid employment. They will also emphasise the degree of control they can exercise over the terms, price, and clientele of their sexual services. In a recent study of working street prostitutes the authors note how the women in negotiation with potential clients 'adopt an assertive, businesslike stance. . . . As vendors of a desired service, the women consider themselves to be in a position to dictate the terms and conditions of that sale'.[13]

If prostitution of itself or at least some of prostitution as it can be practised escapes censure by the terms of the Principle of Consensuality, is that enough to show its permissibility? Remaining worries about prostitution may usefully be divided into three broad categories: a worry about the *sale* of sex, a worry that it is not simply sex which is on sale, and a worry about the role of selling whatever it is that the prostitute sells in supporting broader social understandings of sexuality and gender. Let me take each in turn.

Some things, it might be said, should just not be for sale. One might say this for two kinds of reason, one having to do with the proper ends of that thing, the other having to do with the inherent nature of the thing. Political power could be, is, and has been bought and sold. It should not be because it will then be exercised in morally undesirable ways inconsistent

with the proper exercise of power. We could say similar things about criminal justice or freedom of speech. There are also some things which cannot
both be bought or sold and remain the things that they are. Friendship or
love just is without price. Neither can be purchased and remain genuine
love or friendship. One might buy the outward displays of such a feeling,
but it is of the nature of such a feeling to be given spontaneously and freely
or not at all.[14]

What of sex? It does not seem that there is anything intrinsic to the nature of sex which makes it impossible to sell and yet remain sex. This might
be true of sexual love or sexual intimacy, but the prostitute most certainly
does not sell *that*, and the very distinction between sex and love is acknowledged in a standard critique of prostitution.[15] What of reasons having to do
with the ends of sex? Does the sale of sex mean that bought and sold sex is
practised in morally undesirable ways inconsistent with the proper conduct
of sexual relationships? One argument to show that bought and sold sex is
morally undesirable understands morally desirable sex in terms other than
those provided for by the Principle of Consensuality. For instance, one
might consider prostitution as incompatible with the procreative function
of sex or with sex as only properly a loving activity.[16] This kind of argument begs the question against the permissibility of consensual prostitution
so that the present discussion must put it to one side.

The more interesting possibility is an argument conducted in terms of
what are thought to be properly only gifts. To Richard Titmuss is owed the
influential claim that a system in which blood for transfusion is freely given
is preferable to one in which there is a market for such blood.[17] One reason
for claiming this is that the blood that is bought and sold is more likely to
be contaminated. The more interesting reason is that a system of gifted
blood helps to promote and sustain a society in which altruism and concern
for others predominate over selfish indifference to the interests of others.
Allowing a market in blood does not deny people the freedom to give blood
if they choose. However, the existence of such a market devalues the free
gift. Being able to choose to make the gift in the market's absence can be
seen as representing a 'deeper' and more valuable freedom than that of selling.[18] One might think of sex as Titmuss and his defenders do about
blood.[19] If sex can be sold, then the 'deeper' choice freely to give it is lost.

The problems with this argument against prostitution are several. Sex is
not a gift in the way that blood is. It does not seem that there is an altruis-
tic motive for 'giving' sex which could be eroded by permitting its sale. Sex
is not life saving, nor need it be a one-way donation. Evidence suggests that

where a market in blood replaces free donation, there is a decline in the number of people who are prepared to give blood. There is no reason to think that a similar story could be told in the case of sex. The value of giving sex is surely as much lowered by its being given away without thought or care as it is by its being sold. Promiscuity is as damaging in this context as prostitution.

There are also general considerations that appear to tell against this argument from the nature and value of gifts. Talk of a 'deeper' freedom (of gift) which is protected by denial of a freedom (to sell) invokes the ideal of 'positive' freedom, that is, a freedom defined in terms of the quality, not quantity, of options it can realise. And there are standard arguments against any such understanding of freedom.[20] That something is given when it could be sold might be thought to make the gift more, not less, valuable.[21] Moreover, it seems perfectly possible to retain a sense of the value of what it is that you are doing in freely giving another something when others are buying and selling that same thing. The disvalue of the sold item does not, as it were, transfer to that of the gift. Why should someone think that the sex she gives in love is devalued by the fact that another person could lovelessly sell hers? If the thought is along the lines of 'But how can my gift of sex mean as much to him when he could buy it?' then the reply is 'What is freely given is precisely what he could not buy—sex without a price tag'.

Perhaps the worry about prostitution is not that sex is sold but that it is and cannot just be sex that is sold or that something is implicated in the sale of sex which makes its sale a morally graver matter than the sale of some other service or commodity. A familiar defence of prostitution insists that selling sex is just like selling anything else. Whatever suffices to make the sale of things in general acceptable will also suffice to make the sale of sex in particular acceptable. There is nothing about sex as that which is voluntarily exchanged at an agreed price between buyer and seller to make its sale more objectionable than that of anything else which might be so exchanged.[22] In reply it will be said that more is up for sale in the case of prostitution than in any other sale. The 'more' is variously expressed as the prostitute's body, or self, or person. Carole Pateman, for instance, argues that the 'prostitute cannot sell sexual services alone; what she sells is her body', and the body is 'inseparably connected to the sense of the self'.[23]

Arguably the artist also sells herself when she sells a unique piece of her own artistic creation, for she is implicated in, her sense of self is inseparably connected to, that work of hers. The case of the prostitute differs in two ways. First, the sense of self she sells is pejorative. Second, it is tied to her identity as a woman. I will turn later to the idea that prostitution reinforces certain understandings of gender. Let me pause here to examine the claim that the prostitute cannot but sell a demeaning sense of herself. The idea is that she sells to the man a sense of herself as his inferior, as the servant is hired not just to supply services to the master but to do so in a servile fashion.

Three points should be made in response to this criticism. First, there are surely forms of prostitution in which the prostitute exhibits superiority and dominance within the contracted relationship. Here it is the client who abases himself at the behest and under the direction of the prostitute. Second, prostitution does not differ from many other professions in respect of supplying a service wherein seller and buyer display such asymmetrical attitudes. Consider what is implied if one takes seriously every salesperson's motto that the customer is always right. Third, the prostitute in performing the role required of her need not really alienate herself and become that which she is seen to be by her client. There is all the difference between a butler, such as P. G. Wodehouse's Jeeves, who can perfectly perform the duties of obedient personal valet while remaining his master's better and the butler of Kazuo Ishiguro's *The Remains of the Day* (1989), who is so taken over by his role as to have no sense of himself and his relationships to others beyond that role and its performance.

Of course it is of moral concern that someone should even 'play' at being another's servant. It is not just that they are complicit in practices based upon assumptions of human superiority and inferiority. It is also that they avoid personal responsibility for their own actions. Sartre's waiter 'plays' the part of being a waiter, but he is in bad faith nonetheless.[24] It may also be insisted that if the prostitute avoids her sense of self being implicated in the performance of her duties, then she suffers a different loss, that of the opportunity to define and individuate herself through intimate sexual encounters with others.[25] But there are many ways in which such an opportunity can be lost—celibacy, a loveless marriage, repression of one's homosexuality, an insuperable distaste for sex, and so on. It is not clear that the prostitute loses this opportunity in any more decisive or irreparable fashion than people do in these other cases. Moreover, it needs to be shown that it is only through sexual intimacy that a person may individuate herself, or that the manner in which such self-definition is achieved through sex is incomparably better than is possible by any other non-sexual means. This is doubtful.

The third area of worry about prostitution is the role that it may play in reinforcing certain understandings of sexuality and gender. The prostitute, it will be alleged, sells an image not just of the individual prostitute but of womanhood in general. Carole Pateman writes that prostitution is the 'public recognition of men as sexual masters; it puts submission on sale as a commodity in the market'.[26] Similarly Debra Satz claims that prostitution represents women as the 'sexual servants of men'.[27] These assertions are ambiguous between the claim that 'what is sold is woman as inferior' and the distinct claim that 'the very fact of being sellable constitutes the sold woman as inferior'. If it is the second claim that is being made, then it would follow that the existence of male prostitution is sufficient to represent men as the servants of women. In general, the sale of *any* service in which deference or submission to the wishes of the buyer is an essential part of the service could be represented in the same way.

If the claim is in fact the first one, then two responses are in order. First, much may depend on the cultural context, the background values, and the general social understandings of sexuality and gender. Presumably male prostitution could represent women as the sexual masters of men only within a matriarchal society, that is, one whose understanding of relative gender status was the exact mirror image of a patriarchal one. The feminist critique of prostitution is in fact a critique of female prostitution within a patriarchal society. Since it will not also be a critique of male prostitution, it is not a critique of prostitution as such. Second, the wrongness of prostitution derives from the wrongness of those understandings of women of which prostitution is, in some fashion, a 'representation' or 'public recognition'. But then women who voluntarily fulfil those roles which feminism pejoratively characterises as damagingly stereotypical of submissive womanhood—domestic helpmate, happy housewife, or whatever—are as guilty as the prostitute—and perhaps more so inasmuch as the prostitute makes money from a gender for which, the anecdotal evidence suggests, she has little respect.

Sado-masochism

In 1990 five men were convicted of assault occasioning actual bodily harm and unlawful wounding under the 1861 British Offences Against the Person Act. They pleaded guilty after the judge ruled that the prosecution did not have to prove that the victims of the offences did not consent to the infliction of harm and wounding. In 1992 the Court of Appeal dismissed their appeals, and in 1993, by a three to two majority, that conviction was upheld by the House of Lords. The case *Regina* v. *Brown* is notable for the following reason:[28] The five men were convicted of their offences for engaging in sado-masochistic activity which the Principle of Consensuality would judge entirely permissible. The nature of the case as well as the judicial reasoning to the convictions and dismissed appeals thus sheds valuable light on the limits of these principles.

The following four features of the case are undisputed. First, the men had engaged in consensual sado-masochistic acts. Indeed they belonged to a nation-wide group that had enthusiastically participated in such activities over a ten-year period, on occasion in rooms specially prepared for these activities. Not one member of that group had dissented from the practices. Second, the group's practices were private and were discovered by the police only by chance. The activities were video-taped, but the video was for viewing only by group members. No unwilling third parties were involved at any stage. Third, the sado-masochism in question was of an extreme kind, involving genital torture. Yet no permanent injury was suffered, and no party to these activities was hospitalised or sought medical attention. Fourth, there was no commercial exploitation of their practices. Although a video was made, its distribution was restricted to group members and was not sold. The convicted men appealed their conviction on the grounds, fully consistent with the Principle of Consensuality, that a person could not be guilty of assault or wounding in respect of acts carried out in private with the consent of the victim.

What reasons could be given for disputing their claim? Let me suggest there are three which might be, and were, offered, although not always in a clear and distinct fashion.[29] These have to do with the degree of harm occasioned, the fact that the activities were sexual, and the basic wrongness of deliberately hurting another person. It might be urged, first, that there must be a point at which the injury inflicted by one person on another is so great as to make the victim's giving of their consent to this injury besides the point. Raymond Belliotti, for example, thinks that *'thoroughly* sado-masochistic sex, which inevitably involves *significant* harm' is inherently morally wrong.[30] Yet it is hard to see by what principles, explicitly outlined, he judges this to be the case. Moreover, the only imagined example of sado-masochism which he does offer is evidently wrong for its commercial exhibitionism and reinforcement of oppressive gender roles.[31] Belliotti, who is generally sympathetic to a Principle of Consensuality, still clearly thinks that beyond a certain point the occasioning of consensual injury is not only not permissible but also is evidently wrong in itself.

How might and why should this point be fixed? In the case of *Rex* v. *Donavan*, which was frequently cited in discussion of *Brown*, the relevant degree of bodily harm was defined as that which, while it need not be permanent, should 'be more than merely transient and trifling'.[32] But why should such a definition mark the boundary within the category of consensual harms between permissible and impermissible? It should be evident that there are many apparently morally unproblematic instances of consensual harms which lie beyond (often well beyond) the 'transient and trifling'—for instance, boxing and other contact sports injuries, medical treatment, and body alteration such as tattooing, ear-piercing, and circumcision. Licit chastisement is even an instance of such a harm which need not be consensual.

It cannot be thought that harms which are not transient and trifling are *so* serious as to go off the consensual-as-permissible scale, as it were. There is merit in the idea that some harms do go off such a scale. But if they do, they surely do so in virtue of some combination of their permanence or irreversibility and the material difference they make to the quality of life that can be led by the person who suffers them. In this spirit, L. H. Leigh would confine acts which are illegal, even if there is consent, to conduct resulting in mutilation, disfigurement, or serious impairment of a person's mental or physical powers.[33] Yet the kinds of harm which are involved in even thoroughly sado-masochistic sex need not be permanent. Nor do they substantially damage (or seriously risk so damaging) the health of the person who suffers them. Someone can endure such harms, need no doctor, and subsequently bear no scars.

Perhaps the idea is that beyond a certain point of injuriousness someone cannot really be consenting to the infliction of a harm. Two thoughts which might be a source of confusion at this point should be identified. The first (the 'wince factor') is a natural disinclination to believe on a reading of the facts of a case like *Brown* that anyone could possibly consent to these kinds of harming. That many could not and most certainly do not consent does not mean that no one in fact can and does. To repeat, no hearing of the case disputed the fact which lay at the heart of the defence case, namely, that the practices were consensual. The second confusing thought is that the more serious the harm inflicted, the more stringent should be any requirement that it be consensual to be permissible. It is perfectly consistent with the Principle of Consensuality to insist that the more injurious a consensual activity is, the more important it is that the person really does consent. However, this, if true, does not show the Principle of Consensuality to have a limited scope whose boundaries are fixed by a certain degree of harmful-ness. It is not that beyond a certain point consent does not count; it is that because it does count, even beyond such an imagined point, it is all the more important to be assured that it really is consent.

It is also salutary to point out the very great plausibility of the following claim: that sado-masochists will give their consent to only and just those practices the extent of whose harmfulness is limited by the nature of their desires and projects. As was mentioned in Chapter 2, sado-masochists are careful to ensure that the boundaries of any activity are agreed in advance and that participants have the means, for instance, by using code words, to terminate an activity if and when they desire. Sado-masochists practise sado-masochism not for the purpose simply of occasioning or receiving harm but for the pleasure which is derived from inflicting and/or enduring such harm.[34] No sado-masochists, mindful of their own future pleasure, will willingly submit to harms which are so lasting and severe as to jeopar-dise further sado-masochistic enjoyment.[35]

A distinct idea evident in the reasoning of the judges in the *Brown* case was that there is something wrong with causing harm, even if with the con-sent of the victim, when it is motivated by sexual pleasure. Commentators on the case noted a significant shift in the judicial argument from a pre-sumption that the consensual infliction of harm is prima facie lawful to the presumption that it must be shown to be in the public interest to legalise such behaviour.[36] On the first presumption the prosecution would have to demonstrate it was in the public interest to criminalise the otherwise lawful behaviour. On the second presumption the defence must show that it is in the public interest to permit such behaviour. Such a shift is of course a move away from the use of the Principle of Consensuality as a first and per-haps decisive test of an activity's permissibility. It puts the onus upon the agents to demonstrate that their doing what it is they want freely to do serves some valuable social purpose.

Moreover, the judges endorsed the view that whereas in a sporting activ-ity such as boxing there is a 'good reason' that people should try and harm one another, there is no such 'good reason' in the case of sado-masochism. The Appeal Court judge, Lord Lane, endorsed the lower judge's judgement that 'the satisfying of sado-masochistic libido does not come within the cat-egory of good reason'.[37] It is at least arguable whether public interest con-siderations do decisively favour boxing.[38] It is also plausible to think that the consensual satisfaction of sexual desires *is* a good reason to tolerate an activity whose end that is. Curiously the judges consistently refused to give any positive weight to considerations of sexual self-expression.[39] It seems also evident that negative weight was given to the fact that the activities' end was the satisfaction of *sado-masochistic* libido. Indeed Lord Lane thought it proper that the court 'mark its disapproval' of the activities in question.[40] Such reasoning indicates not so much a shift away from the Principle of Consensuality as a decisive preference for some other principles of evaluating sexual conduct.

The third reason for thinking thorough sado-masochism wrong is just that there is something basically and deeply wrong with hurting people. Perhaps it is true that 'a fundamental building block of our moral society is the social taboo against the infliction of injury on another'.[41] In this vein one British Law lord, Lord Templeman, commented: 'Society is entitled and bound to protect itself against a cult of violence. Pleasure derived from the infliction of pain is an evil thing. Cruelty is uncivilised'.[42] We might readily grant the truth of these thoughts but simply dispute that the sado-masochism in question can properly be described as a 'cult of violence' or 'cruelty'. To repeat an earlier point, sado-masochists give and receive pleasure from their activities. The point is not to be pleased at another's pain but to be pleased at the same time as one is giving pleasure through pain. The true sadist would be disappointed to learn that his victim enjoyed the harms inflicted. He would also discount the wishes of his victim. Indeed it is the fact that the pain he inflicts is unwanted which gives him pleasure. For their part sado-masochists time and again emphasise the centrality of mutual consent to their activities.

Perhaps the thought is that such activities are 'unpredictably dangerous' where this has a double implication[43]—that they might escalate to the point of undisputed cruelty and that they might corrupt or unduly influence persons outside the group into the performance of truly violent acts. The significant risk of such an outcome would be a weighty consideration against tolerance. Yet it needs to be shown that such a risk exists. After all the group prosecuted in *Brown* engaged in their activities over a period of ten years without any sign of these activities degenerating in the manner feared. Moreover, the group was scrupulously careful to keep their activities private. It took ten years, and even then completely by chance, for the police to discover their occurrence. It may be that there are activities which can, in the sense suggested, be thought of as constituting a 'cult of violence'. It is very doubtful that consensual sado-masochism is such an activity.

Before leaving the topic of consensual sado-masochism, I should briefly consider a quite distinct line of criticism, one which has been developed by feminists. This is a critique of lesbian sado-masochism for replicating, in its structure of dominance and submission, patriarchal understandings of women.[44] That such activity is consensual and respectful of the pleasures of its participants is besides the point. The activity in question is to be condemned for the fact that one of those taking part plays the very role—of woman as degraded, humiliated, and pained victim—which women in general are compelled to assume under the oppressive rule of men. Feminist critiques of this kind discount the presumption in favour of tolerating the 'private'.

Interestingly the claim is not that within such a structured activity of dominance and oppression the participants do not and cannot really consent—for reasons which were reviewed in Chapter 6. For of course the structure is not really, as is that of the relationships within patriarchy between men and women, one of domination and oppression. But then if the activity of lesbian sado-masochism is playful, mock, simulated, fantasised, role-playing dominance, it is hard to see how it reproduces actual dominance any more than a game of chess is or reproduces actual warfare.[45] The powerlessness and submission of the masochist are not the real powerlessness and submission of a woman under patriarchy.

But does such play acting nevertheless harmfully endorse or contribute to the reproduction of the real thing? It is arguable that even simulations of some evil can contribute to the perpetuation of that evil. Such anyway is a familiar claim about artistic representations of violence. However, such a claim is deeply contentious. Moreover, it is significant that those who participate in the disputed activity do not themselves endorse the patriarchal power structures they are alleged to assist in reproducing. Again what women do to and with women cannot unproblematically model what men do to and with women. A black employer who badly mistreats his black employee does not mirror the role of a white racist in the same position. The background conditions of power are entirely different, as are the motivations of the actors within the two situations.

◀ **8** ▶

The Limits of Consensuality II: The Age of Sexual Consent

IN THIS CHAPTER I DEAL WITH the age of sexual consent. This topic, like the crime of rape to be discussed in the next chapter, displays features which go beyond the terms of the Principles of Consensuality and Dissent. The worry to be addressed is that the Principles of Consensuality and Dissent do not provide a comprehensive moral evaluation of all the aspects of these cases. My concern is to make clearer what these principles do and do not commit us to saying in each of these instances, and to do so by a careful disentangling of issues.

For consent to legitimate that to which it is given, it must be given by someone capable of giving their consent. Chapter 3 described children as those who are judged to lack such a capacity. They are not permanently disabled since they will (normally) acquire this capacity with age. There is, in short, an age of majority above which are adults presumed capable of consent and below which are children presumed incapable of consent.

All jurisdictions fix an age of majority. Or rather they fix various ages of majority. For the consent to different activities or practices will probably be judged to require different kinds or levels of competence, and the appropriate age for each competence will be set at a higher or lower point. It is unlikely that there will be a single age at which persons can, for instance, legally have sex, marry, inherit property, make wills, buy alcohol, drive cars, and travel abroad. Sticking to the age at which a child is judged able to consent to sexual activity distinctions can be (and are sometimes) made between males and females, and between homosexual and heterosexual activity. Different jurisdictions set the various possible ages of sexual majority at different points. However, within a broad European context the following is true. Most fix the age of homosexual and heterosexual majority at the same point, though some do not. The average age is around fifteen, the lowest being twelve (subject to certain qualifications), and all jurisdictions set the age at which persons can marry some years higher (normally eighteen). Some include in their penal codes specific provisions relating to the difference in ages or to the nature of the relationship between the child and a person who would be guilty of an offence in having sex with that child.

I propose, first, making some general comments about the background to any debate about an age of majority and, in particular, to those features of this background which make discussion of this issue very difficult. Second, I will try to illuminate what is at stake in fixing an age of majority. Third, I will suggest four kinds of consideration which should enter into a discussion of how and where to fix the age of majority. Finally, I briefly consider ways in which one might go beyond the idea of a simple, single age of majority to take adequate account of these considerations.

The Background to the Debate

One very important feature of the background to any debate on an age of majority is a concern about child abuse. The questions of whether or not child abuse is now more prevalent or is merely more readily noticed and reported, and of whether or not the definition of child abuse has been progressively broadened so as now to include any form of less than ideal treatment or remains a significant category of avoidable harm, are moot.[1] The fact is that contemporary Western society is presently alert to the possibility of child abuse and is committed to its prevention in a way that was not previously the case. Child sexual abuse is recognised to be an especially insidious and damaging form of abuse. It is, in consequence, impossible to broach the question of children's sexual activity without taking proper account of the possibility of such abuse.

It might seem an easy matter to characterise the sexual abuse of a child as violative and non-consensual, thus distinguishing it from any other kind of sexual interaction. However, a child is deemed incapable of offering real consent, and abuse is frequently defined in terms of an exploitation of that very fact. Consider a standard definition of child sexual abuse: 'The involvement of dependent, developmentally immature children and adolescents in sexually abusive activities they do not fully comprehend, and to which they are unable to give informed consent, or that violate the social taboos of family roles'.[2] It is not entirely clear whether its authors intend there to be any possibility of sexually *non*-abusive activities. This is because abusive activities are those which the child involved in them cannot fully comprehend or give informed consent to. And what it is to be a child is to fail, as yet, fully to understand or be able fully to consent to any sexual activity.

We are properly horrified by any incidence of child sexual abuse. We are right to do everything we can to prevent its occurrence. We are understandably contemptuous of anything that seems to offer an apology for or justification of it. Yet such strong emotions make it difficult rationally to discuss childhood sexuality and the sexual activity of children—especially when these very terms seem automatically and immediately to connote abuse. It is desirable that one be able to distinguish abusive from non-abusive instances of children's sexual activity, and that one be prepared dispassionately to discuss the latter without losing hold of one's abhorrence of the latter (and resolve to eradicate it).

However, a further complicating feature of the background to discussion of the age of sexual majority is the prevailing understanding of childhood. Much of the debate on our contemporary Western understanding of childhood was provoked by, and greatly influenced by, Philippe Ariès's *Centuries of Childhood,* which argued that the notion of childhood is a uniquely modern one.[3] Notwithstanding the merits of Ariès's claim, it does seem true that we—that is, we of the modern Western world—have a particular understanding of childhood as a period of incompetence and innocence.[4] In such a context it is very difficult to discuss the existence and nature of childhood sexuality. It is to Freud that we conventionally attribute the discovery of the child as a libidinous creature whose sexuality must be constrained and directed to ensure a healthy psychological development into adult normality. Yet it would be mistaken to think that children had, prior to the late nineteenth century, been thought of as sexless angels. Indeed, as Michel Foucault in particular has pointed out, the extreme concern to discipline and suppress a precocious childhood sexuality is evident in eighteenth-century educational discourse.[5]

Indeed it can seem as if the existence of such sexuality is acknowledged only for it more effectively to be concealed and curbed in the interests of preserving the ideal of childhood as a period of asexual innocence. Child sexual abuse is frequently represented as being horrific precisely for robbing children of that innocence which properly defines childhood. Such an understanding is problematic for at least three reasons. First, it obfuscates the reality of a child's actual sexual development. Second, it is an unhelpful self-sustaining ideology of childhood: One acts in denial of the facts to maintain the appearance of what is wanted from the child, namely, a 'natural' innocence adults cannot have. Third, such an ideology may be dangerously sexual. A child's innocence is rather like the purity of the virginal woman which is the object of a certain male sexual desire—attractive for being that which is not yet but can be corrupted.[6]

These remarks about child abuse and child sexuality have been very brief and schematic. They are intended only to indicate the difficulties in discussing an age of sexual majority. The problem is that one cannot suggest what it might be proper for a child to do sexually without immediately implicating deep-lying and incredibly powerful sentiments about the abuse of children and the innocence of childhood. When we return from the background to the foreground of the discussion, however, it is important for us to be clear what is at stake in the fixing of any age of majority.[7]

What Is at Stake in Fixing the Age of Sexual Majority?

Those below the legal age of sexual majority can engage in sexual activity. They can even give their 'consent' to that activity, if we understand by 'consensual' something minimal like 'done willingly and knowingly in the absence of coercion or deliberate deception'. However, sexual activity by someone below the age of majority is characterised as non-consensual. Non-consensual here means not so much that the child's participation is unwilling, but rather that the child's 'consent' is viewed as not consent proper and is thus discounted. A child does not have a consent to give or to withdraw. Moreover, someone who engages in sexual activity with a minor, even if it is voluntary, is guilty of an offence. In the United States the crime is 'statutory rape'.

Consider a pair of heterosexual fifteen-year-olds in a steady heterosexual relationship who sleep together. Neither puts the other under any pressure to do so, and both understand what it is that they are doing. Nevertheless, such a pair would, under British law, be acting illegally. The import of the law is such that their 'consent' does not count. Further, this will be true of any and all forms of sexual activity. A child who cannot exercise her sexual freedom is disabled from engaging in each and every form of activity that the law construes as sexual in the relevant sense. Most criminal law systems distinguish degrees of seriousness in sexual offences. These will depend on aggravating factors, such as the accompanying use of violence, and the very nature of the act perpetrated, whereby sexual assault may be viewed as a lesser offence than penetrative rape. However, below the age of majority a child cannot, even consensually, engage in any act of sexual familiarity with another. Of course the manner of activity makes a difference to the seriousness of the offence of those who engage in sexual activity with a minor. But for the minor it makes no difference to their freedom to so engage with someone else.

Someone who does not have the right to make sexual choices is effectively considered to be a person without sexual desires, an asexual being. Whatever sexual wishes a minor might have, they are, in practice, discounted. They are given no weight. They are insufficient, most obviously, to acquit any chosen sexual partner of a criminal offence. To prosecute someone for engaging in voluntary sexual activity with a person below the age of majority, and not to prosecute this latter person, is to acknowledge that sexual activity has occurred and yet refuse to acknowledge the expressed sexuality of one party to the activity. We can see in operation here the background view of children as essentially innocent inasmuch as defenders of a sexual age of majority often rely on a presumption that children are without sexual desires and lack a sexuality.[8] In similar fashion, some American feminists have worried about statutory rape laws which criminalise the sexual acts of male minors but not those of complicit female minors. They do so because such a distinction derives from a view of young women as passive, asexual victims of male sexuality.[9]

In short, the import of an age of sexual majority for those below it is that they lack the right to do what it is they may consider themselves to be doing (willingly have sex), they expose themselves and/or their partners to prosecution for willingly doing what they want to, and more generally they may be represented as not even being sexual beings with sexual desires they know themselves to feel.

Four Considerations in Determining the Age of Consent

Let me next suggest four considerations which should enter into any determination of where the age of sexual majority should fall. They are the nature of sexual activity, the age of the consenting party, the age differential between the parties, and the existence, if any, of a special relationship between the parties.

Different Ages for Different Sex?

It is arguable and is, as we have seen, normally presumed by the law that any form of sexual activity is forbidden when one of its parties is below the age of consent. Nevertheless, it could be argued in reply that the age of consent should vary in accord with the character of the sexual activity to which consent is being given. Let me consider two versions of this claim—one with respect to levels of sexual activity, and the other concerning homosexual, as opposed to heterosexual, sexual activity.

As for the first, it might seem evident that there is a difference between two thirteen-year-olds kissing and cuddling, and those same two individuals having full sex. However, the issue, to be clear, is not whether some slight form of sexual intimacy with a person below the age of consent is less morally grave than full penetrative sexual intercourse with the same person. That much can be conceded. The issue rather is whether the age of consent for the former should be lower than is appropriate for the latter. The reasons which dictate that those below a certain age should not have full sex will also surely dictate that they should not engage in sexual activity which is less than coitus but still beyond some point of intimacy. That point will be hard to fix with precision but will surely have much to do with the sexual explicitness of the behaviour in question. No one regards a kiss or a hug as beyond the pale for those who are under age. But mutual masturbation is, and it is for the same sort of reason that penetrative sex is.

What of the difference between heterosexual and homosexual sexual activity? Most European jurisdictions mark no distinction. The United Kingdom is, at present, one that does. There are at least three arguments for maintaining two separate ages of sexual consent—that for homosexual activity being later than that for heterosexual activity. The first is that homosexuality is an unnatural or immoral form of human sexuality, a perversion, the abhorrence of which society can appropriately express by fixing a later age of consent. Notwithstanding the contentiousness of the evaluative characterisation of homosexuality, a differential age of consent is a curious and unsatisfactory way to express societal disapproval. It concedes the legality of the activity beyond some age, and it is unlikely to act as a significant deterrent to the commission of homosexual acts.

The second argument is that sexual preferences are not determined until comparatively late in a young person's development and that it is, in consequence, important to protect that person from making premature choices which would have long-term consequences. Expressed more baldly the claim is that allowing young persons below a certain age to engage in homosexual activity will result in them becoming homosexual. This is presumed to be a deleterious outcome. In response three things need to be said. First, the evidence strongly suggests that sexual orientation is fixed early. The British Wolfenden Report of 1957 reported its medical witnesses as being 'unanimously of the view that the main sexual pattern is laid down in the early years of life and the majority of them held that it was usually fixed in main outline by the age of 16. Many held that it was fixed much earlier'.[10] A similar conclusion was reached by the 1969 Dutch Speijer Committee.[11]

Second, it is implausible and contrary to the known facts to presume that adult sexual orientation is somehow irreversibly fixed by those sexual acts which were engaged in when young. A conclusion familiar from most studies of psycho-sexual development is that a significant number of males who will later be exclusively heterosexual in their preferences engage in some form of homosexual experimentation while adolescents. Again the Speijer Committee concluded that 'contact between adult homosexuals and predominantly heterosexual adolescents would not result in an adolescent's conversion to homosexuality, nor would it have a damaging effect on his or her personality'.[12]

Third, even if it were the case that young persons could somehow be 'converted' to a sexual life that went against the grain of their true nature, this would tell as much against premature heterosexual activity by homosexuals as it is claimed to do against premature homosexual activity by heterosexuals. For it could be argued that those who otherwise would be lifelong homosexuals were being converted to heterosexuality by adolescent heterosexual contacts. The conversion claim only supports the claim that a differential age of consent is needed if homosexuality can be characterised as a less desirable sexual orientation than heterosexuality. If that is being assumed or claimed, then the second argument for a higher age of consent for homosexuals is yoked to the first.

The third argument is that the consequences of engaging in homosexual conduct are more serious than those of engaging in heterosexual conduct. A greater maturity is required to understand the former implications than is needed for the latter, and so the age should be set appropriately higher. The Wolfenden Committee employed this argument, claiming that 'a boy is incapable at the age of 16 of forming a mature judgement about actions of a kind which might have the effect of setting him apart from the rest of society'.[13] The European Commission, the forum where challenges to differential ages of consent under the European Convention on Human Rights have taken place, has also given credence to this argument. In a 1978 report it concluded that eighteen- to twenty-year-olds could be exposed to 'substantial social pressures which could be harmful to their psychological development' if permitted to engage in homosexual activities.[14] It should be noted that this argument does not rely on the presumption that homosexuality is wrong, only that there are adverse consequences for the individual of being homosexual. These may, of course, be due to society's judgement that homosexuality is wrong, a judgement which is no less effective, if generally believed, for being false.

Three replies are in order. First, heterosexual sexual activity has very serious possible consequences, chiefly pregnancy. And for the young these may be viewed as being at least as serious as those attaching to homosexual activity. Second, the adverse consequences of homosexual activity may be attributed to society's pejorative understanding of homosexuality. Setting a clear differential in ages of consent between homosexual and heterosexual activity can only play its part in endorsing that understanding. The third argument for an age differential is thus unsatisfactorily self-confirming. Third, the consequences of having an age differential are themselves serious. Young homosexual persons criminalised for acting on their sexual desires, at an age when their heterosexual peers are free to do so, are stigmatised, isolated, prey to fears of prosecution, and denied the possibility of developing meaningful relationships with partners. It should be added that sexual education, counselling, and the provision of contraceptives to those below the age of consent are forbidden. To deny young homosexuals such services when the risks posed by HIV infection are serious is an unacceptable public health policy.

The three arguments for an age of consent differential between homosexuals and heterosexuals are clearly unsatisfactory. Moreover, each of them would still need to meet the challenge of a Principle of Equality, which requires that the fixing of an age of consent should not unfairly distinguish between persons on the basis of their sexual orientation. They all fail to do so satisfactorily.

Sexual Maturity

A second consideration in the debate on an age of sexual majority is age itself. Now, of course, age *simpliciter* is not the decisive consideration. Rather, it is age as a marker for those features of an individual which are thought decisive in the allocation of a permission to engage in sex. There are familiar arguments for and against using age in this way which turn on the apparent arbitrariness of age as a factor and on the failure of alleged correlations between age and possession of the decisively relevant features. I shall ignore these arguments here,[15] and I shall concentrate instead on three features which might be thought relevant to a permission to have sex with others.

The first of these is physical maturity. We might, for instance, set the age of majority at the onset of puberty. There is some merit in the straightforward thought that girls should be able to consent to sex at that point at which they are capable of procreating. It is surely relevant to any current debate on the age of consent to note that girls and boys are now maturing at an earlier age than previously. The average age of a girl's first period has, for instance, dropped from sixteen to seventeen in 1860 to twelve to thirteen a hundred years later. However, physical maturity on its own cannot be the sole relevant feature any more than should the ability to be intoxicated determine the age at which one is allowed first to consume alcohol. What matters is not just that one can have sex but that one has some understanding or appreciation of what is involved in having sex.

So a second, and more plausible, feature of individuals at the age of majority is what John Stuart Mill called the 'maturity of their faculties'.[16] I take this to comprise a certain level of cognitive development—that is, an ability to understand the relevant facts, a certain degree of acquired knowledge (since an ability to understand facts is nothing without the provision of those very facts), and a certain level of temperamental maturity, that is, the possession of a character which both permits a proper appreciation of these facts and is able to determine appropriate choices in the light of such an appreciation. The idea here is that it is not enough that someone simply know the relevant facts about sexual activity. She should also appreciate what having sex means and be able to choose sensibly in consequence of that appreciation. Such a characterisation of 'maturity of faculties' is necessarily vague, but it points us in a direction which all can surely recognise as the right one.

Where a society may choose to fix the age at which it deems that maturity to be acquired is not of course settled by the preceding characterisation of the maturity. However, the sorts of factors which should enter into that determination of age are evident. Let me make just two points. First, a society should strive to be consistent in its judgements of maturity. The reasoning by which it sets the age of sexual consent should not be at odds with that by which it sets other ages of majority. It is reasonable to think someone is mature enough to have sex before they are mature enough to marry; it is not so reasonable to think them mature enough to consume alcohol before they are mature enough to have sex.

Second, it is evident that education must play its part in the acquisition of the maturity. In the matter of sexual education things can be difficult. Here it seems to be the case that children are often denied both the right to make sexual choices and the sexual education which is a condition of their acquiring that right. This simultaneous denial derives, once again, from the belief that a certain sexual 'innocence' marks the child and disqualifies her both from being sexually active and from being sexually well informed.

There is a further related belief that to acquire the knowledge is at the same time to acquire the disposition to engage in the activity. To know what can be done disposes whoever knows to do it. Sexual education, or at least to be fair a premature education in sexual matters, is thus thought of as a double corruption of innocence. It brings to an end both sexual ignorance and sexual indifference or unwillingness. These sorts of belief are deeply rooted in a prevalent, long-standing understanding of sexuality and innocence whose most powerful metaphor is to be found in the Christian narrative of the Fall. Yet the facts gainsay this understanding. In those countries, such as the Scandinavian ones, where children are provided with an earlier and more comprehensive sexual education than is the case in Britain, the age of the first experience of intercourse is significantly higher. There are also lower rates of teenage pregnancy and abortions.

There is a final point that needs to be made about the child's acquisition of the requisite 'maturity'. There are different models of cognitive development. One influential model should be indicated. This is the understanding of a child's development both as endogenous and culturally invariant. The child's gaining of some ability develops at its own internal rate, barely altered by outside factors. This model's most celebrated defender is obviously Jean Piaget. The import of the model is that no significant difference is made to the child's acquisition of a competence either by social context or by society permitting the child to engage in some appropriate activity. The child will not become any more capable of doing X through making it possible for the child to do or to practise X. This model is open to serious criticism.[17] The more damaging these criticisms are, the further support is given to the need to acknowledge a role for sexual education in the acquisition of the relevant maturity.

In addition to physical adulthood and the 'maturity of their faculties', it is also possible to take note of prevailing social patterns. What, for instance, is the age at which young persons are as a matter of fact engaging in sexual activity? It is evident that this age is declining.[18] This is probably a decisive and irreversible trend. It may, incidentally, be historically inaccurate to appeal to the example of Romeo and Juliet in arguing that earlier times also tolerated young love and child brides.[19] Both liberals and conservatives may regret the contemporary prevalence of premature sexual activity. Yet determining a proper age of consent in the light of such facts, even if they are displeasing, is not an easy matter. A legal age of consent should not simply and blindly follow social trends. Nor however should it be thought that trends of behaviour can be decisively affected by a law of consent. The comparative evidence from European countries suggests a complicated picture in which general social attitudes to sex and sexuality, public sexual education, and the provision of sexual health services all play their part in determining what young people do. Any fixing of the proper age of consent should seek neither simply to reflect nor on its own to determine the reality. It should take account of the broader social picture.

Intergenerational Sex

A third consideration in the debate on the age of sexual consent is the age difference between the parties. As a matter of fact most young people seek sexual relationships with persons of their own age. One year is the average age gap between partners at their first sexual experience. Nevertheless, there should be legitimate worries about a sexual relationship between persons of significantly disparate ages. Most people would agree that there is an evident difference between two fourteen-year-olds having sex and a thirty-four-year-old having sex with a fourteen-year-old. The moral worry here is best expressed in terms of an exploitation of someone which is possible because of a substantial difference in sexual knowledge and appreciation. Richard Card, for instance, writes that a disparity of age between older man and young girl is, if 'consensual' sex between them occurs, 'presumptively deserving of punishment because he has abused the disparity in experience, maturity and understanding between them; in short he has taken "advantage of her"'.[20] It is hard also to ignore the disparity in power, influence, social resources, and economic resources between an adult and youth—even if we set aside the existence of any special relationship between them.

Notably there has been intense debate about 'intergenerational' sex within both the gay and feminist movements. Gays in particular are acutely conscious of prevailing prejudices against gay sexuality. Their starting point is an insistence that the consensual pursuit of sexual pleasure should not be constrained by mistaken or moralising conceptions of normal sex. At the same time gays are alert to the dangers of 'moral panics' about homosexuality and paedophilia. Ironically while homosexuals are most frequently depicted as corrupters of youth, the majority of illicit paedophilia concerns adult males and young girls. For their part feminists insist upon the non-neutrality of sexual pleasure and the importance of situating sexuality within what need to be acknowledged as social relationships of unequal power and influence.

Those who have offered a defence of paedophilia may thus begin by insisting that whatever feels good is okay so long as it is consensual. They will further maintain that children are sexual creatures and that they are fully able to communicate their willingness to participate in sexual activity.[21] Feminist and gay critics of paedophilia will respond in the following vein: 'Fundamentally, there are issues of disparity of experience, needs, desires, physical potentialities, emotional resources, sense of responsibility, awareness of consequences of one's actions, and, above all, power between adults and children'.[22]

The response by defenders of paedophilia is weak. They may insist that a sexual relationship can be insulated from the social roles of its participants. This seems deeply implausible. Moreover, its contrary—the view that sex and sexuality are constituted by social relationships—is central to the thinking of most within the gay and feminist movements. Or the defenders of paedophilia may resort to a defence of paternalism. This either takes the weak form of requiring that adults should be, and assuming that they also can be, sensitive to the proper needs and desires of children. Let us simply observe that this is a very generous understanding of those adults who pursue sexual gratification with children. Or the defence of paternalism takes the stronger form of the 'Greek love' thesis, namely, that adults may have a legitimate role to play as a young person's sexual mentor or teacher.[23] This does seem to be self-serving rationalisation. It is also contradictory to assert both that children are sufficiently mature to know what they sexually want and yet sufficiently immature to require the guidance of an adult in their sexual initiation. Above all there is the danger of imposing adult understandings of sex and adult sexual needs upon those of children. It is right to insist that sex in itself is not wrong; it is correct and salutary to remember that the particular forms it takes as a result of the social roles and identities of its participants may be. As Jeffrey Weeks observes, 'It is not sex that is dangerous but the social relations which shape it'.[24]

Sexual Abuse of Authority

A fourth and final consideration in any debate on the age of sexual consent is the possible existence of some particular relationship between a child and an adult. Most obvious here is a relationship of authority such as that between guardian and child, or teacher and pupil. The particular features of such a relationship, especially the dependence of any minor upon the adult, can be abstracted from the facts of any probable disparity in ages. These features are of a kind such that it is unlikely there could be any genuine consent to sex on the part of the minor. Indeed an adult within such a relationship who secures 'consent' to sex is guilty of an abuse or exploitation of that relationship. Some have argued that what is wrong with incest can be captured by such an abuse, and have proposed that any law on incest should be replaced by one of the 'sexual abuse of authority'. This could apply to all persons in charge of children and not simply parents or guardians.[25] A number of jurisdictions already make some such provision. For instance §212 of the Austrian Penal Code (1975) punishes a 'misuse of a position of authority', and Spanish law specifies that sexual abuse (*estrupo*) occurs when a person has carnal knowledge of someone between twelve and eighteen 'by taking advantage of a position of superiority or dominance'.

A Single Age of Sexual Consent?

Let me conclude this chapter by briefly suggesting ways in which the fixing of any age of consent should take account of the four considerations discussed. I concluded that the fixing of the age should not distinguish among forms of explicit sexual conduct, or between homosexual and heterosexual activity. I tried to specify the terms of a 'maturity' whose acquisition the age of majority marked. I also commended the view that a disparity of age or the existence of some relationship of authority between the parties should significantly influence our evaluation of what the fixing of an age of consent is designed to legislate against.

We might thus modify a single age of consent for sex, whether homosexual or heterosexual, with provisions prohibiting sex above that age where there is a significant age disparity or an 'abuse of authority'. Let us say we fix the age of consent at fourteen. We might then add that sex with someone over fourteen but below eighteen remains illicit if the other party is significantly older (say, over twenty-one) or if the other party occupies a special role of authority over the person. An adult is responsible for having wrongful sex with a minor when he knows her to be underage or when it is reasonable to judge that he should have known her to be so.

These kinds of provision may be such that we feel confident in lowering the age of consent below the European average of fifteen. For so long as we are excluding exploitative intergenerational sex, we may be less troubled by sex between two minors both of whom do 'consent'. Tony Honoré, for instance, recommends that the 'law should be altered so that a boy under the age of majority is not liable to be prosecuted for having sexual intercourse with a girl of 13 or over, but under 16, at least if she is not more than a year or two younger'.[26] More radically still Holland in 1990 amended §245 of its Criminal Code to decriminalise consensual sexual activity by twelve- to sixteen-year-olds—a move which greatly occupied the British tabloid press.[27] The amendment was carefully hedged however. The sexual act remained, in principle, forbidden to boys and girls between twelve and sixteen. The law simply stated that if there were no complaints—by either party, a parent, or a child welfare organisation—then there would be no prosecution.

Such a provision might be thought realistic in acknowledging that young teenagers do have sex, humane in not denying them access to sexual health and educational facilities or in criminalising their consensual behaviour, and yet judicious enough to provide them with protection against exploitation. The provision also illustrates an important truth: A simple age of sexual consent is by itself inadequate. Provisions which recognise the facts of social relationships, such as disparate age or authority, which can subvert consent are necessary. At the same time any age of consent can only be fixed with a clear eye on the social context—general attitudes to sex, the provision of sex education, sexual health services, understandings of childhood and children's sexuality, and so on. This context should play a role in determining how an appropriate age is fixed. Further, only within such a context can the influence of that age of majority upon the extent and nature of the sexual behaviour of the young be properly appreciated.

9

The Limits of
Consensuality III: Rape

THIS CHAPTER DISCUSSES THE crime of rape. Rape is non-consensual sex, and discussion of the crime thus provides an opportunity to apply the understanding of consent and consensuality which has been gained so far. At the same time a full definition of the crime and a specification of what shall count as acceptable evidence for its commission take us some way beyond what has been considered up until now. This is useful. However, any further discussion of rape is constrained by the need first to acknowledge the significance of rape within feminism.

The Feminist Critique of Rape

Feminism, as a theory and a practice, has been developed out of and in direct response to the concrete experiences of women.[1] In this context certain phenomena assume a considerable significance and symbolic importance. Rape, like domestic violence and pornography, is such a phenomenon.

It is not just that rape is deeply significant for feminism; it is also that feminism invests rape with a certain significance. Chiefly this is that rape displays, in an especially clear and revealing way, the role of gender and the structure of gender relations within the society which feminism criticises. As we saw in Chapter 6 some feminists, such as MacKinnon and Dworkin, charge that the significance of rape is that it displays itself to be indistinguishable from 'normal' heterosexual intercourse. Reasons were given for my being sceptical of this claim.

Other feminists have argued that rape is a distinct and horrendous act but one whose prevalence nevertheless says something general about the way in which women are treated by men. Thus for Susan Brownmiller, 'From prehistoric times to the present rape has played a critical function', namely, 'to keep all women in a constant state of intimidation', thereby keeping them in their 'proper place' of submissive sexual service.[2] Whether or not all men are, in the familiar contentious claim, potential rapists, it can still be argued, as a separate matter, that all men benefit from the climate of fear for which some of their gender are directly responsible and thus that they all share responsibility for the harms rape causes to women.[3]

In addition to claims about what rape represents, feminists have also sought to expose the way in which the law of rape as it has been defined and enforced conforms to male expectations at the expense of women and their desires.[4] Thus Susan Estrich writes of the history of rape law in the United States that it has been a history of sexism.[5] Attention has been drawn to evidence suggesting that rape is a significantly under-reported crime or one with a considerably lower rate of conviction than other crimes. It has been argued that the treatment of rape within the judicial system is prejudicial to its women victims and unfairly predisposed in favour of accused rapists. This prejudice extends from the processing of any original complaint, the chances of a subsequent charge being laid, to the conduct and reporting of any subsequent trial.[6]

Feminists have tried to show how a society's understanding of rape (and consequently its legal understanding of the crime of rape) is crucially informed by myths about rape itself, but also by prejudicial stereotypes of male and female sexuality. Myths of rape include the view that women fantasise about being rape victims;[7] that women mean 'yes' even when they say 'no'; that any woman could successfully resist a rapist if she really wished to; that the sexually experienced do not suffer harms when raped (or at least suffer lesser harms than the sexually 'innocent'); that women often deserve to be raped on account of their conduct, dress, and demeanour; that rape by a stranger is worse than one by an acquaintance.[8] Stereotypes of sexuality include the view of women as passive, disposed submissively to surrender to the sexual advances of active men, the view that sexual love consists in the 'possession' by a man of a woman, and that heterosexual sexual activity is paradigmatically penetrative coitus.[9]

For some feminists the general social understanding of rape is such that it would be better if it were not treated as a sexual crime. Viewing it in this way, so the argument may run, assimilates rape to a continuum of sexual behaviours and somehow helps to represent it as a deplorable but understandable departure from the norm. Instead, once the surface or apparent sexual character of rape is set aside, it should be seen simply as a species of violent assault, a violation of another's personal integrity. Rape is of course this, but it is also evidently true that rape is a sexual crime. It is a sexual violation of another, a violation of their sexual identity and self-esteem. It is an assault upon someone as a sexual being. One does not have to believe that sexual gratification is the sole or even chief end of the rapist or that women may secretly derive pleasure, despite their protestations, from a violent 'possession' of their bodies. That myths of sex and sexuality are implicated in prevailing attitudes about rape is not sufficient to justify treating rape as a non-sexual crime. Indeed its seriousness as a crime is to be explained in significant part by the mistaken and harmful understandings of sexuality which inform its commission.[10]

In their efforts to expose those representations of rape which have understated its significance, prevalence, and seriousness, feminists have been accused of overstating their own case. They have been charged with extending the category of rape to include many forms of sexual activity which do not properly belong there and, in consequence, with devaluing the coinage of rape discourse. The campaign to gain recognition for 'date' or 'acquaintance' rape has been accused of trivialising the crime of rape and blurring an important distinction between it and sex which is simply unwanted or regretted.[11] The categorisation of rape as a crime of male power and domination has been charged with leading, alongside similar understandings of sexual harassment, to a dangerously false, and possibly self-confirming, picture of women as powerless victims of predatory men.[12]

This is not the place to assess the charges and counter-charges in what is already a charged debate. Moreover, some parts of this debate are not strictly relevant to the discussion of this chapter. However, it is entirely proper to take account of the feminist critique in the assessment of what understandings of consent are appropriate in a full and proper appreciation of the crime of rape. To gain such an appreciation, it should be remembered that the two essential elements of any crime are an *actus reus* and a *mens rea,* that is, both a conduct which is contrary to the law and a 'guilty mind' in the commission of that conduct. Someone commits the crime of rape if he has sexual intercourse with a woman who does not consent to it, and if his disposition in regard to her lack of consent is of a certain nature. A more precise definition of the *mens rea* required for rape is avoided at this point since, as will be seen, it is a matter of serious contention. The respects in which the feminist critique touch on this appreciation concern the criteria of and evidence for non-consent and consent, the possibility of prior or implied consent, and the definition of *mens rea*. I will turn to a consideration of each of these aspects after first, briefly, discussing the *actus reus* of rape.

The Act of Rape

The act of rape is normally defined as 'sexual intercourse' with a person who, at the time of the intercourse, did not consent. British law has qualified this definition with 'unlawful' where this adjective functions principally to exclude marital sexual intercourse. Understood in this way a husband could not be guilty of raping his wife since the intercourse in question even if non-consensual was not 'unlawful'. Reasons for thinking the exemption of marital sexual relations from the scope of the crime of rape justified will be considered and rejected later. British law, it should be noted, is changing so as no longer to recognise the marital exemption.

What is 'sexual intercourse'? The law has tended to consider this to be penile penetration of the vagina, however slight and short of duration. Two comments are in order. First, it seems arbitrary to effect any sharp distinction between vaginal and anal or oral penetration. Anal penetration of a man, as well as of a woman, should be accounted rape. Relatedly, it can seem arbitrary to distinguish too sharply between penile penetration and the use of a hand or object. This criticism is not that the law does not treat these actions as other than serious sexual assaults. It is that reliance on any implied notion of 'natural' intercourse may help to reinforce the understanding of rape as on the end of some continuum of normal sexual behaviours. The penis is no less of a weapon of assault in a rape than a bottle for being other times deployed in 'normal' sexual relations. In the same vein the vagina is not, somehow, a more 'natural' orifice for penetration than the mouth.

The second comment is directed at the view, operative in British law, that 'intercourse' may be considered to be 'complete' upon penetration alone. In the New Zealand case of *Regina* v. *Kaitamaki* the defendant asserted that the young woman initially consented to a second act of intercourse which took place after a first act of intercourse, followed by the woman's departure from and return to the room in which he was.[13] He did not also deny that during this second act he became aware that she was not consenting, though he did not desist. He appealed his initial conviction on the grounds of an alleged misdirection on the basis of that section (127) of the (New Zealand) Crimes Act of 1961 which states that 'for the purposes of this Part of the Act, sexual intercourse is complete upon penetration'.[14]

What might justify the law in this view? It might hold to this view in consequence of an understanding of the sexual act as 'indivisible'. That is evidently false. It is possible to distinguish between moments of the sexual act and, in particular, between penetration and emission. On the other hand, the law may take the view that it can justifiably 'deem' the sexual act to be indivisible. That is, although the act is divisible, it should not be thought so for the purposes of determining what has been consented to. The claim is that in consenting to penetration, a woman may be judged to be consenting to the 'completion' of intercourse. That again is without warrant. A woman may consent to penetration but not consent to full coitus. She may indeed explicitly dissent from the latter. A favoured form of contraception adopted by couples without recourse to artificial contraceptives has been penile withdrawal prior to ejaculation. Intercourse could be and has been engaged in with prior agreement on such a precaution against unwanted pregnancy being taken.

But if the women does not explicitly dissent from full intercourse and consents to initial penetration, may she be deemed to consent to the former? At the end of the first chapter it was argued that a woman can change her mind. The question raised there was whether she can revoke her consent. That is, is her dissent during intercourse sufficient to negate her initial consent to the 'completion' of that which initial penetration began? Appeal might be made here to the notion of indirect consent to that which is the inevitable outcome of that to which direct consent has been given. Even if the sexual act is divisible into separate moments, each subsequent moment follows inescapably from the preceding one. In Chapter 2 reasons were given for us to be deeply suspicious of a 'climactic' model of sexual activity in terms of a certain natural end, marked by an increasing intensity and involuntariness. The familiar idea of a man's sexual passion being unstoppable once suitably aroused is a dangerous one which needs to be subverted. It can and should be challenged, for if it is allowed to operate unchallenged, it helps to shift the burden of responsibility for unconsented sex onto women. Women, it will be said, cannot revoke their consent to that which, once it has begun, is unstoppable. 'It' is stoppable, and a request to stop that which has only been started should not be deemed without force simply because a start has been agreed.

It is arguable that a man has good reason to think that a woman who consents to penetration thereby consents to full intercourse. However, he has such good reasons only in the absence of signs to the contrary. In *Kaitamaki* the defendant did not deny that the woman dissented during intercourse from its continuation. Persistence in the face of such protest is unreasonable. It might be thought that the wrong done to a woman who consents to penetration but dissents from 'completion' is considerably less than the wrong done to a woman who does not even consent to penetration. That can be a dangerous assumption. As was argued at the end of Chapter 1 the character of the sexual activity may change radically. Proceeding with intercourse which is extremely painful or deeply unwelcome to the woman is not to be thought less costly to her on account of her initial agreement. Overriding the wishes of a woman in these circumstances need not be any less of a violation of her person than an initial unconsented penetration.

Finally it might be argued that allowing for the revocation of consent during intercourse panders to the quixotic and changeable temperament of a woman.[15] Such prejudicial characterisations are unhelpful. At issue is the force of a woman's sincere and genuine dissent from continued sexual activity. That dissent should have force at whatever point of the sexual intimacy it is expressed. It is no less serious for being expressed at a later stage of such intimacy. The thought that it should not may, in the final analysis, be due only to the already criticised assumption that the further on a sexual encounter is, the less reason its parties can have for bringing it to a halt.

The other element of the criminal act of rape, besides its being 'sexual intercourse', is that it was not, at the time of the intercourse, consented to. In past British law lack of consent has been regarded as established 'by force, fear or fraud'. That view is recognised now to be mistaken. In the case of *Regina* v. *Olugboja* the British Court of Appeal maintained that 'the question now is simply: "At the time of sexual intercourse did the woman consent to it?" It is not necessary for the prosecution to prove that what might otherwise appear to have been consent was in reality merely submission induced by force, fear or fraud, although one or more of these factors will no doubt be present in the majority of cases of rape'.[16]

This change is to be welcomed. The *actus reus* of rape is unconsented sex. What matters then is simply and solely whether the women did or did not give her consent. It is unnecessary and misleading to construe sex without consent as sex 'against the will' of the woman, as sex obtained 'forcefully' or despite 'utmost resistance'. However, there is now a problem which was acknowledged in general terms at the outset of Chapter 7. This is that the morally impermissible and the illegal do not and should not always coincide.

In particular, rape is a crime. It is more than morally impermissible; it is deserving of criminal sanctions and not just moral reprobation. In Chapter

4 I raised worries about cases where the consent given might not be considered valid even though it would be thought so on the standard account of consent. I concluded that the real issue was not whether the consent was valid or 'real', but whether it was valid *enough* to legitimate the behaviour to which the consent is given. Now it is plausible to think that some giving of consent should fail to be valid enough to legitimate the behaviour but be at the same time not invalid enough to warrant criminalising the behaviour in question.[17] In other words not all instances of non-consensual sex, on the broad construal of consensuality which serves as a ground for moral permissibility in this book, should be counted as instances of rape.

The law needs to agree and define conventions which make precise what conditions and circumstances determine what is sufficient consent for its absence to constitute the *actus reus* of rape. The law, in short, would need to mark the boundary between the lack of consent which suffices morally to condemn and that which must suffice to render criminal. There is no ready answer to the question of where this boundary should be fixed. It is implausible to think that rape is only sexual intercourse obtained by 'force, fear or fraud'. But it is also arguable that a doctor should be professionally sanctioned but not criminally liable for seducing his patient. We should try to recognise that it uses the law ill, as it also does little to change patterns of behaviour and underlying attitudes, to criminalise all activities to which the consent of one party is less than 'real'. The arguments of this book have been intended to give a clearer picture of what 'real' consent looks like. They do not settle, they merely better inform, the further discussion of what should be 'real enough' for the law's purposes.

What the Law Counts as Evidence of Consent

Central to the feminist criticism of the law's treatment of rape has been a contestation of the evidential criteria for the giving of consent which courts have been prepared to admit. In what follows it should be borne in mind that there is a distinction between evidence that consent has been given and evidence that shows a defendant's belief that it has been given to be reasonable. The issues raised by the second will be considered when the topic of *mens rea* is discussed.

The disputed criteria touch on past behaviour, dress and demeanour at the time of the alleged rape, and any relationship with the accused. The effect of feminist criticisms has been to change the law in desirable ways. For instance, 'rape-shield statutes' narrow the range of admissible evidences concerning the plaintiff's past sexual history. Concerns remain about the extent to which residual legitimate grounds for admitting such evidence are exploited in ways the statutes were intended to eliminate.[18] However, my concern here is not to review or evaluate these changes. It is rather briefly to assess the various claims that certain facts, if proven, do bear on the question of whether consent has been given.

The fact that a woman has in the past consented to sexual relations with men does not of itself constitute consent, in whole or some measure, to sex with a man now. Her past givings of consent do not, as it were, carry over into the present, being somehow additive and counting towards a giving of current consent. Of course a man who is aware of the woman's sexual history may be disposed to believe that she is more or less likely to give her consent to him. His belief is not reasonable if he simply judges past sexual activity as making present indiscriminate sexual activity more probable. He can have good reason to make *some* kind of prediction about what she may agree to on the basis of what she has previously agreed to. However, the key point is that from her previous behaviour alone he has reason only to judge that she might consent, not to conclude that she does consent.

More objectionable is the view that past sexual behaviour stains a character in such a way as to discount the validity or value of its owner's consent. The view is that an 'unchaste' woman no longer has any consent to give or withhold. If she says 'no', it cannot be taken as really meaning 'no'. And even if she does say and mean 'no', her refusal need not be taken as seriously as that of an 'innocent' or less sexually experienced woman. A related but also objectionable view is that an 'unchaste woman' is untrustworthy in general. Her testimony in defence of the charge that she was raped should thus be taken less seriously. No one, it should be noted, normally takes a sexually active man to have less moral integrity simply in virtue of his promiscuity.

The charge that a woman who dresses or behaves in a sexually explicit way is thereby giving her consent to sex is open to the same kinds of criticism. 'Sexually explicit' should be understood as characterising behaviour outside the context of a sexual interaction which has been initiated and which is already intimate to some degree. If, after mutual kissing and caressing, a woman changes the character of that intimacy—by, for instance, removing her or the man's clothes, moving her or his hands to the genitals—then such behaviour may be judged both as sexually explicit and as constituting a willingness to be more intimate. That much can be conceded with the caution, expressed previously, that consent to a higher level of sexual intimacy need not and should not be taken as consent to complete intercourse.

However, sexually explicit behaviour outside such a context should not be interpreted as consent to sexual intimacy. 'Sexually explicit' may here cover a range of behaviours—by some of which women are expressing themselves as sexual beings, by some of which they are expressing an interest in sex, by some of which they are expressing a sexual desire for someone, and by some of which they are just enjoying themselves without any sexual intentions or meanings. None of these behaviours constitutes a consent to have sex as such. At most some of them express a wish to begin a process of interaction that may be sexually intimate to a greater or lesser degree. Hopefully enough was said in Chapter 2 to subvert the assumption that such behaviours conform to conventions whereby women give their consent to sex.

Consider, however, the following difficult question. Feminists have rightly criticised those, including on notorious occasions certain judges, who have accused women of 'inviting' or 'provoking' rape by their conduct or dress. It is important to separate the question of whether women can be held responsible for contributing to the situation in which their rape is an outcome from that of whether such contributory negligence lessens the blame-worthiness of the rapist. A defensible general rule is that a person who knows that some harm will probably befall her (or is much more likely to do so) under a specifiable set of circumstances, and who can reasonably avoid those circumstances, may be held in part responsible for the harm that is caused her if and when she does not avoid those circumstances. By extension if it is reasonable for someone to know the foregoing, then she is negligent in not avoiding those circumstances.

If I enter a neighbourhood I know to be the site of regular muggings when I do not have to do so, then I play some part in bringing it about that I am mugged, if I am. My responsibility is the greater if I make several unnecessary strolls through the neighbourhood, if I dress conspicuously, walk alone, take out and display my wallet, and so on. Now it is easy to see how the argument might extend to cover the case of dressing or behaving in a sexually explicit manner under circumstances where that may make it more likely that rape will be attempted. Does it follow that such behaviour 'invites' the rape?

Five replies are in order. First, the relationship between the behaviour and the crime it 'invites' needs carefully to be specified. A thief does not take a solitary and evidently rich stroller to be consenting to the theft of his money. He simply exploits an occasion which the solitary stroll presents. A rapist may allege that sexually explicit behaviour is evidence of consent to sex. But it is not—for reasons already given—and such behaviour no more 'invites' rape than a bulging wallet invites robbery. Second, rapists do not follow the rule that only women who are evidently 'inviting' sex are to be raped. Rapes may occur when women 'provoke' the sexual interest of their attackers. But such stereotypical scenarios are by no means typical. Rapists target women for reasons other than their evident sexual attractiveness, these reasons most often having to do with the exercise of power by the rapist and his exploitation of the victim's vulnerability.

Third, the rich person may walk through another less dangerous neighbourhood without significant cost to himself. Women are, similarly, asked to bear the cost of dressing and behaving in ways that do not 'invite' rape. They may justifiably insist that it is unreasonable to impose such costs upon them. Such costs are serious in that they involve a denial of free self-expression. They are unreasonably imposed because they are the price of avoiding a harm occasioned by the unjustifiable actions of some men. It is more reasonable, then, to think that the costs of making rape less likely should be borne not by women but by society at large, indeed by men in general. These costs would be incurred in securing higher conviction rates and instituting more effectively deterrent punishments for rape, and in changing the prevailing social understandings of sex and sexuality which may underpin male sexual aggression.

Fourth, there is a danger of having a zero-sum picture of responsibility for a crime. This picture imagines that the more that a person contributes by her behaviour or negligence to bringing about the circumstances in which she is a victim of a crime, the less responsible is the criminal for the crime he commits.[19] A crime is no less unwelcome or serious in its effects, or need it be any the less deliberate or malicious in its commission, for occurring in circumstances which the victim helped to realise. Yet judges who spoke of women 'inviting' or 'provoking' a rape would go on to cite such contributory behaviour as a reason for regarding the rape as less grave or the rapist as less culpable. It adds judicial insult to criminal injury to be told that one is the part author of a crime one did not seek and which in consequence is supposed to be a lesser one.

Fifth, it does not follow from the fact a woman knows her attacker that she is now consenting to sex with him. It is equally mistaken to believe that rape by an acquaintance is less serious than rape by a stranger. Indeed the gross breach of trust which the former represents constitutes it as a grave offence.[20] A woman's present consent should not be inferred from the fact that she has shared a sexual history with some person. As before, it must not be thought that any past givings of consent add up to a present consent or that the question of whether consent is or is not being given now may be discounted or a positive answer assumed simply because the question was answered positively in the past. The pattern of past sexual behaviour between two persons may have evidentiary significance in consideration of a present case of alleged rape. But the presumption that a couple will always negotiate their sexual relations in the same way is a defeasible one. It is an especially unsafe presumption to rely on once a relationship is over. It is also unsafe if there are features of the present case which, in the absence of any previous relationship, would lend weight to the alleged victim's claim of rape. A woman may have had 'consensual' sex within a violent relationship with a man who regularly beat her, often doing so as prelude to sex. That is not evidence that, the relationship over, she consents to sex with the same man after the use or threat of violence against her.[21]

What the Law Counts as Evidence of the Absence of Consent

Feminists have charged that the law's understanding not only of what shall count as consent but also of what shall count as the absence of consent is defective. Most strikingly the law has frequently been prepared only to see resistance to force as evidence of non-consent. There is a double error here. First, it is mistaken to think that consent can be negated only by a use or threat of force. That much has already been established in previous chapters. Second, it is a mistake to think that the only evidence of such force could be resistance to it. A judgement that passive submission is the prudent response to a threat of overwhelming superior force is more reasonable, on many occasions, than a decision to resist. As Susan Estrich notes, 'Rape is most assuredly not the only crime in which consent is a defence; but it is the only crime that has required the victim to resist physically in order to establish non-consent'.[22] Others have rightly criticised the equation of non-consent with resistance to superior force.[23]

There are a number of reasons for this equation, none of them satisfactory. There is the thought that women so prize their 'virtue' that if they were truly unwilling, they would resist to the utmost, to the point of death even. There is the assumption that many women mean 'yes' when they say 'no', and may even engage in token resistance to a man's advances which they secretly welcome. They do so insofar as their gender role requires that they appear chaste even while they collude in their own 'possession'. Only strenuous resistance could persuade that a woman is really refusing and not playing out her part in the sexual game. And, finally, in the background is Hale's infamous view that 'rape is . . . an accusation easily to be made and hard to be proved, and harder to be defended by the party accused, tho never so innocent'.[24] Such a view requires much clearer evidence both of non-consent on the part of the victim and of evident culpability on the part of the defendant in the case of rape than would be needed for any other crime. Only extreme physical resistance fits the bill.

All these views rely upon prejudicial understandings of the two genders and their appropriate behaviour in sexual contexts. Once such views are set to one side, it is hard to see what warrant there is for the law taking 'utmost resistance' as the only admissible evidence of non-consent. Of course the broader one's understanding of what should count as consent as a defence to the crime of rape, the more difficult it may be to agree what shall count as evidence of its absence. I defer consideration of the view that a failure to give affirmative consent (by a woman saying 'yes' or some uncontroversial verbal equivalent) should count. Certainly the weaker view, that dissenting (by a woman saying 'no' or some uncontroversial verbal equivalent) should count, most certainly must apply. The slogan that '"No!" means no' is important not least for directly disputing the suggestion that, on occasion, 'no' may not mean no. For dissent to have force, it is, however, arguable that its contrary should also. It would be curiously asymmetrical to think that women should be believed when they say 'no' but disbelieved when they sincerely say 'yes'. That is another reason to doubt a feminist claim that a woman's 'no' means just that, but that her 'yes' does not signify true consent.[25]

Prior or Pre-consent

Could a woman give her consent to the future discounting of her consent or dissent? That is one interpretation of the marriage contract which supplies an influential reason for believing that a husband cannot rape his wife. For in marrying her husband, a woman is said irrevocably to agree henceforward to be sexually accessible to her husband. Hale is, once again, the source of an infamous quotation: '[A] husband cannot be guilty of a rape committed by himself upon his lawful wife, for by their mutual matrimonial consent and contract the wife hath given up herself in this kind unto her husband which she cannot retract'.[26] Prior or implied pre-consent is not the only basis for the marital-rape exemption,[27] but it is the most interesting and salient one, certainly within the context of a discussion of sexual consent.

The obvious response to this view is that it misunderstands the nature of marriage and the marital contract. This is to say that marriages either do not or should not involve that kind of contractual agreement. Of course a man and a woman do enter into a contractual arrangement whereby they willingly constrain themselves in respect of future conduct. The pledge of mutual fidelity, agreeing to 'forsake all others', is a kind of self-binding, a foreclosing of future sexual conduct outside the marriage. However, agreeing that one will not do certain things henceforward is very different from agreeing to have things done to one by another, especially when the agreement is a 'blanket' one. It would be easy then simply to conclude that a prior, exceptionless agreement by one party to sexual access by the other is inconsistent with a proper understanding of the marital relationship.

But—notwithstanding its impropriety as a constituent part of *marriage*—should some such agreement be morally permissible? Ought a person to be allowed to agree to give themselves over totally to sexual use by another? The question, in effect, is whether a sexual slavery contract is allowable. There has been considerable debate as to whether a slavery contract is tolerable. Much of this has grown out of John Stuart Mill's assertion that individuals should not be allowed to use their freedom to alienate their freedom, as would be the case with such a contract. My own view, defended elsewhere,[28] is that Mill is right, in the terms of a principle protecting the exercise of freedom, to forbid uses of freedom which abrogate or abridge its future exercise. If freedom is valuable, then it is right to stop people freely giving up that which is valued. Someone should not then be allowed to give their consent to a relationship in which their future consent or dissent is discounted as of no value.

The *Mens Rea* of Rape

To be guilty of rape, a man must not only have sexual intercourse to which the woman, at the time of the intercourse, was not consenting. He must also have had a certain disposition in regard to her lack of consent. The clearest instance of such a disposition is that he knew that she did not consent (and persisted nonetheless). But what if he did not know she was not consenting? What, in this instance, must be the case for him to be possessed of a 'guilty mind'? British law has required only that he act 'recklessly'. It has not punished negligence. The question of whether the law should hold a man culpable for negligently having unconsented sex with a woman broaches the broader issue of what should constitute criminal guilt and was also raised, in a particular and controversial manner, by the case of *Director of Public Prosecutions* v. *Morgan*.[29]

In *Morgan* several men had sex with Morgan's wife in the sincere but unreasonable belief that she consented to the sex despite her clear protestations to the contrary. Morgan had informed them that his wife actually welcomed rough sex and that they should discount her violent objections and struggling. The British House of Lords rejected the argument that an unreasonable belief in consent could not be a defence. That decision caused widespread concern. For it is arguable that someone should be held culpable for a rape, as they would for other crimes, if they could have but failed to prevent what a reasonable person should have foreseen would be the outcome of their actions. Someone should be guilty of rape if he had sex with a woman to which a reasonable man would have known she did not consent. The man would be guilty of negligent rape.

The difference between negligence and recklessness is as follows: One acts negligently in not taking the precautions that a reasonable person should; one acts recklessly in deliberately taking risks one ought not. A negligent person is not aware of the harms he risks, but he should be. A reckless person does not care what harms he risks. In *Morgan* the men sincerely but mistakenly believed that the wife gave her consent. They were not reckless since they were not conscious of any possible risk of non-consent which they then disregarded. Rather, they negligently failed to recognise what any reasonable person could have seen, namely, that she was not consenting. The law might stipulate that what a reasonable person could have foreseen is presumptive evidence of what the person *did* foresee. But such evidence is only presumptive—to be set beside other evidence from what he said and did—and the stipulation does not amount to making negligence culpable. The fact that someone may well foresee what he, if reasonable, should foresee does not mean that he would be culpable if he did not foresee what he ought, if reasonable, to have foreseen.

The general issue at law is whether persons should be held liable and punished only for criminal acts towards which they had the appropriate subjective state of mind—that is, that they deliberately intended or consciously disregarded the risk of the harms which the act occasioned. The dispute is between 'subjectivists' who hold such a state of mind to be a necessary condition of the requisite *mens rea* and 'objectivists' who hold such a state of mind not to be a necessary condition.[30] Of course it may be said that the dispute is not one that can be settled with respect to all crimes. One might be 'subjectivist' with regard to some crimes, 'objectivist' with regard to others. But what should one say about rape? Should a man be guilty of rape if he made an honest mistake about the woman's consent?

Rather than argue from the terms of the general dispute between 'subjectivists' and 'objectivists' or from the comparability of rape as a crime with other serious crimes in terms of the required *mens rea,* I will advance several considerations which tell in favour of the law requiring that a man form a reasonable and not just honest belief in the woman's consent. These considerations tell against the view that a mere mistake-of-fact about consent should be a defence to the crime of rape.

The first consideration is that sexual intercourse is not unwitting. A man knows that he is having sex with a woman. Further, men cannot but be unaware of the particular character of any sexual intercourse. Instances of sex can be and are differentiated by their parties in terms of pleasurability, ease, duration, awkwardness, and so on. I do not mean to suggest that both parties form the *same* judgement about any sex or that each correctly apprises the other's judgement. I mean only that it is important to recognise that persons do not engage in simple sex which is indifferent to its parties. They engage in this sexual encounter with *this* person on *this* occasion.

Second, the nature of any sexual encounter is such that it is hard normally to miss signs of non-consent. A lack of consent insinuates into a person's behaviour, is worn on her body, in a way that is not true of some other facts regarding that person about which the opposite party could be mistaken. A man could fail to know another was just below the age of sexual consent. A woman could fail to know her long-missing husband was still alive when she re-married.

Third, a man can desist from intercourse at little or no cost to himself. It is not only possible for him to do so, but it also can be done without serious harms befalling him. To think otherwise may be to endorse the 'climactic' model of sexuality criticised throughout. In desisting, he does of course fail to secure a satisfaction. But he is not denied the possibility of other future satisfactions of a comparable kind. The loss to him is only of this one instance of sexual satisfaction.

Fourth, the costs to a woman of unconsented sex are considerable. They are evident and well attested by the victims of non-consensual sex. While a man might claim with some merit to be honestly mistaken about whether this woman is giving her consent, he cannot with similar warrant claim to be ignorant of the serious harms occasioned to women who do not consent. These considerations suggest that men have a duty to take reasonable care lest women do not consent. The costs of taking such care are not great and are certainly insignificant when compared with the costs that are avoided by such care being taken. Men can exercise such care by being sensitive to the evidence of a lack of consent on the part of women. Such evidence is palpable, or it can be made so if men take certain measures. That is, men should not only take care to be sure that women do consent; they should also take care to be sensitive to the evidential grounds of any assurance. Discharging such a duty is not only warranted on the grounds of avoiding serious harms. It is also consonant with a view of men and women as equal, knowing partners in any sexual encounter. Such a view regards women not simply as beings whose non-consensual involvement in sex must be avoided, but as persons without whose free and equal involvement sex is a merely a one-sided, exploitative pursuit of selfish pleasure. In Chapter 5 I argued that some instances of sexually 'using' another should not, if consensual, be morally condemned, even if they could be negatively evaluated on non-moral grounds. The point made here is not that, on the contrary, one-sided sexual encounters are wrong. It is that it is wrong to regard women, as a class, as not deserving of anything other than such encounters. It demeans persons to think of them as never having any claim to be treated as an end, or to discount their claim to be so treated, even if, on occasion, they agree to be treated as a means. In summary, if the duty to take reasonable care is acknowledged as appropriate, then the *mens rea* of rape should be broadened beyond 'subjectivist' terms.[31]

Should Only 'Yes' Mean Yes?

As has been noted feminists have long insisted that a woman's 'no' means no. Explicit avowals of dissent should be taken as dissent. But does the contrary hold? Is consent given only if it is explicitly avowed? Should nothing less than a 'yes' or its unambiguous verbal equivalent be taken as indicating consent? In Chapter 2 it was noted that some have defended the 'affirmative verbal standard' of consent. It was argued there that there is a bad reason for not adopting such a standard—the view that women are or should be essentially demure and sexually non-explicit creatures—and a good reason for adopting it—namely, the dangers of reliance upon conventions whereby women are understood to give their sexual consent merely by some instance of non-verbal behaviour. However, it was concluded that it would be wrong to think that it is necessary to say 'yes' to everything with anything less than 'yes' counting as non-consent. The conclusion was drawn as a result of the discussion distinguishing between different kinds of relationship and of specifying the different presumptions that should be made in each.

It is worth re-emphasising this point. It seems absurd to require of an intimate, loving couple that in every one of their sexual encounters they should seek the explicit consent of one another, either's failure to do so being culpable since the absence of explicit consent shall count as non-consent. The absurdity lies in the extension to one type of relationship—characterised by love, long familiarity, mutual understanding, and trust—of presumptive standards which are certainly appropriate to another type, that, for instance, between strangers. Of someone I do not know it does seem right that in a first sexual encounter I should seek to know that her consent is given and that I can satisfactorily learn this only through explicit verbal statements on her part.

The extension of the 'affirmative verbal standard' of consent to all sexual relationships is a mistake. Further, there are two different general grounds for thinking that such a standard should apply even in some cases. The first of these is that men are under a duty to take reasonable care that women do give consent to sex. This duty has already been defended. The second ground is what has been called a 'communicative' model of sexuality.[32] This is an understanding of sex as an activity engaged in by equals, intent on the mutual satisfaction of each other, and in which the desires and intentions of each party are communicated clearly to the other. It contrasts with a model of sex in which wordless contact progresses through unresisted physical exploration and escalating intimacy.

The 'communicative model' comprises two desirable features—that it sees sex as an activity of equal and reciprocal intentions to satisfy, and that it views sex as an activity in which the desires of each are clearly communicated to each other. The model is an ideal. Instances of sexual behaviour which conform to the model are to be commended. But it cannot be the case that any instance of sexual activity which falls short of the ideal is to be morally condemned. I have already argued, in Chapter 5, and repeated earlier that the sexual use of another, with their consent, is not to be condemned. It would also surely be absurd to condemn those whose loving, mutually respectful sex is wordless, progressing through unresisted physical exploration and escalating intimacy. The communicative model errs if it requires that such sensitivity and responsiveness to the wishes of the other can only and on every occasion be expressed in the form of explicit verbal statements.

The importance of the communicative model is that it is possible to engage in sex which conforms to its requirements. Some will suggest a contrast between the reality of sex and the implausibly 'contractualist' character of the model. Sex, it will be said, cannot be negotiated like a commercial exchange. It is spontaneous, desirous behaviour. It does not, cannot, and should not be required to pause for question-and-answer sessions about the permissibility of any next stage.

This characterisation of the contrast is pejorative and mistaken. Parties to a sexual encounter can take care to seek the views of the other. The dynamics of any such encounter are not such that someone, chiefly the male, is so taken over by his desire as to be incapable of controlling his actions and of controlling them in ways that are responsive to the expressed wishes of the woman. They should do so precisely in those circumstances where discharging the duty to take care that consent is being given requires that they do so.

The general point is this: The duty upon men to take reasonable care in being sure that consent is given combines with a view that sexuality can and should be understood in 'communicative' terms to yield the thought that the duty can be discharged only if men seek and secure a verbal affirmation of consent. While that is plausible in cases where the duty presses hardest—where a couple are strangers or uncertain about themselves as sexual partners—it loses plausibility in other cases where the level of familiarity is greater. That should not lead us, however, to think the duty does not oblige all men or that the communicative model is not ideal for all sexual relationships.

◀ 10 ▶

Conclusion

THIS BOOK OPENED WITH A CONCISE EXPRESSION of a common and popular view about sexual matters, namely, that 'there is only one rule on the sex game, and that's consent'. The book has, hopefully, demonstrated both that the rule is a far from simple one and that it is not so evident that it is or should be the only rule of the game. In other words, the problems for the common view—that whatever sexual activity is consented to and harms no one else should be permitted—are of two kinds. The first set of problems, which could be called 'internal', are about how consent should be understood insofar as consent does provide a warrant for what is consented to. They might be summed up by means of the question 'When is consent real or valid enough to legitimate the behaviour to which consent is given?' The second set of problems, which could be called 'external', are about the overall plausibility of the common view. They might be summed up by means of the question 'Is consent, even if real and valid, always enough to legitimate the behaviour to which it is given?'

The first set of problems arises from worries about whether there is a robust and plausible understanding of consent which can then play its appropriate role in the Principle of Consensuality. These problems were raised by the kinds of cases discussed in Chapter 4. The feminist critique, examined in Chapter 6, provides a radical statement of the view that there just is no such thing as a woman's giving of her consent to sex or at least none such that it is possible to derive the permissibility of the sex to which it is given from its being given. The second set of problems arises from worries about whether, however consent is understood, the Principle of Consensuality supplies a sufficient or adequate moral evaluation of all sexual activity. These worries were raised in Chapter 5 when the putative wrongfulness of consensually 'using another' was considered. The final three chapters also pressed the question of whether, in various particular instances of sexual interaction, consensuality is enough.

These two sorts of problems, which I hope have been given a fair hearing in the book, may be regarded by some as sufficiently weighty and intractable to persuade them to give up on the common view. There are, of course, other accounts of what forms of sexual behaviour should be permitted other than that provided in terms of consent. These have been alluded to on occasion. However, there is a line of criticism against the common view which has not thus far been explicitly discussed—although it does inform the feminist critique considered in Chapter 6. Its defenders might well say that the 'internal' and 'external' problems for the common view are to be explained by a more fundamental failing, that of the very notion of individual consent as any kind of foundation for a theory of the sexually permissible. Such a criticism attacks the project of construction of such a theory on the basis of an irredeemably and necessarily flawed concept.

Let me briefly outline the nature of this criticism.[1] Consent, it will be said, can have the normative significance the common view attributes to it only on the basis of a suspect theory of the individual and society. Such a theory is atomistic; it views society as a voluntary and equal association of self-sufficient individuals. Each is deemed capable of making free decisions about how best to lead her life. Her 'private' decisions are hers alone to make, and she should be held accountable only for those of her actions which are 'public' in the stipulated sense. The criticism of this view holds that individuals are socially situated agents whose identities are crucially determined by that fact; that society is structured by significant inequalities—especially relevant being those between the genders; that there are collectives or groups within society with a significance obscured by the view's individualist presuppositions; and that the distinction between a 'public' and 'private' realm of conduct is a false, ideologically constructed one.

Here is an exemplary instance of this kind of criticism. It comes within the context of a critique of the idea that consensual, private lesbian sadomasochism should be condoned by feminists:

> The question of consent also assumes and exacerbates a misleading distinction between private and public spheres of behavior. Consent is conceived as the private exchange of permissions between isolated individuals. Yet little about the permitted behavior is private, nor are the effects of sadomasochism. . . . Our 'consent' to sexual activity is not really free: it is not free in the sense of being the autonomous choice of an atomic individual. . . . The social and cultural nature of choice, per se, is not problematic, nor is it specific to sadomasochism, for we are social creatures. What is crucial is to acknowledge that 'private consen' is nonexistent and go on from there.[2]

This line of criticism shares much with a familiar critique of 'liberalism' which can be found within contemporary social and political philosophy, especially feminist and communitarian writings. A proper general consideration of it can be found in surveys of political philosophy.[3] The proper question to ask here is whether such a line of criticism is fatally damaging to any version of the common view about consensuality.

The criticism maintains that it is a mistake to think of consent as a foundation for sexual morality because of how consent must be conceived. The quoted instance of the criticism does, however, indicate a crucial ambiguity. It is one which can be found in many other versions of the criticism. This is between the concept of consent and that conception of 'consent' which is underpinned and informed by certain assumptions. The distinction between 'concept' and 'conception' is a familiar one. Rawls speaks of a concept of justice which is 'specified by the role which . . . different conceptions of justice have in common'.[4] As H.L.A. Hart, whom Rawls acknowledges as sharing his distinction in this context, makes plain, there is a 'general principle latent in [the] diverse applications of the idea'.[5] It would follow that criticism of some particular 'application' of an idea did not impugn the underlying principle, or show the impossibility of defending some other application of the idea.

The quotation attacks a conception of consent, not the concept as such. Thus it criticises how consent is 'conceived', for what it 'assumes'. 'Consent' is not free 'in the sense of' presuming a certain understanding of the individual and her choices. What, it is concluded, does not exist is not consent per se, but rather 'private consent'. The very use of scare quotes and a qualifying adjective confirms, it would seem clear, the fact that what is problematic is only a specific conception of consent.

If this is so, then it would seem fair to ask of those who defend this line of criticism whether they are prepared to offer a revised conception of 'consent', one which does not make the 'atomistic' assumptions of which the liberal conception is accused, which acknowledges that we are 'social creatures' and that our choices have a 'social and cultural nature'. If the word 'consent' is substituted for that of 'rights', then the following provides an admirable statement of just such a view: 'At the same time, a critical stance toward liberal formulations of individual rights does not mean *abandoning* "rights" discourse but rather pushing it to its logical conclusion. It is important to be very clear about this in order to differentiate the socialist-feminist position on "a woman's right to choose" from bourgeois notions of "privacy"'.[6]

The other option for defenders of the line of criticism under review is explicit abandonment of any notion of consent playing a legitimating role in sexual conduct. But then it must be made clear both what, if anything other than the consent of individuals, does legitimate conduct, and what are the implications of refusing consent, in any form, such a legitimating role. Does the consent of individuals to sexual relations with others who also consent to these relations count for nothing? What weighs more heavily in the evaluation of such relations than the consent of its parties? Is nothing appropriately described as 'private' where that means only that something qualified as such is an inappropriate subject for collective or 'public' control? There may be answers that can be given to these questions. But the need to answer them should not be avoided by the disguising of a general abandonment of the Principle of Consensuality as a critique of an allegedly ideological conception of 'consent'.

The common view about sexual consensuality—'there is only one rule on the sex game, and that's consent'—is understandably a popular one. It fits with other views about the importance of voluntary choice in what are properly to be regarded as essentially 'private' matters. It provides a simple alternative to other more traditional and conservative views about sexual morality. It supplies a manifesto of sexual freedom and tolerance. The common view may not be defensible. Nor may there may be any defensible understanding of 'consent' which can play its required role within that view. However, the view should not lightly be abandoned. This book has indicated the scope and depth of the problems facing those who would wish to continue resisting the view's abandonment.

Notes

Preface

1. David Archard, 'Sex for Sale: The Morality of Prostitution', *Cogito* 3 (1989):47–51; David Archard, 'Exploited Consent', *Journal of Social Philosophy* 25 (1994):92–101.

2. David Archard, '"A Nod's as Good as a Wink": Consent, Convention, and Reasonable Belief', *Legal Theory* 2 (1997):273–290.

Chapter One

1. *Independent on Sunday*, 26 June 1994.

2. An excellent account of consent is provided by John Kleinig, 'The Ethics of Consent', *Canadian Journal of Philosophy* (supplementary volume) 8 (1982):92–118.

3. The phrase 'moral magic' comes from Heidi M. Hurd, 'The Moral Magic of Consent', *Legal Theory* 2 (1996), Special Issue: Sex and Consent, Part 1:121–146. Alan Wertheimer, 'Consent and Sexual Relations', ibid., 89–112, speaks of consent as 'morally transformative'.

4. This is sometimes expressed as the view that consent is 'performative' and not 'attitudinal'. For a defence of the view that this is how John Locke understood consent, see Frank Snare, 'Consent and Conventional Acts in John Locke', *Journal of the History of Philosophy* 13 (1975):27–36.

5. The example is from A. John Simmons, *Moral Principles and Political Obligations* (Princeton: Princeton University Press, 1979), 79–80. Simmons adds that silence can be taken as consent only if it is clear that this is how it is to be understood, there is a reasonable period whose limits are clearly signalled during which dissent can be expressed, the dissent can reasonably be expressed, and the consequences of such an expression are not 'extremely detrimental' to the individual.

6. Joseph Raz, *The Morality of Freedom* (Oxford: Clarendon Press, 1986), 81.

7. J. L. Austin, *How to Do Things with Words*, ed. J. O. Urmson (Oxford: Clarendon Press, 1962), 15, 18, 39, 50.

8. Searle titles these, respectively, the 'sincerity' and the 'essential' conditions of promising. See John Searle, 'What Is a Speech Act?', in John Searle (ed.), *The Philosophy of Language* (Oxford: Oxford University Press, 1971), 50.

9. John Locke, *Two Treatises of Government,* ed. Peter Laslett (Cambridge: Cambridge University Press, 1988), 2, 8, §119.

10. S. Gardiner, 'The Law and the Sportsfield', *Criminal Law Review* (1994):513.

11. Craig L. Carr, 'Tacit Consent', *Public Affairs Quarterly* 4 (1990):335–345, defends tacit consent in this fashion.

12. I. Eibl-Eibesfeldt, 'Expressive Movements', in R. A. Hinde (ed.), *Non-verbal Communication* (Cambridge: Cambridge University Press, 1972), 303–304.

13. D. A. Lloyd-Thomas, *Locke on Government* (London: Routledge, 1995), 35.

14. C. S. Nino, 'A Consensual Theory of Punishment', *Philosophy and Public Affairs* 13 (1984):295, who quotes in support Hobbes, 'Whoever voluntarily doth any action, accepteth all the known consequences of it'. Thomas Hobbes, *Leviathan*, ed. Michael Oakeshott (Oxford: Basil Blackwell, 1955), 218.

15. Act 4, Scene 1, 301–302, 319–327.

16. John Plamenatz, *Man and Society: A Critical Examination of Some Important Social and Political Theories from Machiavelli to Marx* (London: Longman, 1963), 1:239.

17. For an exchange on these matters, see Frederick Siegler, 'Plamenatz on Consent and Obligation', *Philosophical Quarterly* 18 (1968):256–261; and John J. Jenkins, 'Political Consent', *Philosophical Quarterly* 20 (1970):60–66.

18. Peter Singer, *Democracy and Disobedience* (Oxford: Clarendon Press, 1973), 47.

19. Ronald Dworkin, 'The Original Position', in N. Daniels (ed.), *Reading Rawls: Critical Studies on Rawls' A Theory of Justice* (Oxford: Basil Blackwell, 1975), 18.

20. Compare Malm, who argues with respect to the use of 'nonparadigmatic' signs to signify consent that we should use paradigmatic signs for 'activities that have significant consequences and are such that a mistake about consent cannot be corrected prior to the realisation of the consequences' and that 'as a general rule, the more the nonparadigmatic act is open to other interpretations . . . the less justified we are interpreting it as an act of consent'. H. M. Malm, 'The Ontological Status of Consent and Its Implications for the Law of Rape', *Legal Theory* 2 (1996), Special Issue: Sex and Consent, Part 2:154–155.

21. See Martha Chamallas, 'Consent, Equality, and the Legal Control of Sexual Conduct', *Southern California Law Review* 61 (1988):816–817.

Chapter Two

1. Onora O'Neill, 'Between Consenting Adults', *Philosophy and Public Affairs* 14 (1985):252–277, emphasises the importance of consent within sexual relationships at 268–272.

2. Tony Honoré, *Sex Law* (London: Duckworth, 1978), 78.

3. H.L.A. Hart, *Law, Liberty, and Morality* (Oxford: Oxford University Press, 1963), 22.

4. Irwin Altman, 'Privacy Regulation: Culturally Universal or Culturally Specific?' *Journal of Social Issues* 33 (1975):66–84.

5. Extracts from testimony to the Law Commission quoted in its *Consent in the Criminal Law: A Consultation Paper* (London: HMSO, 1995), 137–138.

6. Alan Goldman, 'Plain Sex', *Philosophy and Public Affairs* 6 (1977):267–287, has criticised the communicative model of sexuality which is evident in much influential philosophical writing on sexual morality, such as Thomas Nagel, 'Sexual Perversion', *Journal of Philosophy* 66 (1969):5–17; and Robert Solomon, 'Sexual Paradigms', *Journal of Philosophy* 71 (1974):336–345. All three pieces are reprinted in A. Soble (ed.), *Philosophy of Sex: Contemporary Readings* (Totowa, N.J.: Rowman and Littlefield, 1980), 119–138 (Goldman), 76–88 (Nagel), 89–98 (Solomon).

7. For a critique of this 'insidious assumption' about the male sex drive in the context of sexual discrimination, see Jane H. Aiken, 'Differentiating Sex from *Sex*: The Male Irresistible Impulse', *New York University Review of Law and Social Change* 12 (1984):357–383.

8. For critiques of such models in the context of legal thinking about rape, see Bernadette McSherry, 'No! (Means No?)', *Alternative Law Journal* 18 (1993): 27–30; and Ngaire Naffine, 'Possession: Erotic Love in the Law of Rape', *Modern Law Review* 57 (1994):10–37.

9. This kind of example and the line of thinking it illustrates were suggested to me by perceptive comments of Sue Mendus.

10. Most famously, and influentially, as a contrast between 'community' (*Gemeinschaft*) and 'association' (*Gesellschaft*), which is due to the work by Ferdinand Tönnies, *Community and Association*, trans. Charles P. Loomis (London: Routledge and Kegan Paul, 1955).

11. To Marx is owed the understanding of communism as a society in which the 'narrow horizon of bourgeois right' will be crossed. Karl Marx, *Critique of the Gotha Programme*, in Karl Marx and Friedrich Engels, *Selected Works* (Moscow: Foreign Languages Publishing House, 1969), 2:24.

12. Michael Sandel, *Liberalism and the Limits of Justice* (Cambridge: Cambridge University Press, 1982), 28–40, criticises Rawls for not recognising that 'justice' is a remedial, not the first virtue, of any society and argues that 'when I act out of a sense of justice in inappropriate circumstances, say in circumstances where the virtues of benevolence and fraternity rather than justice are relevantly engaged, my act may not merely be superfluous, but might contribute to a reorientation of prevailing understandings and motivations, thereby transforming the circumstances of justice in some degree' (34–35).

13. Among those who have defended such a standard are Lois Pineau, 'Date Rape: A Feminist Analysis', *Law and Philosophy* 8 (1989):217–243; Lani Anne

Remick, 'Read Her Lips: An Argument for a Verbal Consent Standard in Rape',
University of Pennsylvania Law Review 141 (1993):1103–1151; and Stephen J.
Schulhofer, 'The Gender Question in Criminal Law', *Social Philosophy and Policy* 7
(1990):105–137.

14. 'Even if it could be denied that a special sentiment of chasteness was natural
to women, would it be any the less true that in society . . . they ought to be raised in
principles appropriate to it? If the timidity, chasteness, and modesty which are
proper to them are social inventions, it is in society's interest that women acquire
these qualities'. Jean-Jacques Rousseau, *Politics and the Arts: A Letter to M.
d'Alembert on the Theatre*, trans. A. Bloom (Ithaca: Cornell University Press,
1968), 87. Quoted, along with other revealing remarks, by Carole Pateman, '"The
Disorder of Women": Women, Love, and the Sense of Justice', *Ethics* 91 (October
1980):25.

15. For a study of how such an attitude operates in everyday, non-coercive sexual
scenarios, see Leslie Margolin, 'Gender and the Stolen Kiss: The Social Support of
Male and Female to Violate a Partner's Sexual Consent in a Noncoercive Situation',
Archives of Sexual Behavior 19 (1990):281–291.

16. Douglas N. Husak and George C. Thomas III, 'Date Rape, Social Convention, and Reasonable Mistakes', *Law and Philosophy* 11 (1992):5–126.

17. As we shall also see, the *mens rea*, or guilty intent, required of the crime of
rape has been argued to be constituted by recklessness in respect of likely non-consent, negligence in determining whether there was consent, or an unreasonable belief that consent was forthcoming. The precise definition of the *mens rea* is a matter
of deep contention.

18. Husak and Thomas, 'Date Rape', 109.

19. At one point they speak of 'the dangers of trying to resolve these matters
without consulting empirical data' (ibid., 110).

20. A classic article is Antonia Abbey, 'Sex Differences in Attributions for
Friendly Behavior: Do Males Misperceive Females' Friendliness?' *Journal of Person-
ality and Social Psychology* 42 (1982):830–838. See also Spencer E. Cahill, 'Cross-
Sex Pseudocommunication', *Berkeley Journal of Sociology* 26 (1981):75–88; Char-
lene L. Muehlenhard, 'Misinterpreted Dating Behaviors and the Risk of Date Rape',
Journal of Social and Clinical Psychology 6 (1988):20–37; R. Lance Shotland and
Jane M. Craig, 'Can Men and Women Differentiate Between Friendly and Sexually
Interested Behavior?' *Social Psychology Quarterly* 51 (1988):66–73; Tracy D. Bost-
wick and Janice L. Delucia, 'Effects of Gender and Specific Dating Behaviors on
Perceptions of Sex Willingness and Date Rape', *Journal of Social and Clinical Psy-
chology* 11 (1992):14–25; and Robin M. Kowalski, 'Inferring Sexual Interest from
Behavioral Cues: Effect of Gender and Sexually Relevant Attitudes', *Sex Roles* 29
(1993):13–36.

21. Consider the following footnoted paragraph from Abbey, 'Sex Differences':
'The research described in this article grew out of the observation that females'

friendly behavior is frequently misperceived by males as flirtation. Males tend to impute sexual interest to females when it is not intended. For example, one evening the author and a few of her female friends shared a table at a crowded campus bar with two male strangers. During one of the band's breaks, they struck up a friendly conversation with their male table companions. It was soon apparent that their friendliness had been misperceived by these men as a sexual invitation, and they finally had to excuse themselves from the table to avoid an awkward scene. What had been intended as platonic friendliness had been perceived as sexual interest. After discussions with several other women verified that this experience was not unique, the author began to consider several related, researchable issues' (830 n. 17).

22. The classic study of conventions as a solution to co-ordination problems is David K. Lewis, *Convention: A Philosophic Study* (Cambridge, Mass.: Harvard University Press, 1969).

23. Husak and Thomas, 'Date Rape', 124.

24. Ibid., 124–125.

Chapter Three

1. 'Every human being of adult years and sound mind has a right to determine what should be done with his body'. *Schloendorff* v. *Society of New York Hospital* 105 NE 92, 933 (1914) *per* Cardozo, J.

2. This kind of an example is put to just such a use by Douglas N. Husak and George C. Thomas III, 'Date Rape, Social Convention, and Reasonable Mistakes', *Law and Philosophy* 11 (1992):119–120.

3. What follows is indebted to the work of Cohen, who has long worried over the foundational status of a principle of self-ownership (especially inasmuch as it might appear to legitimate significant inequality of condition). See G. A. Cohen, *Self-Ownership, Freedom, and Equality* (Cambridge: Cambridge University Press, 1995). Cohen points out that for the most celebrated defender of a principle of self-ownership, Robert Nozick, self-ownership is basic and freedom (independently conceived) is not (68).

4. John Locke, *Two Treatises of Government*, ed. Peter Laslett (Cambridge: Cambridge University Press, 1988), 2, §95.

5. The standard account is set out with exemplary lucidity and comprehensiveness by one of its best defenders, Joel Feinberg, in *Harm to Self,* vol. 3 of *The Moral Limits of the Criminal Law* (Oxford: Clarendon Press, 1986).

6. Quoted in the Policy Advisory Committee on Sexual Offences, *Report on the Age of Consent in Relation to Sexual Offences* (London: HMSO, April 1981), §35.

7. Allen E. Buchanan and Dan W. Brock, *Deciding for Others: The Ethics of Surrogate Decision Making* (Cambridge: Cambridge University Press, 1989), 78.

8. Sue Lees, *Carnal Knowledge: Rape on Trial* (London: Hamish Hamilton, 1996), 81.

9. Section 36, Crimes (Rape) Act 1991 for the State of Victoria, Australia, includes among those circumstances in which a person does not freely agree to an act that 'the person is asleep, unconscious, or so affected by alcohol or another drug as to be incapable of freely agreeing'.

10. In *Regina* v. *Elbekkay* (1995) Crim LR 163, a woman consented to sexual intercourse in the false belief that it was her regular male partner who had got into bed with her.

11. 'A person is guilty of an offence if he procures a woman by deception to have sexual intercourse in any part of the world'. Section 91 of the Draft Code recommended in Criminal Law Revision Committee, *Fifteenth Report: Sexual Offences* (London: HMSO, 1984).

12. In *Regina* v. *Linekar* (1995) QB 250, the Court of Appeal held that the prostitute whose client promised but had no intention of paying for her services was not raped. Joel Feinberg considers the case of payment with counterfeit notes and favours the view that it does not merit being considered rape. See Feinberg, *Harm to Self*, 295.

13. Feinberg, *Harm to Self*, 300.

14. Ibid., 296.

15. Ibid., 299. Compare 'It is implausible . . . to think that a woman who consents because of a false promise of a cash gift has suffered a grievous harm consistenting [*sic*] in "unwanted sexual intercourse as such"' (300).

16. Glanville Williams, *Textbook of Criminal Law*, 2d ed. (London: Stevens, 1983), 562.

17. Feinberg, *Harm to Self*, 301.

18. Robert Nozick, 'Coercion', in Peter Laslett, W. G. Runciman, and Quentin Skinner (eds.), *Philosophy, Politics, and Society, Fourth Series* (Oxford: Basil Blackwell, 1972), 101–135.

19. Australian Capital Territory, Crimes (Rape) Act 1900, §92P.

20. The first case is reported in *Regina* v. *Willard* (1978) 67 Cr App Rep 364 at 368; the second case is *Regina* v. *Harold* (1984) 6 Cr App Rep (S) 30, CA.

21. 'If one were met in a lonely place by four big men and told to hold up his hands or do anything else, he would be doing the reasonable thing if he obeyed, even if they did not say what they would do to him if he refused'. The judge in *People* v. *Flores* (1944), 145 P(2d) 320, cited as the 'four big men' argument by Brenda M. Baker, 'Consent, Assault, and Sexual Assault', in Anne Bayefsky (ed.), *Legal Theory Meets Legal Practice* (Edmonton, Alberta: Academic Printing and Publishing, 1988), 235.

22. For the threat to negate consent in the context of the crime of rape, it 'must be of such a nature as to overbear the mind of a woman of normal stability and courage'. J. C. Smith and B. Hogan, *Criminal Law: Cases and Materials*, 5th ed. (London: Butterworths, 1993), 487.

23. This elegant way of putting it is due to Anne C. Minas, 'Coercion and Consciousness', *Canadian Journal of Philosophy* 10 (1980):302.

24. See Harry Frankfurt, 'Coercion and Moral Responsibility', in Ted Honderich (ed.), *Essays on Freedom of Action* (London: Routledge and Kegan Paul, 1973), 65–86.

25. These four ways are usefully distinguished and discussed by Feinberg under the descriptions 'coercive force', 'coercive minimum', 'differential coercive force', and 'total coercive burden'. Feinberg, *Harm to Self,* 203–210.

Chapter Four

1. Raymond A. Belliotti, *Good Sex: Perspectives on Sexual Ethics* (Lawrence: University Press of Kansas, 1993), argues for a modified contractarianism which takes due account of those circumstances where the parties to the contract 'may have radically unequal bargaining power' and where 'one of the parties may bargain under the oppression of destitute circumstances' (p. 89). In effect he accepts what I give as the third and fourth reasons for thinking Mary's agreement to sleep with Richard is not valid.

2. 'The important thing for our purposes, however, is to determine what sorts of influence do invalidate consent, not deciding what word to apply to these influences'. Joel Feinberg, *Harm to Self*, vol. 3 of *The Moral Limits of the Criminal Law* (Oxford: Clarendon Press, 1986), 248.

3. Ibid., 244.

4. Ibid., 233.

5. Ibid., 253.

6. Amartya Sen, *Inequality Reexamined* (Oxford: Clarendon Press, 1992), 54–55, 149–150.

7. For a discussion of sexual harassment in a university context and the means of dealing with it, see Judith Berman Brandendburg, 'Sexual Harassment in the University: Guidelines for Establishing a Grievance Procedure', *Signs* 8 (1982):320–336.

8. 'Whatever houses I visit, I will come for the benefit of the sick, remaining free of all intentional injustice, of all mischief and in particular of sexual relations with both female and male persons, be they free or slave'. 'Oath of Hippocrates', in Warren T. Reith (ed. in chief), *Encyclopaedia of Bioethics* (New York: Free Press, 1978), 3:1731.

9. The Honourable Mr. Justice Thorpe, 'The Relationship Between Lawyer and Client: Legal Professional Privilege and Other Matters', An address to the American Inns of Court Association, June 1993, *Family Law* (December 1993):683.

10. See Pam Carter and Tony Jeffs, *A Very Private Affair: Sexual Exploitation in Higher Education* (Ticknall, England: Education Now Books, 1995), for evidence of this among university lecturers.

11. Ibid. See also Pam Carter and Tony Jeffs, 'The Hidden Curriculum: Sexuality in Professional Education', in Pam Carter, Tony Jeffs, and Mark K. Smith (eds.), *Changing Social Work and Welfare* (Buckingham, England: Open University Press, 1992), 231–244.

12. I originally defended this view in David Archard, 'Exploited Consent', *Journal of Social Philosophy* 25 (1994):92–101.

13. The approach to exploitation outlined here is due to the work of Roemer. See John Roemer, *A General Explanation of Exploitation and Class* (Cambridge, Mass.: Harvard University Press, 1982).

14. Yet it remains surprisingly common. Five to 7 percent of American physicians surveyed in 1973 indicated that they engaged in sexual intercourse with their patients. Sheldon H. Kardener, Marielle Fuller, and Ivan N. Mensh, 'A Survey of Physicians' Attitudes and Practices Regarding Erotic and Noneroterotic Contact with Patients', *American Journal of Psychiatry* 130 (1973):1077–1081.

15. In the case of psychoanalysis there is under the heading of 'transference' a theory of how and why an analysand is likely to form certain feelings towards the analyst and a prescriptive account of the role that these feelings should play in the progress of the analysis.

16. Australian Capital Territory Crimes Act 1900, §92P, (h).

17. Canadian Criminal Code, §273.1 (2) (c).

18. John Kleinig, 'The Ethics of Consent', *Canadian Journal of Philosophy* (supplementary volume) 8 (1982):110–111.

19. Ibid., 111.

20. For a good defence of the view that manipulation involves the complex motivation of another's behaviour through the manipulator playing on a supposed weakness of the other, see Joel Rudinow, 'Manipulation', *Ethics* 88 (1978):338–347.

21. Most famously, Harry Frankfurt, 'Freedom of the Will and the Concept of a Person', *Journal of Philosophy* 68 (1971):5–20.

Chapter Five

1. Of course 'Harry' is, strictly speaking, a party to the bestial practice, but the point of our considering bestiality is to understand better whether, in general, animals have interests and thus can be affected third parties. Similar remarks apply to the subsequent discussion of necrophilia.

2. *Regina* v. *Bourne* (1952) 36 Cr App Rep 125.

3. This is how Feinberg defines interests. See Joel Feinberg, *Harm to Others,* vol. 1 of *The Moral Limits of the Criminal Law* (Oxford: Oxford University Press, 1984), 34.

4. See Tony Honoré, *Sex Law* (London: Duckworth, 1978): Animals have a right 'not to be treated with cruelty. They cannot claim not to be touched', 176.

5. Robert Nozick, *Anarchy, State, and Utopia* (Oxford: Basil Blackwell, 1974), considers the merits of the position 'utilitarianism for animals, Kantianism for people' (35–47).

6. Raymond A. Belliotti, *Good Sex: Perspectives on Sexual Ethics* (Lawrence: University Press of Kansas, 1993), 232.

7. This view is defended by Feinberg, *Harm to Others,* 83–95; and George Pitcher, 'The Misfortunes of the Dead', *American Philosophical Quarterly* 21 (1984):183–188; and endorsed by Belliotti, *Good Sex,* 239–241.

8. Belliotti provocatively argued as much in his early piece 'A Philosophical Analysis of Sexual Ethics', *Journal of Social Philosophy* 10 (1979):8–11. In his later *Good Sex,* 241–242, he repeats this view but more guardedly and with the proviso that any 'consensual' necrophilia have no significant adverse societal effects.

9. Joel Feinberg, *Offense to Others,* vol. 2 of *The Moral Limits of the Criminal Law* (Oxford: Oxford University Press, 1985), 1–3.

10. Ibid., chap. 8.

11. Ibid., 33–35, 47–48.

12. Richard Wasserstrom, 'Privacy: Some Arguments and Assumptions', in Ferdinand David Schoeman (ed.), *Philosophical Dimensions of Privacy: An Anthology* (Cambridge: Cambridge University Press, 1984), 317–332. The counter-cultural argument is considered at 329–332.

13. The Judeo-Christian tradition within which the notion of the 'natural' is prominent is carefully considered by Belliotti, *Good Sex,* chap. 2. Understandings of the 'natural' and the 'perverse' are also intelligently examined in Robert Gray, 'Sex and Sexual Perversion', *Journal of Philosophy* 75 (1978):189–199; and Donald Levy, 'Perversion and the Unnatural as Moral Categories', *Ethics* 90 (1980):191–202. Both pieces are reprinted in A. Soble (ed.), *Philosophy of Sex: Contemporary Readings* (Totowa, N.J.: Rowman and Littlefield, 1980), 158–168 (Gray) and 169–189 (Levy).

14. There has been extensive philosophical discussion of paternalism. An excellent and much-cited discussion of the topic can be found in Gerald Dworkin, 'Paternalism', in Richard A. Wasserstrom (ed.), *Morality and the Law* (Belmont, Calif.: Wadsworth, 1971), 107–126. A useful collection of pieces (including Dworkin's own 'second thoughts' on the issues) can be found in Rolf Sartorius (ed.), *Paternalism* (Minneapolis: University of Minnesota Press, 1982). As always Feinberg is a brilliant and illuminating guide through the material. See Joel Feinberg, *Harm to Self,* vol. 3 of *The Moral Limits of the Criminal Law* (Oxford: Oxford University Press, 1986).

15. This view was of course most notably defended by Patrick Devlin, *The Enforcement of Morals* (London: Oxford University Press, 1965); and criticised by H.L.A. Hart, *Law, Liberty, and Morality* (Oxford: Oxford University Press, 1963). It is of course a further question whether the harms done in a person behaving immorally by the lights of society are sufficiently serious to warrant their legal proscription as Devlin believes. A more recent sophisticated defence of the view that the law may legitimately play a role in enforcing morality is provided by Robert

George, *Making Men Moral: Civil Liberties and Public Morality* (Oxford: Clarendon Press, 1993).

16. Joel Feinberg, *Harmless Wrongdoing*, vol. 4 of *The Moral Limits of the Criminal Law* (Oxford: Oxford University Press, 1988), 201.

17. In similar terms Blum argues that deception can be explained by, rather than itself explain, the wrongness of using someone: 'It is because being used is something objectionable to the person being used that the deception is required'. Larry Blum, 'Deceiving, Hurting, and Using', in Alan Montefiore (ed.), *Philosophy and Personal Relations* (London: Routledge and Kegan Paul, 1973), 48.

18. Feinberg, *Harmless Wrongdoing,* 181, cites John Kleinig as defending such a view in 'Consent as a Defence in Criminal Law', in *Archives for Philosophy of Law and Social Philosophy* (Wiesbaden: Franz Steiner Verlag GMBH, 1979), 65:3.

19. Blum, 'Deceiving, Hurting, and Using', 34–61.

20. Nancy Davis, 'Using Persons and Common Sense', *Ethics* 94 (1984):387–406.

21. Bernard H. Baumrin, 'Sexual Immorality Delineated', in R. Baker and F. Elliston (eds.), *Philosophy and Sex*, 2d ed. (Buffalo, N.Y.: Prometheus Books, 1984), 300–311.

22. Thomas Nagel, 'Sexual Perversion', *Journal of Philosophy* 66 (1969):17.

23. Don E. Marietta, Jr., 'On Using People', *Ethics* 82 (1971–1972): 'Forbidding all use of people is an unsatisfactory moral standard, not simply because it is too difficult, but because it carries altruism to the point of gross unfairness and disutility', 233.

24. Onora O'Neill, 'Between Consenting Adults', *Philosophy and Public Affairs* 14 (1985): esp. 268–272.

25. Samuel Scheffler, *Human Morality* (Oxford: Oxford University Press, 1992), 18–19, who quotes Wolf: 'It is misleading to insist that one is *permitted* to live a life in which the goals, relationships, activities, and interests that one pursues are not maximally morally good. For our lives are not so comprehensively subject to the requirement that we apply for permission, and our nonmoral reasons for the goals we set ourselves are not excuses, but may rather be positive, good reasons which do not exist *despite* any reasons that might threaten to outweigh them'. Susan Wolf, 'Moral Saints', *Journal of Philosophy* 79 (1982):436.

26. John Rawls, *A Theory of Justice* (Oxford: Oxford University Press, 1972), 48–51; N. Daniels, 'Wide Reflective Equilibrium and Theory Acceptance in Ethics', *Journal of Philosophy* 76 (1979):256–282.

Chapter Six

1. The main relevant texts by Catharine MacKinnon are 'Feminism, Marxism, Method, and the State', *Signs* 7 (1982):515–554; 'Feminism, Marxism, and the

State', *Signs* 8 (1983):635–658; *Toward a Feminist Theory of the State* (Cambridge, Mass.: Harvard University Press, 1989), esp. chap. 9; and 'Sexuality, Pornography, and Method: "Pleasure Under Patriarchy"', *Ethics* 99 (1989):314–346. The main relevant works by Carole Pateman are 'Women and Consent', in Carole Pateman, *The Disorder of Women: Democracy, Feminism, and Political Theory* (Cambridge: Cambridge University Press, 1989), 71–89; and *The Sexual Contract* (Cambridge: Polity Press, 1988).

2. MacKinnon, 'Sexuality, Pornography, and Method', 340.

3. Pateman, 'Women and Consent', 72.

4. *Regina* v. *Olugboja* (1981), 1 QB (CA), 320, at 332.

5. For a critical discussion of Carole Pateman's understanding of the 'sexual contract' along these kinds of lines, see Moira Gatens, 'Sex, Contract, and Genealogy', *Journal of Political Philosophy* 4 (1996):29–44.

6. Elizabeth Rapaport, 'Generalizing Gender: Reason and Essence in the Legal Thought of Catharine MacKinnon', in Louise M. Anthony and Charlotte Witt (eds.), *A Mind of One's Own: Feminist Essays on Reason and Objectivity* (Boulder: Westview Press, 1993), 127–143.

7. The further critical claim that what it is to be a woman in general is based purely upon the experiences of white middle-class women, and thereby excludes other groups of women, is made by Elizabeth V. Spelman, *Inessential Woman: Problems of Exclusion in Feminist Thought* (Boston: Beacon Press, 1988).

8. Pateman, 'Women and Consent', 83–84.

9. '[Sexual politics] obtains consent through the "socialisation" of both sexes to basic patriarchal policies with regard to temperament, role and status'. Kate Millett, *Sexual Politics* (London: Abacus, 1972), 26.

10. Pateman, 'Women and Consent', 84.

11. 'Male and female are created through the erotization of dominance and submission'. MacKinnon, 'Feminism, Marxism, Method, and the State', 635. '. . . Sex—that is, the sexuality of dominance and submission— . . . '. MacKinnon, 'Sexuality, Pornography, and Method', 316.

12. MacKinnon, 'Feminism, Marxism, Method, and the State', 646–647.

13. Andrea Dworkin, *Pornography: Men Possessing Women* (New York: Perigree Books, 1981), 69.

14. Andrea Dworkin, *Intercourse* (London: Arrow, 1988), 73.

15. Ibid., 143.

16. Of course Dworkin's language would apply also to male homosexual anally penetrative sex.

17. Moria Gatens, 'Sex, Contract, and Genealogy', 32 n. 17, notices the obvious military metaphors in Dworkin's language.

18. MacKinnon, 'Feminism, Marxism, Method, and the State', 516.

19. Ibid., 516, 531. 'The claim is that men, women, and the social relations they engage in are *all* constructed by sex, the activity, rather than the other way round'.

Susan E. Bernick, 'The Logic of the Development of Feminism; or, Is MacKinnon to Feminism as Parmenides Is to Greek Philosophy?' *Hypatia* 7 (1992):7.

20. MacKinnon, 'Sexuality, Pornography, and Method', 541.

21. 'MacKinnon's concept of sexuality parallels Schelling's concept of the Absolute Spirit as described by Hegel, that is "the night in which all cows are black"'. Marina Valverde, 'Beyond Gender Dangers and Private Pleasures: Theory and Ethics in the Sex Debates', *Feminist Studies* 15 (1989):242.

22. MacKinnon, 'Sexuality, Pornography, and Method', 336.

23. Emily Jackson, 'Catharine MacKinnon and Feminist Jurisprudence: A Critical Appraisal', *Journal of Law and Society* 19 (1992):203; Valverde, 'Beyond Gender Dangers and Private Pleasures', 243.

24. MacKinnon, 'Feminism, Marxism, Method, and the State', 647.

25. MacKinnon, 'Sexuality, Pornography, and Method', 317.

26. MacKinnon, 'Feminism, Marxism, Method, and the State', 537.

27. Ibid., 638–639.

28. 'MacKinnon's legacy to feminism is the impossibility of any future feminism. Her account makes feminism theoretically impossible'. Bernick, 'The Logic of the Development of Feminism', 12.

29. Valverde, 'Beyond Gender Dangers and Private Pleasures', 241.

30. 'MacKinnon's work is infused with a paradoxical mix of debilitating pessimism and unfathomable optimism'. Jackson, 'Catharine MacKinnon and Feminist Jurisprudence', 211.

31. This claim has been most influentially expressed by Adrienne Rich, 'Compulsory Heterosexuality and Lesbian Existence', *Signs* 5 (1980):631–660. It is also argued by Christine Overall, 'Heterosexuality and Feminist Theory', *Canadian Journal of Philosophy* 20 (1990):1–17.

32. Rich, 'Compulsory Heterosexuality and Lesbian Existence', 648.

33. Overall, 'Heterosexuality and Feminist Theory', 3.

34. Rich, 'Compulsory Heterosexuality and Lesbian Existence', 653.

35. Ibid., 638–639.

36. A classic study of adaptive preference formation is to be found in Jon Elster, *Sour Grapes: Studies in the Subversion of Rationality* (Cambridge: Cambridge University Press, 1983), chap. 3.

37. This is argued succinctly by John D. Walker, 'Liberalism, Consent, and the Problem of Adaptive Preferences', *Social Theory and Practice* 21 (1995):457–471.

Chapter Seven

1. James B. Twitchell, *Forbidden Partners: The Incest Taboo in Modern Culture* (New York: Columbia University Press, 1987), 128–129.

2. Raymond A. Belliotti, *Good Sex: Perspectives on Sexual Ethics* (Lawrence: University Press of Kansas, 1993), 246.

3. For suggestions that any law on incest might be subsumed under a general law proscribing the abuse of authority, see Tony Honoré, *Sex Law* (London: Duckworth, 1978), 81; and Victor Bailey and Sarah McCabe, 'Reforming the Law of Incest', *Criminal Law Review* (1979):762.

4. Temkin, for instance, appears concerned to represent incest as child abuse, albeit with some possible attendant genetic risks. See Jennifer Temkin, 'Do We Need the Crime of Incest?' *Current Legal Problems* 44 (1991):185–216.

5. 'The incest taboo is enforced in societies that have no knowledge of reproductive causality, let alone of genetic complexity'. Twitchell, *Forbidden Partners,* 11.

6. Moreover, the use of animal husbandry suggests that regulated inbreeding within a controlled population may be improving.

7. Bolingbroke wrote of the abhorrence of incest that it is 'artificial, and . . . has been inspired by human laws, by prejudice and by habit'. Bolingbroke, *Works* (London, 1809), 7:495, quoted in Alfred Owen Aldridge, 'The Meaning of Incest from Hutcheson to Gibbons', *Ethics* 61 (1951):309–313.

8. This is the claim of Jerome Neu, 'What Is Wrong with Incest?' *Inquiry* 19 (1976):27–39.

9. David Cox, 'Justice and Philosophical Method: Prostitution as an Illustration', *Journal of Social Philosophy* 11 (1980):12, where he cites the pejorative language of the British Wolfenden Committee on Homosexual Offences and Prostitution (1957) as an example.

10. Joseph Kupfer, 'Prostitutes, Musicians, and Self-Respect', *Journal of Social Philosophy* 26 (1995):77. Kupfer instances ancient Babylonian culture, which ascribed a sacred role to reproductive sexuality and hence regarded prostitution as a 'valuable social service'. Laurie Schrage, 'Should Feminists Oppose Prostitution?' *Ethics* 99 (1989):347–361, also sets prostitution and its valuation within a social context.

11. Mark R. Wicclair, 'Is Prostitution Morally Wrong?' *Philosophy Research Archives* 7 (1981):349.

12. This is the argument of Karen Green, 'Prostitution, Exploitation, and Taboo', *Philosophy* 64 (1989):525–534.

13. Neil McKeganey and Marina Barnard, *Sex Work on the Streets: Prostitutes and Their Clients* (Buckingham, England: Open University Press, 1996), 32.

14. Both kinds of unsaleable good are discussed by Walzer under his list of 'blocked exchanges'. Michael Walzer, *Spheres of Justice* (New York: Basic Books, 1983), 100–103.

15. It is frequently reported that prostitutes do not kiss their clients—not because of health reasons but because that would be to display an affection or intimacy which is inconsistent with the terms of their transaction.

16. These are the terms under which Primoratz considers and criticises the 'not for sale' claim. See Igor Primoratz, 'What's Wrong with Prostitution?' *Philosophy* 68 (1993):165–171.

17. Richard Titmuss, *The Gift Relationship: From Human Blood to Social Policy* (London: Allen and Unwin, 1970).

18. Which is how Peter Singer defends Titmuss. Peter Singer, 'Altruism and Commerce: A Defense of Titmuss Against Arrow', *Philosophy and Public Affairs* 2 (1973):312–320.

19. As does Loren E. Lomasky, 'Gift Relations, Sexual Relations, and Freedom', *Philosophical Quarterly* 33 (1983):250–258, but in order to rebut Titmuss's claim.

20. Both Loren Lomasky, 'Gift Relations, Sexual Relations, and Freedom'; and Robert M. Stewart, 'Morality and the Market in Blood', *Journal of Applied Philosophy* 1(1984):227–237, criticise Singer's defense of Titmuss in these terms.

21. Stewart, 'Morality and the Market in Blood', 231.

22. Janet Radcliffe Richards, *The Sceptical Feminist* (Harmondsworth: Penguin, 1980), 243; Mark Wicclair, 'Is Prostitution Morally Wrong?' 358; Lars O. Ericsson, 'Charges Against Prostitution: An Attempt at a Philosophical Assessment', *Ethics* 90 (1980):338–339.

23. Carole Pateman, 'Defending Prostitution: Charges Against Ericsson', *Ethics* 93 (1983):562. I have similarly argued, in an earlier article, that one's whole person is implicated in the exchange of sex for money. David Archard, 'Sex for Sale: The Morality of Prostitution', *Cogito* 3 (1989):47–51.

24. Jean-Paul Sartre, *Being and Nothingness: An Essay on Phenomenological Ontology*, trans. Hazel Barnes (London: Methuen, 1957), 59.

25. This is the argument of Kupfer, 'Prostitutes, Musicians, and Self-Respect'.

26. Pateman, 'Defending Prostitution', 564.

27. Debra Satz, 'Markets in Women's Sexual Labour', *Ethics* 106 (1995):78.

28. *Regina* v. *Brown* (1992) 2 All ER CA, 552; (1993) 2 All ER HL, 75.

29. My concern here is not with the actual judicial reasoning in the case—which many commentators are inclined to think confused and deeply flawed—but with the moral reasoning to which such judicial argument gives voice.

30. Belliotti, *Good Sex,* 226, 228 (emphasis added).

31. Ibid., 215–216. In this example a husband sadistically brutalises his willing wife before a paying audience.

32. *Rex* v. *Donavan* (1934) 2 KB 498, at 500.

33. L. H. Leigh, 'Sado-masochism, Consent, and the Reform of the Criminal Law', *Modern Law Review* 39 (1976):30–146.

34. Lois Bibbings and Peter Alldridge, 'Sexual Expression, Body Alteration, and the Defence of Consent', *Journal of Law and Society* 20 (1993):360.

35. This point is made by David Kell, 'Social Disutility and the Law of Consent', *Oxford Journal of Legal Studies* 14 (1944):125.

36. Marianne Giles, 'R. v *Brown:* Consensual Harm and the Public Interest', *Modern Law Review* 57 (1994):101–111.

37. *Regina* v. *Brown* (1992), at 559.

38. See Michael Gunn and David Ormerod, 'The Legality of Boxing', *Legal Studies* 15 (1995):191–193.

39. Kell, 'Social Disutility and the Law of Consent', 130–131.

40. *Regina* v. *Brown* (1992), at 560.

41. William Wilson, 'Is Hurting People Wrong?' *Journal of Social Welfare and Family Law* 5 (1992): 395.

42. *Regina* v. *Brown* (1993), at 84.

43. This, again, was Lord Templeman's thought; ibid., at 82, 83.

44. See, for instance, Lorena Leigh Saxe, 'Sadomasochism and Exclusion', *Hypatia* 7 (1992):59–72.

45. 'SM sexual activity does not replicate patriarchal sexual activity. It simulates it. Replication and simulation are very different'. Patrick D. Hopkins, 'Rethinking Sadomasochism: Feminism, Interpretation, and Simulation', *Hypatia* 9 (1994):123.

Chapter Eight

1. For a general survey of the main ethical issues raised by child abuse, see David Archard, 'Child Abuse', in Ruth Chadwick (ed.), *Encyclopedia of Applied Ethics* (San Diego: Academic Press, forthcoming), vol. 3.

2. M. D. Schecter and L. Roberge, 'Sexual Exploitation', in R. E. Helfer and C. H. Kempe (eds.), *Child Abuse and Neglect: The Family and the Community* (Cambridge, Mass.: Ballinger, 1976), 129.

3. Philippe Ariès, *L'Enfant et la vie familiale sous l'ancien régime* (Paris: Librarie Plon, 1960). Translated by Robert Baldick as *Centuries of Childhood* (London: Jonathan Cape, 1962).

4. For further discussion of these ideas, see David Archard, *Children, Rights, and Childhood* (London: Routledge, 1993), chaps. 2–3.

5. Michel Foucault, *Histoire de la sexualité, 1, La Volunté de savoir* (Paris: Gallimard, 1976), esp. 38–42. Translated by Robert Hurley as *The History of Sexuality: An Introduction* (Harmondsworth: Penguin, 1981), esp. 27–30.

6. Jenny Kitzinger, 'Defending Innocence: Ideologies of Childhood', *Feminist Review* 28 (1988):77–87.

7. For a slightly more extended discussion of these matters through a contrast between an age of sexual majority and one of political majority, see David Archard, 'The Age of Majority', in Iain Hampsher-Monk and Jeffrey Stanyer (eds.), *Contemporary Political Studies 1996* (Nottingham, England: Political Studies Association of the United Kingdom, 1996), 1:520–528.

8. Richard Davenport-Hines, 'Too Young to Know?' *The Times Saturday Review,* 9 February 1991, 10–12.

9. See, for instance, Frances Olsen, 'Statutory Rape: A Feminist Critique of Rights Analysis', *Texas Law Review* 63 (1984):387–432.

10. Wolfenden Committee, *Report of the Committee on Homosexual Offences and Prostitution* (London: HMSO, 1957), §50.

11. Report of the Council of Health, 'Advice Concerning Homosexual Relations with Minors 22–25' (1969), cited in Laurence R. Helfer, 'Finding a Consensus on Equality: The Homosexual Age of Consent and the European Convention on Human Rights', *New York University Law Review* 65 (1990):1083 n. 271.

12. Ibid., 1082 n. 262.

13. Wolfenden Committee, *Report of the Committee on Homosexual Offences and Prostitution*, §71. Interestingly the British home secretary, Michael Howard, made great use of this argument in the British Parliament in 1994 when resisting a move to reduce the age of consent for homosexuals. See *Hansard*, 21 February 1994, 92ff.

14. *X. v. United Kingdom*, App. No. 7215/75, European Commission on Human Rights, 12 October 1978; quoted in Helfer, 'Finding a Consensus on Equality', 1083.

15. I discuss them in Archard, *Children*, chap. 5.

16. John Stuart Mill, *On Liberty*, ed. Gertrude Himmelfarb (Harmondsworth: Penguin, 1974), 69.

17. For a concise statement of the criticism and its significance, see Priscilla Anderson, 'In the Genes or in the Stars? Children's Competence to Consent', *Journal of Medical Ethics* 18 (1992):119–124.

18. According to the estimates of British studies, 20 percent of young Britons have their first experience of sexual intercourse at fifteen or younger, and 50 percent of the girls questioned in a survey of 400 claimed to have had a sexual experience before the age of sixteen. See Ian Katz, 'Not so Sweet Sixteen', *The Guardian*, 11 January 1991; and Davenport-Hines, 'Too Young to Know?' 10.

19. Bruce W. Young, 'Haste, Consent, and Age at Marriage: Some Implications of Social History for *Romeo and Juliet*', *Iowa State Journal of Research* 62 (1988):459–474, argues that the average age of Renaissance marriage was in the mid- to late twenties, and that in this context Shakespeare's *Romeo and Juliet* may be read as voicing contemporary concern about the dangers of early marriage.

20. Richard Card, 'Sexual Relations with Minors', *Criminal Law Review* (1975):377.

21. See, for instance, Tom O'Carroll, *Paedophilia: The Radical Case* (London: Peter Own, 1980); and the contributions by Jamie Gough, 'Childhood, Sexuality, and Pedophilia', and Pat Califia, 'Man/Boy Love and the Lesbian/Gay Movement', especially, to Daniel Tsang (ed.), *The Age Taboo: Gay Male Sexuality, Power, and Consent* (London: Gay Men's Press, 1981), 65–71, 133–146.

22. Gay Left Collective, 'Happy Families? Paedophilia Examined', in Tsang (ed.), *The Age Taboo*, 60.

23. 'Not withstanding the sexual element of paedophilia, the affectual structure of a paedophiliac relationship, *so far as the child is concerned*, is more like that be-

tween parent and child, or between teacher and pupil, than between lovers'. O'Carroll, *Paedophilia*, 168.

24. Jeffrey Weeks, *Sexuality and Its Discontents: Meanings, Myths, and Modern Sexualities* (London: Routledge, 1985), 230.

25. Tony Honoré, *Sex Law* (London: Duckworth, 1978), 81; and endorsed by Victor Bailey and Sarah McCabe, 'Reforming the Law of Incest', *Criminal Law Review* (1979):762.

26. Honoré, *Sex Law*, 83.

27. The balanced and judicious report by Katz, 'Not so Sweet Sixteen', quotes the British tabloid newspaper the *Sun* as speaking of 'thousands of teenage lovers in the sexual madhouse that is Holland'.

Chapter Nine

1. Michael Freeden, *Ideologies and Political Theory: A Conceptual Approach* (Oxford: Clarendon Press, 1996), 520–525, notes the distinctive 'role of the concrete' in feminism as an ideology.

2. Susan Brownmiller, *Against Our Will* (New York: Simon and Schuster, 1975), 14–15, 209.

3. Keith Burgess-Jackson, *Rape: A Philosophical Investigation* (Aldershot, England: Dartmouth, 1996), chap. 10; Larry May and Robert Strikwerda, 'Men in Groups: Collective Responsibility for Rape', in Hugh LaFollette (ed.), *Ethics in Practice: Anthology* (Oxford: Basil Blackwell, 1997), 418–428.

4. For a good summary of the main charges, see Steven B. Katz, 'Expectation and Desire on the Law of Forcible Rape', *San Diego Law Review* 26 (1989):21–71.

5. And, she adds, a history of racism. Susan Estrich, 'Rape', *Yale Law Journal* 95 (1986):1089.

6. For a damning recent study of the English judicial process in regards to rape, see Sue Lees, *Carnal Knowledge: Rape on Trial* (London: Hamish Hamilton, 1996).

7. For an empirical rebuttal of this particular myth, see Eugene J. Kanin, 'Female Rape Fantasies: A Victimization Study', *Victimology* 7 (1982):114–121.

8. Martha R. Burt, 'Rape Myths and Acquaintance Rape', in Andrea Parrot and Laurie Bechhofer (eds.), *Acquaintance Rape: The Hidden Crime* (New York: John Wiley, 1991), 26–40.

9. For critical discussion of these stereotypes in the context of rape, see Bernadette McSherry, 'No! (Means No?)', *Alternative Law Journal* 18 (1993):27–30; and Ngaire Naffine, 'Possession: Erotic Love in the Law of Rape', *Modern Law Review* 5(1994):10–37.

10. For a review of the arguments for and against seeing rape as the crime of assault *sans phrase*, see Rosemarie Tong, *Women, Sex, and the Law* (Totowa, N.J.: Rowman and Allanheld, 1984), chap. 4.

11. See, for example, Margaret D. Bonilla, 'What Feminists Are Doing to Rape Ought to Be a Crime', *Policy Review* 66 (1993):22–29.

12. See, notably, Katie Roiphe, *The Morning After: Sex, Fear, and Feminism* (London: Hamish Hamilton, 1994).

13. *Regina* v. *Kaitamaki* (1980) NZLR 59.

14. For further details and discussion of the case, see Richard H.S. Tur, 'Rape: Reasonableness and Time', *Oxford Journal of Legal Studies* 1 (1981):432–441.

15. Notice how the word 'sudden' functions in the dissenting opinion of J. Woodhouse in *Kaitamaki*: 'She could transform his innocent and acceptable conduct into criminal activity of the most serious kind should he fail to meet her sudden indication that he must leave her'. Quoted in ibid., 439.

16. *Regina* v. *Olugboja* (1981) 73 Cr App Rep 344, at 350.

17. Emily Sherwin, 'Infelicitous Sex', *Legal Theory* 2 (1996), Special Issue: Sex and Consent, Part 2:230, argues that there is a distinction between an 'infelicity' which negates consent but not sufficiently to invoke the law and an 'infelicity' which amounts to a legal violation.

18. Leon Letwin, '"Unchaste Character", Ideology, and the California Rape Evidence Laws', *Southern California Law Review* 54 (1980):35–89; Sakthi Murthy, 'Rejecting Unreasonable Sexual Expectations: Limits on Using a Rape Victim's Sexual History to Show the Defendant's Mistaken Belief in Consent', *California Law Review* 9 (1991):541–576.

19. As Wertheimer says regarding B's drunken incompetence properly to consent which makes it possible for A to have sex with her: 'Although B's behavior may put her on the moral hook, it does not take A off the moral hook'. Alan Wertheimer, 'Consent and Sexual Relations', *Legal Theory* 2 (1996), Special Issue: Sex and Consent, Part 1:105–106.

20. See Beverly Balos and Mary Louise Fellows, 'Guilty of the Crime of Trust: Nonstranger Rape', *Minnesota Law Review* 75 (1991):599–618; and Laurie Bechhofer and Andrea Parrot, 'What Is Acquaintance Rape?' in Bechhofer and Parrot (eds.), *Acquaintance Rape*, 9–25.

21. Just such a case, *State* v. *Alston*, is cited and discussed by Estrich, 'Rape', 1108–1109.

22. Ibid., 1090. 'No similar effort is required of victims of other crimes for which consent is a defense' (1125).

23. See Donald A. Dripps, 'Beyond Rape: An Essay on the Difference Between the Absence of Force and the Absence of Consent', *Columbia Law Review* 92 (1992):1780–1809; Lucy Reed Harris, 'Towards a Consent Standard in the Law of Rape', *University of Chicago Law Review* 43 (1975):613–645; J. A. Scutt, 'Consent Versus Submission: Threats and the Element of Fear in Rape', *University of Western Australia Law Review* 13 (1977):52–76; and Robin D. Wiener, 'Shifting the Communication Burden: A Meaningful Consent Standard in Rape', *Harvard Women's Law Journal* 8 (1983):143–161.

24. Matthew Hale, *The History of the Pleas of the Crown* (London: Professional Books, 1971; originally published 1736), 214–225.

25. Estrich, 'Rape', 1131–1132.

26. Hale, *The History of the Pleas of the Crown,* 629.

27. Burgess-Jackson, *Rape,* chap. 7, supplies an admirably clear summary, and rebuttal, of the principal grounds offered for such an exemption.

28. David Archard, 'Freedom Not to Be Free: The Case of the Slavery Contract in J. S. Mill's *On Liberty*', *Philosophical Quarterly* 40 (1990):419–432.

29. *Director of Public Prosecutions* v. *Morgan* (1975) 2 All ER 347.

30. For an influential interpretation of the dispute, see Celia Wells, 'Swatting the Subjectivist Bug', *Criminal Law Review* (1982):209–220.

31. For critical discussion of the mistake-of-fact defense to rape, see Leigh Bienen, 'Mistakes', *Philosophy and Public Affairs* 7 (1970):224–245; E. M. Curley, 'Excusing Rape', *Philosophy and Public Affairs* 5 (1976):325–360; Toni Pickard, 'Culpable Mistakes and Rape: Relating Mens Rea to the Crime', *University of Toronto Law Review* 30 (1980):75–98; and T. M. Thornton, 'Rape and Mens Rea', *Canadian Journal of Philosophy* (supplementary volume) 8 (1982):119–146.

32. Lois Pineau, 'Date Rape: A Feminist Analysis', *Law and Philosophy* 8 (1989):217–243, defends such a model.

Conclusion

1. Burgess-Jackson articulates one version of this criticism when he contrasts a 'radical' conception of rape with a 'liberal' one. The latter, of course, is that which accords the disputed normative significance to consent. See Keith Burgess-Jackson, *Rape: A Philosophical Investigation* (Aldershot, England: Dartmouth, 1996), esp. chaps. 2, 6.

2. Lorena Leigh Saxe, 'Sadomasochism and Exclusion', *Hypatia* 7 (1992):61.

3. For an introduction to the relevant debates within contemporary political philosophy, see Will Kymlicka, *Contemporary Political Philosophy: An Introduction* (Oxford: Clarendon Press, 1990); David Archard, 'Social and Political Philosophy', in Nicholas Bunnin and Eric P. Tsui-James (eds.), *The Blackwell Companion to Philosophy* (Oxford: Basil Blackwell, 1996), 257–289; and Stephen Mulhall and Adam Swift, *Liberals and Communitarians,* 2d ed. (Oxford: Basil Blackwell, 1996).

4. John Rawls, *A Theory of Justice* (Oxford: Oxford University Press, 1972), 5.

5. H.L.A. Hart, *The Concept of Law* (Oxford: Clarendon Press, 1961), 155.

6. Rosalind Pollack Petchesky, *Abortion and Woman's Choice: The State, Sexuality, and Reproductive Freedom* (London: Verso, 1986), xiv.

Bibliography

Abbey, Antonia. 'Sex Differences in Attributions for Friendly Behavior: Do Males Misperceive Females' Friendliness?' *Journal of Personality and Social Psychology* 42 (1982):830–838.

Aiken, Jane H. 'Differentiating Sex from *Sex*: The Male Irresistible Impulse'. *New York University Review of Law and Social Change* 12 (1984):357–383.

Aldridge, Alfred Owen. 'The Meaning of Incest from Hutcheson to Gibbons'. *Ethics* 61 (1951):309–313.

Altman, Irwin. 'Privacy Regulation: Culturally Universal or Culturally Specific?' *Journal of Social Issues* 33 (1975):66–84.

Anderson, Priscilla. 'In the Genes or in the Stars? Children's Competence to Consent'. *Journal of Medical Ethics* 18 (1992):119–124.

Archard, David. 'The Age of Majority'. In Iain Hampsher-Monk and Jeffrey Stanyer (eds.), *Contemporary Political Studies 1996*. Nottingham, England: Political Studies Association of the United Kingdom, 1996, 1:520–528.

_____. 'Child Abuse'. In Ruth Chadwick (ed.), *Encyclopedia of Applied Ethics*. Vol. 3. San Diego: Academic Press, forthcoming.

_____. *Children, Rights, and Childhood*. London: Routledge, 1993.

_____. 'Exploited Consent'. *Journal of Social Philosophy* 25 (1994):92–101.

_____. 'Freedom Not to Be Free: The Case of the Slavery Contract in J. S. Mill's *On Liberty*'. *Philosophical Quarterly* 40 (1990):419–432.

_____. '"A Nod's as Good as a Wink": Consent, Convention, and Reasonable Belief'. *Legal Theory* 2 (1997):273–290.

_____. 'Political and Social Philosophy'. In Nicholas Bunnin and Eric P. Tsui-James (eds.), *The Blackwell Companion to Philosophy*. Oxford: Basil Blackwell, 1996, 257–289.

_____. 'Sex for Sale: The Morality of Prostitution'. *Cogito* 3 (1989):47–51.

Ariès, Philippe. *L'Enfant et la vie familiale sous l'ancien régime*. Paris: Librarie Plon, 1960. Translated by Robert Baldick as *Centuries of Childhood*. London: Jonathan Cape, 1962.

Austin, J. L. *How to Do Things with Words*. Ed. J. O. Urmson. Oxford: Clarendon Press, 1962.

Bailey, Victor, and Sarah McCabe. 'Reforming the Law of Incest'. *Criminal Law Review* (1979):749–764.

Baker, Brenda M. 'Consent, Assault, and Sexual Assault'. In Anne Bayefsky (ed.), *Legal Theory Meets Legal Practice*. Edmonton, Alberta: Academic Printing and Publishing, 1988, 223–238.

Balos, Beverly, and Mary Louise Fellows. 'Guilty of the Crime of Trust: Non-stranger Rape'. *Minnesota Law Review* 75 (1991):599–618.

Baumrin, Bernard H. 'Sexual Immorality Delineated'. In R. Baker and F. Elliston (eds.), *Philosophy and Sex*. 2d ed. Buffalo, N.Y.: Prometheus Books, 1984, 300–311.

Bechhofer, Laurie, and Andrea Parrot. 'What Is Acquaintance Rape?' In Laurie Bechhofer and Andrea Parrot (eds.), *Acquaintance Rape: The Hidden Crime*. New York: John Wiley, 1991, 9–25.

Belliotti, Raymond. *Good Sex: Perspectives on Sexual Ethics*. Lawrence: University Press of Kansas, 1993.

_____. 'A Philosophical Analysis of Sexual Ethics'. *Journal of Social Philosophy* 10 (1979):8–11.

Bernick, Susan E. 'The Logic of the Development of Feminism; or, Is MacKinnon to Feminism as Parmenides Is to Greek Philosophy?' *Hypatia* 7 (1992):1–15.

Bibbings, Lois, and Peter Alldridge. 'Sexual Expression, Body Alteration, and the Defence of Consent'. *Journal of Law and Society* 20 (1993):356–370.

Bienen, Leigh. 'Mistakes'. *Philosophy and Public Affairs* 7 (1970):224–245.

Blum, Larry. 'Deceiving, Hurting, and Using'. In Alan Montefiore (ed.), *Philosophy and Personal Relations*. London: Routledge and Kegan Paul, 1973, 34–61.

Bonilla, Margaret D. 'What Feminists Are Doing to Rape Ought to Be a Crime'. *Policy Review* 66 (1993):22–29.

Bostwick, Tracy D., and Janice L. Delucia. 'Effects of Gender and Specific Dating Behaviors on Perceptions of Sex Willingness and Date Rape'. *Journal of Social and Clinical Psychology* 11 (1992):14–25.

Brandendburg, Judith Berman. 'Sexual Harassment in the University: Guidelines for Establishing a Grievance Procedure'. *Signs* 8 (1982):320–336.

Brownmiller, Susan. *Against Our Will*. New York: Simon and Schuster, 1975.

Buchanan, Allen E., and Dan W. Brock. *Deciding for Others: The Ethics of Surrogate Decision Making*. Cambridge: Cambridge University Press, 1989.

Burgess-Jackson, Keith. *Rape: A Philosophical Investigation*. Aldershot, England: Dartmouth, 1996.

Burt, Martha R. 'Rape Myths and Acquaintance Rape'. In Laurie Bechhofer and Andrea Parrot (eds.), *Acquaintance Rape: The Hidden Crime*. New York: John Wiley, 1991, 26–40.

Cahill, Spencer E. 'Cross-Sex Pseudocommunication'. *Berkeley Journal of Sociology* 26 (1981):75–88.

Card, Richard. 'Sexual Relations with Minors'. *Criminal Law Review* 1975:370–380.

Carr, Craig L. 'Tacit Consent'. *Public Affairs Quarterly* 4 (1990):335–345.

Carter, Pam, and Tony Jeffs. 'The Hidden Curriculum: Sexuality in Professional Education'. In Pam Carter, Tony Jeffs, and Mark K. Smith (eds.), *Changing Social Work and Welfare*. Buckingham, England: Open University Press, 1992, 231–244.

_____. *A Very Private Affair: Sexual Exploitation in Higher Education*. Ticknall, England: Education Now Books, 1995.

Chamallas, Martha. 'Consent, Equality, and the Legal Control of Sexual Conduct'. *Southern California Law Review* 61 (1988):777–862.

Cohen, G. A. *Self-Ownership, Freedom, and Equality*. Cambridge: Cambridge University Press, 1995.

Cox, David. 'Justice and Philosophical Method: Prostitution as an Illustration'. *Journal of Social Philosophy* 11 (1980):10–16.

Criminal Law Revision Committee. *Fifteenth Report: Sexual Offences*. London: HMSO, 1984.

Curley, E. M. 'Excusing Rape'. *Philosophy and Public Affairs* 5 (1976):325–360.

Daniels, N. 'Wide Reflective Equilibrium and Theory Acceptance in Ethics'. *Journal of Philosophy* 76 (1979):256–282.

Davenport-Hines, Richard. 'Too Young to Know?' *The Times Saturday Review*, 9 February 1991, 10–12.

Davis, Nancy. 'Using Persons and Common Sense'. *Ethics* 94 (1984):387–406.

Devlin, Patrick. *The Enforcement of Morals*. London: Oxford University Press, 1965.

Dripps, Donald A. 'Beyond Rape: An Essay on the Difference Between the Absence of Force and the Absence of Consent'. *Columbia Law Review* 92 (1992):1780–1809.

Dworkin, Andrea. *Intercourse*. London: Arrow, 1988.

_____. *Pornography: Men Possessing Women*. New York: Perigree Books, 1981.

Dworkin, Gerald. 'Paternalism'. In Richard A. Wasserstrom (ed.), *Morality and the Law*. Belmont, Calif.: Wadsworth, 1971, 107–126.

Dworkin, Ronald. 'The Original Position'. In N. Daniels (ed.), *Reading Rawls: Critical Studies on Rawls'* A Theory of Justice. Oxford: Basil Blackwell, 1975, 16–53.

Eibl-Eibesfeldt, I. 'Expressive Movements'. In R. A. Hinde (ed.), *Non-verbal Communication*. Cambridge: Cambridge University Press, 1972, 297–314.

Elster, Jon. *Sour Grapes: Studies in the Subversion of Rationality*. Cambridge: Cambridge University Press, 1983.

Ericsson, Lars O. 'Charges Against Prostitution: An Attempt at a Philosophical Assessment'. *Ethics* 90 (1980):338–339.

Estrich, Susan. 'Rape'. *Yale Law Journal* 95 (1986):1087–1184.

Feinberg, Joel. *The Moral Limits of the Criminal Law*. Vol. 1: *Harm to Others*. Oxford: Oxford University Press, 1984.

_____. *The Moral Limits of the Criminal Law*. Vol. 2: *Offense to Others*. Oxford: Oxford University Press, 1985.

_____. *The Moral Limits of the Criminal Law*. Vol. 3: *Harm to Self*. Oxford: Clarendon Press, 1986.

_____. *The Moral Limits of the Criminal Law*. Vol. 4: *Harmless Wrongdoing*. Oxford: Oxford University Press, 1988.

Foucault, Michel. *Histoire de la sexualité, 1, La Volunté de savoir*. Paris: Gallimard, 1976. Translated by Robert Hurley as *The History of Sexuality: An Introduction*. Harmondsworth: Penguin, 1981.

_____. 'Freedom of the Will and the Concept of a Person'. *Journal of Philosophy* 68 (1971):5–20.

Frankfurt, Harry. 'Coercion and Moral Responsibility'. In Ted Honderich (ed.), *Essays on Freedom of Action*. London: Routledge and Kegan Paul, 1973, 65–86.

Freeden, Michael. *Ideologies and Political Theory: A Conceptual Approach*. Oxford: Clarendon Press, 1996.

Gardiner, S. 'The Law and the Sportsfield'. *Criminal Law Review* (1994):513–515.

Gatens, Moira. 'Sex, Contract, and Genealogy'. *Journal of Political Philosophy* 4 (1996):29–44.

George, Robert P. *Making Men Moral: Civil Liberties and Public Morality*. Oxford: Clarendon Press, 1993.

Giles, Marianne. 'R. v. *Brown*: Consensual Harm and the Public Interest'. *Modern Law Review* 57 (1994):101–111.

Goldman, Alan. 'Plain Sex'. *Philosophy and Public Affairs* 6 (1977):267–287.

Gray, Robert. 'Sex and Sexual Perversion'. *Journal of Philosophy* 75 (1978):189–199.

Green, Karen. 'Prostitution, Exploitation, and Taboo'. *Philosophy* 64 (1989):525–534.

Gunn, Michael, and David Ormerod. 'The Legality of Boxing'. *Legal Studies* 15 (1995):181–203.

Hale, Matthew. *The History of the Pleas of the Crown*. London: Professional Books, 1971; originally published 1736.

Harris, Lucy Reed. 'Towards a Consent Standard in the Law of Rape'. *University of Chicago Law Review* 43 (1975):613–645.

Hart, H.L.A. *The Concept of Law*. Oxford: Clarendon Press, 1961.

_____. *Law, Liberty, and Morality*. Oxford: Oxford University Press, 1963.

Helfer, Laurence R. 'Finding a Consensus on Equality: The Homosexual Age of Consent and the European Convention on Human Rights'. *New York University Law Review* 65 (1990):1044–1100.

Hobbes, Thomas. *Leviathan*. Ed. Michael Oakeshott. Oxford: Basil Blackwell, 1955.

Honoré, Tony. *Sex Law*. London: Duckworth, 1978.

Hopkins, Patrick D. 'Rethinking Sadomasochism: Feminism, Interpretation, and Simulation'. *Hypatia* 9 (1994):116–141.

Hurd, Heidi M. 'The Moral Magic of Consent'. *Legal Theory* 2 (1996). Special Issue: Sex and Consent, Part 1:121–146.

Husak, Douglas N., and George C. Thomas III. 'Date Rape, Social Convention, and Reasonable Mistakes'. *Law and Philosophy* 11 (1992):95–126.

Jackson, Emily. 'Catharine MacKinnon and Feminist Jurisprudence: A Critical Appraisal'. *Journal of Law and Society* 19 (1992):95–213.

Jenkins, John J. 'Political Consent'. *Philosophical Quarterly* 20 (1970):60–66.

Kanin, Eugene J. 'Female Rape Fantasies: A Victimization Study'. *Victimology* 7 (1982):114–121.

Kardener, Sheldon H., Marielle Fuller, and Ivan N. Mensh. 'A Survey of Physicians' Attitudes and Practices Regarding Erotic and Nonerotic Contact with Patients'. *American Journal of Psychiatry* 130 (October 1973):1077–1081.

Katz, Steven B. 'Expectation and Desire on the Law of Forcible Rape'. *San Diego Law Review* 26 (1989):1–71.

Kell, David. 'Social Disutility and the Law of Consent'. *Oxford Journal of Legal Studies* 14 (1944):121–135.

Kitzinger, Jenny. 'Defending Innocence: Ideologies of Childhood'. *Feminist Review* 28 (January 1988):77–87.

Kleinig, John. 'The Ethics of Consent'. *Canadian Journal of Philosophy* (supplementary volume) 8 (1982):92–118.

Kowalski, Robin M. 'Inferring Sexual Interest from Behavioral Cues: Effect of Gender and Sexually Relevant Attitudes'. *Sex Roles* 29 (1993):13–36.

Kupfer, Joseph. 'Prostitutes, Musicians, and Self-Respect'. *Journal of Social Philosophy* 26 (1995):75–88.

Kymlicka, Will. *Contemporary Political Philosophy: An Introduction.* Oxford: Clarendon Press, 1990.

Law Commission. *Consent in the Criminal Law: A Consultation Paper.* London: HMSO, 1995.

Lees, Sue. *Carnal Knowledge: Rape on Trial.* London: Hamish Hamilton, 1996.

Leigh, L. H. 'Sado-masochism, Consent, and the Reform of the Criminal Law'. *Modern Law Review* 39 (1976):130–146.

Letwin, Leon. '"Unchaste Character", Ideology, and the California Rape Evidence Laws'. *Southern California Law Review* 54 (1980):35–89.

Levy, Donald. 'Perversion and the Unnatural as Moral Categories'. *Ethics* 90 (1980):191–202.

Lewis, David K. *Convention: A Philosophic Study.* Cambridge, Mass.: Harvard University Press, 1969.

Lloyd-Thomas, D. A. *Locke on Government.* London: Routledge, 1995.

Locke, John. *Two Treatises of Government.* Ed. Peter Laslett. Cambridge: Cambridge University Press, 1988.

Lomasky, Loren E. 'Gift Relations, Sexual Relations, and Freedom'. *Philosophical Quarterly* 33 (1983):250–258.

MacKinnon, Catharine. 'Feminism, Marxism, Method, and the State'. *Signs* 7 (1982):515–554.

_____. 'Feminism, Marxism, and the State'. *Signs* 8 (1983):635–658.

_____. *Sexual Harassment of Working Women: A Case of Sex Discrimination.* New Haven: Yale University Press, 1979.

_____. 'Sexuality, Pornography, and Method: "Pleasure Under Patriarchy"'. *Ethics* 99 (1989):314–346.

_____. *Toward a Feminist Theory of the State.* Cambridge, Mass.: Harvard University Press, 1989.

Malm, H. M. 'The Ontological Status of Consent and Its Implications for the Law of Rape'. *Legal Theory* 2 (1996). Special Issue: Sex and Consent, Part 2:147–164.

Margolin, Leslie. 'Gender and the Stolen Kiss: The Social Support of Male and Female to Violate a Partner's Sexual Consent in a Noncoercive Situation'. *Archives of Sexual Behavior* 19 (1990):281–291.

Marietta, Don E., Jr. 'On Using People'. *Ethics* 82 (1971–1972):232–238.

Marx, Karl, and Friedrich Engels. *Selected Works.* 2 vols. Moscow: Foreign Languages Publishing House, 1969.

May, Larry, and Robert Strikwerda. 'Men in Groups: Collective Responsibility for Rape'. In Hugh LaFollette (ed.), *Ethics in Practice: Anthology.* Oxford: Basil Blackwell, 1997, 418–428.

McKeganey, Neil, and Marina Barnard. *Sex Work on the Streets: Prostitutes and Their Clients.* Buckingham, England: Open University Press, 1996.

McSherry, Bernadette. 'No! (Means No?)'. *Alternative Law Journal* 18 (1993):27–30.

Mill, John Stuart. *On Liberty.* Ed. Gertrude Himmelfarb. Harmondsworth: Penguin, 1974.

Millett, Kate. *Sexual Politics.* London: Abacus, 1972.

Minas, Anne C. 'Coercion and Consciousness'. *Canadian Journal of Philosophy* 10 (1980):301–309.

Muehlenhard, Charlene L. 'Misinterpreted Dating Behaviors and the Risk of Date Rape'. *Journal of Social and Clinical Psychology* 6 (1988):20–37.

Mulhall, Stephen, and Adam Swift. *Liberali and Communitarians.* 2d ed. Oxford: Basil Blackwell, 1996.

Murthy, Sakthi. 'Rejecting Unreasonable Sexual Expectations: Limits on Using a Rape Victim's Sexual History to Show the Defendant's Mistaken Belief in Consent'. *California Law Review* 9 (1991):541–576.

Naffine, Ngaire. 'Possession: Erotic Love in the Law of Rape'. *Modern Law Review* 57 (1994):10–37.

Nagel, Thomas. 'Sexual Perversion'. *Journal of Philosophy* 66 (1969):5–17.

Neu, Jerome. 'What Is Wrong with Incest?' *Inquiry* 19 (1976):27–39.

Nino, C. S. 'A Consensual Theory of Punishment'. *Philosophy and Public Affairs* 13 (1984):289–306.

Nozick, Robert. *Anarchy, State, and Utopia.* Oxford: Basil Blackwell, 1974.

_____. 'Coercion'. In Peter Laslett, W. G. Runciman, and Quentin Skinner (eds.), *Philosophy, Politics, and Society, Fourth Series*. Oxford: Basil Blackwell, 1972, 101–135.

O'Carroll, Tom. *Paedophilia: The Radical Case*. London: Peter Own, 1980.

Olsen, Frances. 'Statutory Rape: A Feminist Critique of Rights Analysis'. *Texas Law Review* 631 (1984):387–432.

O'Neill, Onora. 'Between Consenting Adults'. *Philosophy and Public Affairs* 14 (1985):252–277.

Overall, Christine. 'Heterosexuality and Feminist Theory'. *Canadian Journal of Philosophy* 20 (1990):1–17.

Pateman, Carole. 'Defending Prostitution: Charges Against Ericsson'. *Ethics* 93 (1983):561–565.

_____. '"The Disorder of Women": Women, Love, and the Sense of Justice'. *Ethics* 91 (1980):20–34.

_____. 'Women and Consent'. In Carole Pateman, *The Disorder of Women: Democracy, Feminism, and Political Theory*. Cambridge: Cambridge University Press, 1989, 71–89.

_____. *The Sexual Contract*. Cambridge: Polity Press, 1988.

Petchesky, Rosalind Pollack. *Abortion and Woman's Choice: The State, Sexuality, and Reproductive Freedom*. London: Verso, 1986.

Pickard, Toni. 'Culpable Mistakes and Rape: Relating Mens Rea to the Crime'. *University of Toronto Law Review* 30 (1980):5–98.

Pineau, Lois. 'Date Rape: A Feminist Analysis'. *Law and Philosophy* 8 (1989):217–243.

Pitcher, George. 'The Misfortunes of the Dead'. *American Philosophical Quarterly* 21 (1984):183–188.

Plamenatz, John. *Man and Society: A Critical Examination of Some Important Social and Political Theories from Machiavelli to Marx*. Vol. 1. London: Longman, 1963.

Policy Advisory Committee on Sexual Offences. *Report on the Age of Consent in Relation to Sexual Offences*. London: HMSO, April 1981.

Primoratz, Igor. 'What's Wrong with Prostitution?' *Philosophy* 68 (April 1993):165–171.

Rapaport, Elizabeth. 'Generalizing Gender: Reason and Essence in the Legal Thought of Catharine MacKinnon'. In Louise M. Anthony and Charlotte Witt (eds.), *A Mind of One's Own: Feminist Essays on Reason and Objectivity*. Boulder: Westview Press, 1993, 127–143.

Rawls, John. *A Theory of Justice*. Oxford: Oxford University Press, 1972.

Raz, Joseph. *The Morality of Freedom*. Oxford: Clarendon Press, 1986.

Reith, Warren T. (ed. in chief). *Encyclopaedia of Bioethics*. New York: Free Press, 1978.

Remick, Lani Anne. 'Read Her Lips: An Argument for a Verbal Consent Standard in Rape'. *University of Pennsylvania Law Review* 141 (1993):1103–1151.

Rich, Adrienne. 'Compulsory Heterosexuality and Lesbian Existence'. *Signs* 5 (1980):631–660.

Richards, Janet Radcliffe. *The Sceptical Feminist*. Harmondsworth: Penguin, 1980.

Roemer, John. *A General Explanation of Exploitation and Class*. Cambridge, Mass.: Harvard University Press, 1982.

Roiphe, Katie. *The Morning After: Sex, Fear, and Feminism*. London: Hamish Hamilton, 1994.

Rousseau, Jean-Jacques. *Politics and the Arts: A Letter to M. d'Alembert on the Theatre*. Trans. A. Bloom. Ithaca: Cornell University Press, 1968.

Rudinow, Joel. 'Manipulation'. *Ethics* 88 (1978):338–347.

Sandel, Michael. *Liberalism and the Limits of Justice*. Cambridge: Cambridge University Press, 1982.

Sartorius, Rolf (ed.). *Paternalism*. Minneapolis: University of Minnesota Press, 1982.

Sartre, Jean-Paul. *Being and Nothingness: An Essay on Phenomenological Ontology*. Trans. Hazel Barnes. London: Methuen, 1957.

Satz, Debra. 'Markets in Women's Sexual Labour'. *Ethics* 106 (1995):63–85.

Saxe, Lorena Leigh. 'Sadomasochism and Exclusion'. *Hypatia* 7 (1992):59–72.

Schecter, M. D., and L. Roberge. 'Sexual Exploitation'. In R. E. Helfer and C. H. Kempe (eds.), *Child Abuse and Neglect: The Family and the Community*. Cambridge, Mass.: Ballinger, 1976, 127–142.

Scheffler, Samuel. *Human Morality*. Oxford: Oxford University Press, 1992.

Schrage, Laurie. 'Should Feminists Oppose Prostitution?' *Ethics* 99 (1989):347–361.

Schulhofer, Stephen J. 'The Gender Question in Criminal Law'. *Social Philosophy and Policy* 7 (1990):105–137.

Scutt, J. A. 'Consent Versus Submission: Threats and the Element of Fear in Rape'. *University of Western Australia Law Review* 13 (1977):52–76.

Searle, John. 'What Is a Speech Act?' In John Searle (ed.), *The Philosophy of Language*. Oxford: Oxford University Press, 1971, 39–53.

Sen, Amartya. *Inequality Reexamined*. Oxford: Clarendon Press, 1992.

Sherwin, Emily. 'Infelicitous Sex'. *Legal Theory* 2 (1996). Special Issue: Sex and Consent, Part 2:209–231.

Shotland, R. Lance, and Jane M. Craig. 'Can Men and Women Differentiate Between Friendly and Sexually Interested Behavior?' *Social Psychology Quarterly* 51 (1988):66–73.

Siegler, Frederick. 'Plamenatz on Consent and Obligation'. *Philosophical Quarterly* 18 (1968):256–261.

Simmons, A. John. *Moral Principles and Political Obligations*. Princeton: Princeton University Press, 1979.

Singer, Peter. 'Altruism and Commerce: A Defense of Titmuss Against Arrow'. *Philosophy and Public Affairs* 2 (1973):312–320.

_____. *Democracy and Disobedience*. Oxford: Clarendon Press, 1973.

Smith, J. C., and B. Hogan. *Criminal Law: Cases and Materials*. 5th ed. London: Butterworths, 1993.

Snare, Frank. 'Consent and Conventional Acts in John Locke'. *Journal of the History of Philosophy* 13 (1975):27–36.

Soble, A. (ed.). *Philosophy of Sex: Contemporary Readings*. Totowa, N.J.: Rowman and Littlefield, 1980.

Solomon, Robert. 'Sexual Paradigms'. *Journal of Philosophy* 71 (1974):336–345.

Spelman, Elizabeth V. *Inessential Woman: Problems of Exclusion in Feminist Thought*. Boston: Beacon Press, 1988.

Stewart, Robert M. 'Morality and the Market in Blood'. *Journal of Applied Philosophy* 1 (1984):227–237.

Temkin, Jennifer. 'Do We Need the Crime of Incest?' *Current Legal Problems* 44 (1991):185–216.

Thornton, T. M. 'Rape and Mens Rea'. *Canadian Journal of Philosophy* (supplementary volume) 8 (1982):119–146.

Titmuss, Richard. *The Gift Relationship: From Human Blood to Social Policy*. London: Allen and Unwin, 1970.

Tong, Rosemarie. *Women, Sex, and the Law*. Totowa, N.J.: Rowman and Allanheld, 1984.

Tönnies, Ferdinand. *Community and Association*. Trans. Charles P. Loomis. London: Routledge and Kegan Paul, 1955.

Tsang, Daniel (ed.). *The Age Taboo: Gay Male Sexuality, Power, and Consent*. London: Gay Men's Press, 1981.

Tur, Richard H.S. 'Rape: Reasonableness and Time'. *Oxford Journal of Legal Studies* 1 (1981):432–441.

Twitchell, James B. *Forbidden Partners: The Incest Taboo in Modern Culture*. New York: Columbia University Press, 1987.

Valverde, Marina. 'Beyond Gender Dangers and Private Pleasures: Theory and Ethics in the Sex Debates'. *Feminist Studies* 15 (1989):237–254.

Walker, John D. 'Liberalism, Consent, and the Problem of Adaptive Preferences'. *Social Theory and Practice* 21 (1995):457–471.

Walzer, Michael. *Spheres of Justice*. New York: Basic Books, 1983.

Wasserstrom, Richard. 'Privacy: Some Arguments and Assumptions'. In Ferdinand David Schoeman (ed.), *Philosophical Dimensions of Privacy: An Anthology*. Cambridge: Cambridge University Press, 1984, 317–332.

Weeks, Jeffrey. *Sexuality and Its Discontents: Meanings, Myths, and Modern Sexualities*. London: Routledge, 1985.

Wells, Celia. 'Swatting the Subjectivist Bug'. *Criminal Law Review* (1982): 209–220.

Wertheimer, Alan. 'Consent and Sexual Relations'. *Legal Theory* 2 (1996). Special Issue: Sex and Consent, Part 1:89–112.

Wicclair, Mark R. 'Is Prostitution Morally Wrong?' *Philosophy Research Archives* 7 (1981):345–367.

Wiener, Robin D. 'Shifting the Communication Burden: A Meaningful Consent Standard in Rape'. *Harvard Women's Law Journal* 8 (1983):143–161.

Williams, Glanville. *Textbook of Criminal Law*. 2d ed. London: Stevens, 1983.

Wilson, William. 'Is Hurting People Wrong?' *Journal of Social Welfare and Family Law* 5 (1992):388–397.

Wolf, Susan. 'Moral Saints'. *Journal of Philosophy* 79 (1982):419–439.

Wolfenden Committee. *Report of the Committee on Homosexual Offences and Prostitution*. London: HMSO, 1957.

Young, Bruce W. 'Haste, Consent, and Age at Marriage: Some Implications of Social History for *Romeo and Juliet*'. *Iowa State Journal of Research* 62 (1988):459–474.

About the Book and Author

A popular belief is that whatever takes place in private between consenting adults should be allowed. This is the first book to offer a systematic philosophical examination of what might be meant by consent and what role it should play in the context of sexual activity.

Investigating the adequacy of standard accounts of consent, the book criticizes an influential feminist critique of consensuality. David Archard then applies this new theoretical understanding of sexual consent to controversial topics, such as prostitution, rape, sado-masochism, and the age of consent.

Written in clear, jargon-free language that combines philosophical analysis with practical discussion of real and imagined legal cases, *Sexual Consent* is both a provocative and fascinating study for philosophers, lawyers, and general readers.

David Archard is Reader in the Department of Moral Philosophy at the University of St. Andrews. He is the author of *Marxism and Existentialism: The Political Philosophy of Jean-Paul Sartre and Maurice Merleau-Ponty* (1980), *Consciousness and the Unconscious* (1984), and *Children, Rights, and Childhood* (1993).

Index